Diseased, Douched and Doctored

Diseased, Douched and Doctored

Thermal Springs, Spa Doctors and Rheumatic Diseases

Roger Rolls

London Publishing Partnership

Published by the London Publishing Partnership
www.londonpublishingpartnership.co.uk

ISBN 978-1-907994-04-3 (pbk.)

A catalogue record for this book is available from
the British Library

This book is composed in Baskerville Old Face

Hydrotherapist giving patient an underwater douche
in the New Royal Baths *(Author's photo)*

Contents

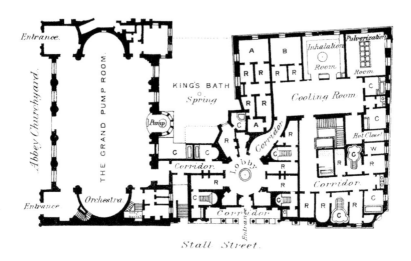

GRAND PUMP ROOM.

KING'S & QUEEN'S PRIVATE BATHS.

WITH THE LATEST ADDITIONS & IMPROVEMENTS

MADE IN 1868, 1869 & 1887.

THE · ROYAL · PUBLIC · & · PRIVATE · BATHS · 1871.

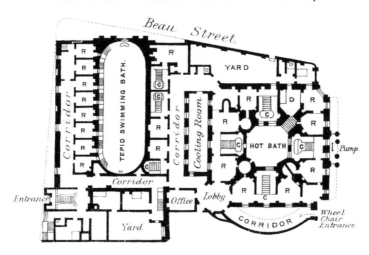

A Aix-les-Bains douche
B Bertholet vapour
C Ordinary Baths
R Dressing Rooms
W Wildbad Bath

Plans of the spa baths in 1890. The Queen's Private Baths suite was redeveloped into a tourist gift shop in the latter half of the 20th century. The Royal Public and Private Baths were redeveloped in the 21st century as part of Thermae Bath Spa.
(From *A Short Manual of the Bath Mineral Waters. London. 1890*)

Preface and Acknowledgements

It is almost 2000 years since the Romans developed the first bathing establishment at *Aquae Sulis*, the Latin name for the Somerset city of Bath. Since then, the thermal waters have been used at various times and in varying ways to treat the diseased and disabled. Bath still has a working spa, although its purpose is primarily for leisure activity. Elsewhere in Europe, thermal waters are still used for treatment and rehabilitation of injury and ill health.

This book considers the rise and fall of thermal waters as a therapeutic facility and the disorders which have been treated in such waters. The focus is on Bath, a city which developed around its hot springs and became the UK's foremost spa. The book examines the way the spa influenced the development of medical practice in the city and how one of the first specialist hospitals in the country is still managing to survive in its original premises after more than a quarter of a millennium.

The history of that hospital has previously appeared in my book, *The Hospital of the Nation*, published in 1988. Much of its contents reappears in this work as the original publication has been out of print for some years. However, the theme has shifted towards the part played by the spa in the history and development of medical practice in the city and beyond. This aims to give the reader a better understanding of the rationale behind spa therapy.

I am indebted to all those who helped with my research on *The Hospital of the Nation* and who are named in the preface to that work, and in particular Clive Quinnell, whose meticulous photography recorded so many of the historical artefacts and paintings associated with the spa and the Royal National Hospital for Rheumatic Diseases (RNHRD). Many of the illustrations in this book derive from Clive's efforts. The hospital had a collection of photographs relating to spa therapies which I have been able to use and my thanks go to Dr John Pauling who rescued some old photographs and press cuttings which were destined for the hospital's refuse collection. I would like to thank all those who helped provide illustrations including Dr Mary Tilley, Amelia Walker and staff at the Wellcome Library, Amina Wright at the Holburne Museum of Art, Helen Daniels at the Victoria Gallery, Gladys Powney at the Roman Baths Museum, and Katie Sandercock of Thermae Bath Spa. Over the years I have had great assistance from the librarians at the Bath Central Library. The enthusiasm of the late Dr George Kersley was an inspiration to me in my quest to uncover the twentieth century history of the spa and hospital. Since then Trevor Fawcett has provided me with much information on local medical personnel, drawing on his extensive knowledge of eighteenth century Bath. Colin Johnson has provided further assistance on my visits to the Bath City Archives. I am indebted to Niall Bowen for proof reading the manuscript. Richard Baggaley, Sam Clark and Jon Wainwright of the London Publishing Partnership have given valuable advice on the book's publication. I would like to thank the members of the former Bath Medical History Group for their support, and particularly Professor Francis Ring and the Friends of the RNHRD who have encouraged me bring this project to fruition and have generously sponsored the publication.

1. Introduction

Visitors to the Royal National Hospital for Rheumatic Diseases in Bath who ascend its main staircase sometimes pause to view the large painting hanging on the wall which depicts two be-wigged gentlemen examining a group of patients. The artist, William Hoare, presented the picture to the hospital in 1762. It is the most impressive of a number of fine eighteenth century paintings which hang in the building. Collections of paintings were common in eighteenth century voluntary hospitals where artists were eager to display their work, not for the benefit of patients,

Painting of *Dr Oliver and Mr Peirce Examining Patients* by William Hoare.
(*RNHRD/ Bath in Time*)

3

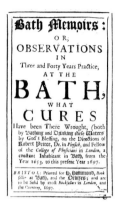

Bath Memoirs:
OR,
OBSERVATIONS
IN
Three and Forty Years Practice,
AT THE
BATH,
WHAT
CURES
Have been There Wrought, (both
by Bathing and Drinking these Waters)
by God's Blessing, on the Directions of
Robert Peirce, Dr. in Physick, and Fellow
of the College of Physicians in London, a
constant Inhabitant in Bath, from the
Year 1653. to this present Year 1697.

BRISTOL: Printed for D. Hammond, Book
seller at Bath, and the Devizes; and are
to be Sold by most Booksellers in London, and
the Country, 1697.

Frontispiece to *Bath Memoirs by Robert Peirce,* first published in 1697

but rather as a means of attracting potential commissions from wealthy benefactors and subscribers.

The painting is entitled *Dr Oliver and Mr Peirce Examining Patients* and subtitled *Rheumatism, Palsy and Leprosy*. The characters in the picture provide a theme for this book which, like the painting, depicts some of the patients who sought a cure for their diseases in the thermal waters at Bath. The book also examines the practitioners who attended them and how the spa influenced the development of medical practice in the city. The events in the painting take place in the Bath General Hospital (later known as the Royal Mineral Water Hospital) which opened in 1742 and was an early example of a voluntary hospital, financed by charitable subscriptions from the more wealthy members of society. Treatment using mineral water was the raison d'être for the hospital and the spa, and the book examines the changing theories and practice of balneology (the name by which this branch of medicine became known).

Hundreds of case descriptions were published in the seventeenth century from which it is possible to gain insight into the way the waters were used therapeutically in those days. Two books are particularly descriptive; one by the Bath physician, Dr Robert Peirce (1622-1710) is entitled 'Bath Memoirs or Observations in three and forty years at the Bath' and contains very detailed medical histories of named patients, many of whom were gentry or nobility. The other publication, known as the Register of Bath, provides the reader with a list of the patients who derived benefit from the waters, together with a brief description of their illness, and was compiled by Dr Thomas Guidott (1638-1706). More publications appeared in the eighteenth century so that there is a large amount of data from which to draw.

Besides published sources, there are some surviving manuscript records now lodged in the Bath City Records Office. The earliest is an admissions book which belonged to Bellott's hospital, an infirmary established in 1609 near the Hot Bath for the poorest of the city's visitors.

The Mineral Water Hospital had a complete set of records dating from its inception but unfortunately, having survived the destruction of the hospital during the Second World War, the records were thrown away just after the end of the war at the behest of the medical committee then in office. The few that did survive, together with the minute books, are now safely stored in the Bath City Records Office. As well as manuscript and printed records, pictures and illustrations provide another rich source of historical material upon which to draw and recently, much of this material has been made available on line by the Bath in Time project[1].

During the twentieth century, spa treatment at Bath became predominantly associated with the developing speciality of rheumatology. This is reflected by the renaming of the Royal Mineral Water Hospital in 1935, since when it has been known as the Royal National Hospital for Rheumatic Diseases. Traditionally rheumatic diseases were only one of many chronic disorders which the Bath waters were reputed to cure. In practice, the types of disease for which spa treatment was deemed suitable applied only to a handful of categories.

In Britain, interest in perpetuating spa treatment waned during the twentieth century and by 1980 all the traditional spas, including Bath had closed. The term 'spa' has been adopted by hotels and health clubs to describe facilities offering beauty treatments and complementary therapies which claim to 'detoxify' their clients or simply offer an opportunity for 'pampering'.

In 2006 a new thermal centre called Thermae Bath Spa opened in the city. Although it has treatment facilities which use water from the hot spring, the therapies on offer are more akin to those in health clubs and hotel spas and its primary purpose is for leisure and pleasure. In that respect, the history of Bath spa has returned to its Roman origins.

Above: Roman Great Bath.
*(Courtesy Bath & North
East Somerset Council)*

Below: Roof-top pool,
Thermae Bath Spa.
*(Photo: Andy Short, courtesy
of Themae Bath Spa)*

2. Douched and Drenched

Although Bath's thermal waters were possibly used for therapeutic bathing before the first century C.E., the Romans developed the first system of swimming baths, hot baths and steam rooms around the sacred spring of the goddess Sul-Minerva. This bathing and religious complex at Aquae Sulis became a healing centre which gained a reputation throughout the Roman Empire. Although the Romans used their public baths mainly for leisure purposes and for social gatherings, the employment of bathing as a therapy is evident in the literature of Roman medical authors like Asclepiades, Celsus, Pliny the Elder and Galen.[2] Pliny wrote in his encyclopaedic work on Natural History that 'beneficial waters gush forth in many lands, some cold, some hot, some tepid and many of them promising relief to the sick'. He recommended thermal springs for soothing painful conditions, promoting good respiration, relieving fatigue, relaxing joints and promoting secretion of urine. Douches or jets of water were thought best for relieving swellings and painful joints, whilst cold springs were often used to treat sore eyes.

Asclepiades, a Greek physician who practised in Rome in the late second century B.C.E., was particularly keen on spa treatment. He advocated cold baths and water drinking, a vogue which became prevalent after the emperor Augustus was cured of a liver abscess, though Asclepiades' popularity probably depended more on his habit of prescribing liberal quantities of wine.

Asclepiades believed that pores, the tiny openings on the surface of the skin, allowed fluids to pass in and out of the body. Acute diseases were caused when there was a constriction of the pores, or when they became blocked by a surfeit of particles from inside the body. Chronic diseases were conversely due to relaxation of the pores causing a deficiency of particles. Asclepiades' remedies supposedly restored harmony by using hot or cold bathing to open or close the pores. (There is no scientific evidence that pores can be made to open and close, nor do they communicate directly with the interior of the body. They are simply the openings of hair follicles, oil glands, and sweat glands.)

Cornelius Celsus, a Roman physician who flourished in the first century C.E., was also a keen advocate of baths, both for maintaining and restoring health. Celsus believed that mineral waters could restore the balance of humours in the body. The humeral theory of disease had been propounded many years before by Hippocrates, Aristotle and others to explain the cause of illness. Each of the four humours had physical properties describing their temperature and humidity. For example, phlegm was cold and moist whilst choler (yellow bile) was hot and dry. In a healthy state, the four humours achieved a steady balance but if one or more became excessive, disease ensued and the symptoms depended on which humour was out of balance.

It was the job of the physician to determine the state of the patient's humours and set up remedies to restore a healthy balance. Jaundice, itching and certain types of fever were due to excess of choler, whereas the cold lifeless limb of a stroke or the swollen legs of dropsy were due to an excess of phlegm. Cataract, literally a cascade of phlegm in the eye, and forgetfulness were due to an accumulation of this humour in the head. Remedies for cold-moist phlegmatic diseases required qualities which were hot and drying. Thermal springs provided an appropriate treatment because the minerals give the water a dry taste and immersion in the water produces a diuresis – an increased output of urine.

Started around 50 C.E., the baths at Aqua Sulis attained their peak in the third century C.E. A visit involved taking a sauna in a room called a *laconicum* with an underfloor heating system known as a *hypocaust*. This was followed by a cold plunge. Visitors also immersed themselves in one of several deep baths supplied with thermal water, or in the

Great Bath which was filled with thermal water reduced to a temperature suitable for swimming. A sluice brought hot water from the temple reservoir above the sacred spring, whilst cold water was fed into a fountain at one side of the bath. Bathers also covered themselves with oil and then scraped it off with a metal instrument known as a *strigil*. Bathing practice varied during the three centuries of Roman occupation, reflecting the influence of emperors. Lascivious and licentious behaviour at the time of Nero and Caligula was displaced by a more ascetic attitude to bathing.

Although there is a degree of rationality evident in Roman medical theory, there was also a large amount of superstition and magic employed in treating illness. The bath complex reflected the sacred nature of the site and the healing aspect of the springs. Votive offerings were thrown into the water, some of which have been recovered in archaeological excavations of the reservoir. Votive offerings could be fashioned to represent parts of the body, for example breasts carved from ivory, thrown in with the hope that the goddess would be directed to heal that particular part of the patient. Some tomb stones found in the city record people who died of wounds or diseases which may have been considered treatable by the water. Religious shrines also existed at the city's other hot springs: the Cross Bath stands on the site of a shrine to Aesculapius, the Roman god of medicine.

The most influential of all ancient medical writers was Claudius Galen, a doctor working in Rome during the second century C.E. In his time, his reputation as both physician and philosopher was legendary, the emperor Marcus Aurelius describing him as first among doctors and unique among philosophers. Galen summarised and consolidated the work of his predecessors so that a comprehensive knowledge of Greek and Roman medicine could be handed down to subsequent generations.

Galen's work was so respected that his theories dominated and influenced European medical science for nearly two millennia. Despite advancing medical practice in late antiquity, Galen's influence stifled further progress in European medicine during the Middle Ages. What progress there was came not from Christendom but from the Islamic world of Asia, North Africa and Spain. Islamic culture revered water and built bath houses which were known as hammams or Turkish baths, whereas the early Christian church discouraged the use of baths. Christians viewed the baths which the Romans had developed across Europe as an immoral and unnecessary indulgence. Cleanliness was equated with the luxury, materialism and excessive sensualism of the Roman lifestyle. Mortifying the flesh by avoiding baths was seen as a penance for sin. As a result baths became unpopular and fell into disrepair, although some monasteries rebuilt them, particularly where there were hot springs with a reputation for healing. This occurred at Bath where, around 1100 C.E., bishop John de Villula repaired the Roman reservoir surrounding the thermal springs and constructed the King's bath above it.

Despite the church's initial disapproval of baths, it was prepared to condone their use for healing and spiritual purification, recognising that in the beginning the spirit of God moved upon the face of the waters.[3] Attitudes to bathing became more liberal during the later mediaeval period. In the twelfth century, the author of the *Gesta Stephani* relates how diseased people from all over England came to wash away their infirmities in the healing waters of Bath[4], although interest seems to have waned in the years leading up to the monastic dissolution when the baths were transferred to the custodianship of the city council.

Within a few years of their transfer, awareness of the baths' healing potential was reawakened by the publication of two books on therapeutic bathing, one by Dr William Turner[5] and the other by Dr John Jones[6]. Turner was born around 1508 at Morpeth in Northumberland. He studied medicine and divinity at Cambridge University. Like many of his fellow students, he was attracted to the growing revolt against the papal control of the church which was gaining momentum in northern Europe under the banner of reformers like Luther, Calvin and Zwingli. These were dangerous times for heretics and Turner's protestant zeal was liable to lead to an unpleasant death by burning. He moved to the safety of Germany and North Italy. The latter was also home to the best medical tuition in Europe and Turner enrolled as a student at the universities of Ferrara and Bologna. Here he could learn about the medical application of mineral water from the works of ancient authors and from lectures on the subject by his contemporaries. Three popular spas lay in the vicinity of Ferrara: Abano, a few miles south of Padua, Caldiero, south of Verona and Porretta, near Bologna. These baths had been described by several Italian physicians who were professors at Padua and Ferrara during Turner's time in Italy.

Even as early as the fifteenth century, there was an attempt to analyse the mineral content of thermal waters. Distilling was used to obtain residues which were identified as iron, sulphur, salt, alum, saltpetre and other minerals. Although knowledge of chemistry was rudimentary, the Abano waters were thought to contain salt and alum and a small amount of sulphur, which made them good for moist diseases because of their dry quality.

Abano was situated on a wind-swept hill which limited the bathing season to the early summer and autumn when the weather was the most calm. One solution to inclement

Below: Illustration showing the bath at Abano from *D. Vandellii. Tractatus de Thermis agri Patavini. Padua. 1761.*

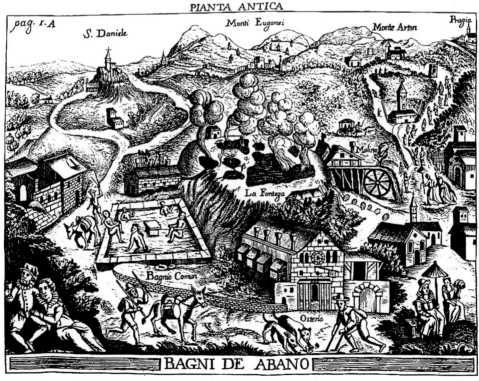

weather was to have the spa water conveyed to the patient's lodgings in a bathtub, although there was concern that it would lose its healing properties once it had been removed from its source.

There were many ways in which the waters could be taken besides bathing. Drinking was advised to 'scour the inside of the body'. Therapy began with a purgative and a day of rest and prayer. On the following day, a patient could drink up to five cups of water, gradually increasing to between ten to twenty cups. This process continued until the urine was virtually colourless. These rules governing bathing practices were to influence Turner when he later came to advise on the medical use of the Bath springs.

After leaving Italy, Turner travelled northwards through Switzerland and into Germany visiting several more spas on the way, including Bad Pfäfers, or the Pepper Bath, near Chur in Switzerland. The controversial physician and alchemist, Paracelsus, had visited Bad Pfäfers in 1535. Paracelsus was particularly interested in mineral waters because he believed that humans had certain balances of minerals in their bodies, and consequently, by choosing the appropriate chemical remedies to counteract the chemical imbalance, they could be cured.

Turner also visited the Swiss resort of Baden and he was given a long list of diseases suitable for treatment there. To cure these maladies it was necessary to stay in the bath for most of the day, that is four hours before dinner and three more after. For women, the recommendations were even longer – nine hours a day.

On his return to England following the death of Henry VIII, Turner was keen to investigate the thermal springs at Bath. The city was then quite small with a population of about 1500 inhabitants, surrounded by mediaeval walls. Its economy rested largely upon the cloth industry rather than tourism. Turner wrote that its baths were little known beyond the West country. After his visit, he was convinced that many persons in the northern and eastern parts of Britain who were 'afflicted with sore diseases' would gladly come to the baths at Bath if only they knew they were there.

Turner lamented how shabby the English baths appeared when compared with those in Germany and Italy. He wrote that 'there is money enough spent upon cockfightings, tennis-playing, parks, banqueting, pageants and plays .... but I have not heard tell that any rich man hath spent upon these noble baths, being so profitable for the whole common wealth of England, one groat in these twenty years'. Such sentiments encouraged the generosity of wealthy visitors like Sir Francis Stonor who, in 1624, paid for an elegant balustrade to be erected around the sides of the bath and for others to finance the facility to draw spring water from a pump rather than have to ladle it out of the bath.

In his publication, *The Book of the Natures and Properties of the Baths of England*, printed in 1562, Turner lists over sixty disorders which could benefit from bathing in the thermal water at Bath, including such diverse conditions as piles, migraine, sciatica, worms in the belly, forgetfulness, dullness of smelling, palsy, cramp in the neck and failure of menstruation. In modern terms, there seems very little to link these conditions but in Turner's day, the majority of diseases in his list were classified as cold-moist disorders. For example, physicians believed that an excess of phlegm

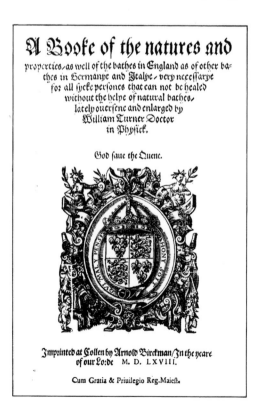

Frontispiece from William Turner's *Booke of the Natures and Properties as well of the bathes in England as of other bathes in Germanye and Italye.*

in the womb could cause sterility. By drying out the womb, the Bath waters were able to restore a woman's fertility and this reputation proved attractive to certain English monarchs. Royal visits helped to popularise the town as a resort. Anne of Denmark, Charles I, Catherine of Braganza and Mary of Modena all visited Bath during the Stuart period in the hope of improving their fecundity.

Turner believed the waters contained sulphur, a misconception perpetuated by certain Bath physicians for at least two centuries after his writings. However sulphur in that era was used more as a term for flammability and was assumed to provide the explanation of the heat in the water and some of its therapeutic action. 'Bathes of brimstone soften the sinews, suage the pain that a man hath in defying the going often unto the stool and when he cometh thither can do little or nothing. They scour and cleanse the skin wherefore they are good for the white and black morphews (i.e.pimples), for leprosy and scabs, scurf, for old sores and blotches and for the falling of humours into joints.'

By the mid-seventeenth century, physicians increasingly challenged the ancient theories of disease causation. After William Harvey's discovery of the circulation of the blood, the old idea of humours ebbing and flowing through the body like the tides had to be abandoned. A new physiological paradigm developed which likened the body to a hydraulic system, although it was based in part on the theories propounded by Asclepiades mentioned earlier in this chapter. Supporters of this theory, known as iatromechanics, held that the main cause of disease was due to different states of elasticity of the solid parts of the body thereby interfering with the movements of the fluids, causing them to stagnate and congest. The fluids themselves could thicken from the accumulation of viscous particles, so compounding the problem. Thermal waters worked by entering the circulation through pores in the skin (or the stomach in the case of drinking), dissolving the viscous particles in the fluids and softening the solids. The waters also stimulated fibres and nerves and cleansed the kidneys, bladder and womb. To prevent the water from washing impurities from the stomach into the blood and from overheating the system, the patient had to be prepared by purging, bleeding and being given emetics. They were then encouraged to drink gradually increasing quantities of water to scour the system. This was monitored by the patient's medical attendant who regularly examined the urine. Once the urine became colourless, the scouring process was deemed complete.

Not everyone believed in this explanation of unblocking obstructions and diluting solid and viscous components. Disciples of Paracelsus, (now known as iatrochemists), likened the body to a chemical laboratory and held that the chemical constituents of the water were able to modify a diseased state. In the seventeenth century chemical analyses were crude and inaccurate, the result of examining the residue of solids remaining after distillation. For example, physicians believed the three principal constituents of the Bath waters were nitre, sulphur and bitumen. Although nitre now refers to naturally occurring potassium nitrate, originally the word was usually applied to sodium carbonate. (The related word natron is a term still sometimes used for this substance.) Sulphur and bitumen were thought to be present because people believed the waters were heated by underground fires of brimstone akin to volcanic activity. Scum, due to growth of algae, frequently formed on the surface of the water in the baths and this was mistaken for bitumen and sulphur but there was considerable scepticism expressed over the presence of these latter two substances, neither of which is present.

During the seventeenth century chemical analysis of mineral waters became more accurate. Dr John Mayow, a brilliant Oxford physician who practised in Bath during the season, managed to get reasonably close to the truth by rejecting the presence of nitre and free sulphur. He also argued about the amount of other constituents, but later physicians preferred to ignore Mayow's work and favoured an earlier writer, Edward Jorden. Dr Jorden published his *Discourse on Mineral Waters* in 1631. It is a general treatise on mineral water therapy but deals specifically with Bath in the final four chapters. It was ironic that one of his sons was drowned in the very water about which Jorden expressed so much enthusiasm. Most of Jorden's book is devoted to the specific properties of various minerals. He classifies them

Portrait of John Mayow from the frontispiece to *Tractatus Quinque*.

into their degree of heat and dryness, and whether they are penetrating, astringent, opening, cleansing or softening. He recommends the Bath waters for heating, drying, softening and cleansing by virtue of their sulphur, nitre and bitumen content, but he was reluctant to recommend their inward use in view of the difficulty of drawing the water in a pure state from the spring.

Like Turner, Jorden spent time in Northern Italy at the universities of Bologna, Ferrara and also at Padua where he obtained his MD degree. He was influenced by the work of Gabriel Fallopio who was a contemporary of Turner at Ferrara and later became professor of anatomy there before being offered the chair of anatomy and surgery at the University of Padua. Fallopio wrote an important treatise on thermal waters[7] but his chemical analysis of the springs at Abano were at odds with those of his contemporaries.

Another influential seventeenth century writer, Dr Thomas Guidott, whose prolific literary outpourings on Bath and its waters followed his flight from London in the wake of the Great Plague of 1665, described the thermal spring water as 'so amicable and balsamick that in conjunction with nitre it penetrates the most intimate recesses of the body in general and the lungs in particular; by the use of which all persons in such distempers may reasonably expect much greater advantage than from any cold Mineral Water or Spaw whatsoever'. Guidott believed the Bath waters contained eight distinct substances, nitre, common salt, vitriol, bitumen, sulphur, freestone, marl and ochre but it is difficult to be certain what he means by some of these terms, particularly nitre.

He enjoyed a high reputation beyond Bath and was offered chairs of physic at Venice and Leiden, but he declined both. He fell out with several of his fellow physicians in Bath, returning to London in 1679. It was perhaps not surprising that when the Oxford physician, John Mayow, arrived in Bath in 1674 refuting the presence of sulphur and nitre, he did not endear himself to Dr Guidott and his Bath colleagues. It would appear that Mayow, who was closely connected to the eminent Oxford physician Thomas Willis, may have influenced Willis's reluctance to recommend the Bath waters to his own patients, preferring to send them to Tunbridge. In turn, Willis seems to have influenced John Radcliffe, whose name will be familiar to anyone from Oxford. Radcliffe was involved in a pamphlet war with the Bath physician William Oliver Senior (not to be confused with a later physician famous for his biscuit) after Radcliffe suggested that Bath waters were good for nothing when bottled. By the end of the seventeenth century, the trade in bottled water was considerable and Radcliffe's remarks provoked a strong reaction from the Bath medics. Radcliffe was accused of wishing to ruin the trade of bottled Bath water by putting a metaphorical 'toad' in the waters.

Despite such adverse publicity, most of the publications were influential in raising the importance of Bath as a health resort and by the seventeenth century there were at least five baths in use, the King's and Queen's Baths, the Cross Bath and the Hot and Leper Baths. The King's Bath was the most popular, as Thomas Johnson's view shows.

Thomas Johnson's view of the King's Bath 1672
(Trustees of the British Museum, London)

The structure in the centre, erected over the hot spring, was known as the kitchen because of the high temperature of the water there and had a habit of gradually subsiding into the bottom of the bath on account of the continual erosion taking place at the spring head. The bathers are crowded with both sexes in the water together, and some are totally naked. Children appear to clamber on the surrounding parapet and dogs, cats and other assorted creatures were, according to John Wood writing a few decades later, often hurled over the side to the amusement of the onlookers and the annoyance of the bathers.[8] A visitor at this time wrote that one could 'see young and old, rich and poor, blind and lame, diseased and sound, English and French, men and women, boyes and girles, one with another, peep up in their caps and appear so nakedly and fearfully in their uncouth postures as would a little astonish and put one in mind of the Resurrection'.[9]

18

There was some attempt to keep order. Each bath was supervised by a Bath Keeper who rented his bath from the city council, the freehold owner of all the baths in the city following the Reformation. The Bath Keeper's business involved allocating duties to a number of lesser officials called Bath Guides and seeing 'that everything in the bath is done peacefully, quietly and modestly.' After the sixteenth century, the Bath Guides were appointed by the city council. There appear to have been eight men and six women for the King's Bath and four men and four women for the other two baths.[10] Ned Ward, a hack writer visiting Bath at the end of the seventeenth century, observed that there were a score or two of guides at work who 'by their scorbutick carcasses and lacker'd hides, you would think they had laid pickling a century of years in the Stygian Lake.'[11] Bathers employed 'those infernal emissaries' to support their limbs or 'scrub their putrefying carcasses like racehorses'.

Bathers were recommended to stay immersed for one or two hours in the water, a considerably shorter period than at some continental spas. Treatment could be directed to specific parts of the body by using buckets. Turner suggests using a bucket with a small hole in the bottom and held above the bather so that a stream of water poured down on the part of the body to be treated. In addition, the bath guides helped move paralysed limbs in the water and stretch contractures. Bath was thus able to offer a treatment, unique in the British Isles, which became increasingly popular with both patients and medical men during the seventeenth century. There was nowhere else in the country with such a large quantity of hot water freely and constantly available. Though Buxton and Matlock attracted patients to their baths at this time, their springs were tepid by comparison with those at Bath. Even at Bristol, although water from the Hotwells spring arises at a temperature of 24°C, the spa was more popular for drinking than bathing. Celia Fiennes described it as 'warm as new milk and much of that sweetness'. In France, spas were little more than muddy pools, sanctuaries of prayer and plain living steeped in the tradition of holy wells. Only in Italy and Germany were there any facilities matching those at Bath and it was

19

not until the nineteenth century that the grand spas were developed in other parts of mainland Europe.

Medical theory as taught by the universities of Oxford and Cambridge was firmly based on age-old paradigms which were so strongly rooted that many physicians continued to ignore the emergent body of new knowledge which was emanating from the experiments and observations of seventeenth century natural philosophers. Despite the influence of foreign universities, which seem to have taught a more pragmatic approach to medicine with greater emphasis on clinical observation, it was not until the second half of the eighteenth century that there was a shift in thinking which ushered in a new attitude to medicine. No longer were age old theories uncritically accepted, though there was great reluctance for many practitioners to depart from traditional therapies.

Charles Lucas, an Irish physician who visited in Bath in 1753, had studied at Leiden university and had investigated the waters at Spa and Aachen. He had been an apothecary in Dublin but had to quit Ireland after he fell into trouble over his attempt to reform the Irish Parliament. On his arrival in Bath, he set about exposing the 'old fashioned errors and abuses' perpetrated by the established physicians in the city. He employed a London specialist in analytical chemistry, Peter Woulfe, to examine the thermal waters. Woulfe was a fellow Irishman who was held in high esteem by the London scientific community. He was elected a Fellow of the Royal Society in 1767, awarded the society's Copley medal in 1768, and delivered the first Bakerian lecture in 1776[12]. Woulfe concluded that the minerals in the Bath waters were 'neither Saponaceous nor Sulphurous, Nitrous nor Alkaline.' The supposed sulphur was actually algae normally associated with stagnant ponds. No nitre or bitumen could be detected and iron sulphate or vitriol, previously thought to be a volatile constituent, remained evident after the water had cooled. He also explained how the practice of gilding silver shillings in Bath water to prove the presence of sulphur was mere trickery whereby the coins were surreptitiously immersed in stale wine or urine.

Lucas's three volume *Essay on Waters*, published in 1756, was dynamite for the established Bath medical fraternity who had recently founded and become involved with the Bath General Hospital. It not only cast doubts on the analytical abilities of the established Bath physicians but called into question the very medicinal virtues of the waters themselves. Dr Rice Charleton, a respected and wealthy physician in the town, was so eager to re-establish sulphur as a constituent that he redefined the word to embrace any oily substance: 'If any such oily substance can be found in these springs, it has all the just right to be called the sulphureous principle however so much it may differ from common brimstone.' In 1757, further publication caused even more stir. William Baylies, another outsider physician who concurred with Lucas's analyses, suggested that the General Hospital was deliberately keeping down the number of honorary physicians on its staff and failing to produce accurate research and statistics. He accused William Oliver of nepotism, and pointed out that some of the mixtures of medicaments and water that were being used were dangerous. He alleged that, at a meeting of the subscribers to another Bath medical charity, he had been told by a surgeon to the hospital that if the case histories of patients in the hospital were to be published in the manner that

Portrait of Dr Charles Lucas (*Wellcome Library, London*)

Baylies suggested, the water would be exposed and that the world would be shown their real insignificance.

Both Lucas and Baylies were ostracised professionally by the triumvirate of influential Bath physicians, William Oliver, Rice Charleton, and Abel Moysey, all of whom refused to consult with them. Moreover, there was a general lack of consensus about the waters composition throughout the mid-eighteenth century but this did little harm to the popularity of the spa. Whatever their mode of action, practitioners and their patients remained convinced about the efficacy of the waters, though the range of diseases amenable to treatment was about to come under the spotlight.

Physicians began to collect statistical data on the outcome of treatment. The emergence of the voluntary hospitals did much to foster this spirit of enquiry. A broadsheet advertising the foundation of the Bath General Hospital reminded potential subscribers that the opportunities for research were far greater than would be available in one physician's practice and there are early examples of numerical analyses of hospital patients' treatment and outcome, though no research was published comparing mineral water treatment with common spring water.

The medical theories of the seventeenth century prevailed well into the next century, though the humoral doctrine was laid to rest by most physicians. The chemical constituents were still seen as an essential property though attention was turned to the newly discovered dissolved gases in the spring water. Dr William Falconer was particularly interested in 'fixed air', the gas we now term carbon dioxide. He made a number of studies on its medicinal effects. Its antiseptic properties led him to postulate that this was the constituent providing the healing nature of the mineral water.

The belief that carbon dioxide was an important therapeutic constituent encouraged the development of artificial mineral water. Natural effervescent waters, like those at Spa, Seltzer and Pyrmont in mainland Europe had long been popular for drinking and large numbers of bottles were imported into England during the seventeenth and eighteenth century. By the time they reached their destination, the bottles had either exploded or much of the gas had leaked away. The marked effervescence of these waters, described variously as *aetherial elastic spirit* or *volatile mineral principle*, was the feature which many physicians believed accounted for their curative properties. The evanescent nature of effervescence and the difficulty of retaining it in a bottle paradoxically proved useful for physicians working in spa towns because they could argue that the benefits of drinking their waters could only be obtained at the source.

William Oliver (senior) noted that the Bath waters contained a 'Chaos of Salt', probably referring to the gaseous bubbles. The word *gas* is derived from *chaos* and was first used by the Flemish physician, Jan Baptist van Helmont in the seventeenth century. However Oliver, who for most of his life practised away from Bath, thought the non-gaseous constituents of the water were as important as its 'elastic spirit'. He implied that they could be drunk away from their source and still be beneficial. [13]

In 1734 Dr Peter Shaw, a physician at Scarborough, published a treatise about his local spa in which he suggested capturing the volatile mineral principle in a sheep's bladder so it could be analysed and reintroduced into ordinary water. This was not long before the volatile principle proved to be carbon dioxide (fixed air) and Joseph Priestley took up Shaw's idea of reintroducing the gas into ordinary water. At first he attempted to dissolve fixed air in spring water suspended over the fermentation vats in his local brewery. He wrote, 'I generally found the next morning that the water had acquired a very sensible and pleasant impregnation'. However, this method failed to achieve any effervescence so he went on to devise an apparatus to artificially impregnate water.

Others were also trying to produce artificial sparkling water at this time. Torbern Bergman, professor of chemistry and pharmacy at Uppsala University, may have made aerated water as early as 1766. His health had been failing for some years and he was drinking imported mineral waters from German spas. In his 1774 publication *De acido aereo commentatio* he writes that by adding suitable salts 'we may perfectly imitate Seltzer, Spa and Pyrmont waters. Such artificial waters I have now been using for eight years with signal advantage.' Certainly Bergman and Priestley were in correspondence together and it is obvious that the interest in producing artificial mineral water was quite widespread at this time.

The medical profession's excitement about carbon dioxide stemmed from a theory propounded in 1764 by an Irish doctor called David MacBride. He had served as a naval surgeon during the war of the Austrian Succession and his seafaring days made him acutely aware of scurvy. MacBride had observed how gas bubbles were released when organic matter decayed and putrefied and he became convinced that the bubbles must act as a bond to maintain substances in a firm and sound state. When it was released as a gas, substances putrefied and fell apart. He postulated that if the fixed air was put back, putrescence should be reversed. Diseases like scurvy, gaol fever, dysentery and fungating ulcers, all of which had putrid qualities, should therefore respond to treatment by giving patients saturated solutions of carbon dioxide.

To achieve maximum therapeutic potential, it was desirable to dissolve as much carbon dioxide as possible in water. Anyone achieving this on a grand scale would reap a handsome profit. One of the criticisms of Priestley's apparatus was that the pig's bladder in which he collected the gas imparted a distinctly unpleasant taste to the water, sometimes so pronounced that it became undrinkable. Priestley vigorously defended his apparatus, reporting that none of his friends, all of whom 'were of the most delicate sensibility', had ever complained about the taste.

One critic was John Mervin Nooth, whose father was an apothecary in the Dorset town of Sturminster Newton. Nooth graduated from Edinburgh in 1766 and appears to have developed an interest in fixed air soon after. In 1774, he delivered a paper to the Royal Society describing his apparatus for impregnating water with fixed air. Although he never worked in the city, Nooth had connections with Bath and retired there. His brother James was a surgeon at the Bath City Infirmary and Dispensary. One of his correspondents was Dr William Falconer, physician to the Bath General Hospital, who experimented with carbonated water using Nooth's apparatus. Falconer tried to dissolve bladder stones in the water.

There were two deficiencies with Nooth's apparatus. It was only possible to produce relatively small quantities of sparkling water without refilling the middle reservoir and there was insufficient pressure of carbon dioxide to produce a decent fizz. Thomas Henry, a Manchester apothecary had been conducting research into various methods of preserving food and water from putrefaction using calcined magnesia and lime, and eventually carbon dioxide. After Priestley's failure to impress the Navy with his prevention of scurvy with aerated water, Henry hoped to interest the Admiralty in preserving drinking water at sea by adding lime to it. Unfortunately this made the water so unpalatable that no sailor could drink it. To overcome this, Henry proposed passing carbon dioxide through the lime water to precipitate the lime and restore the water to its original

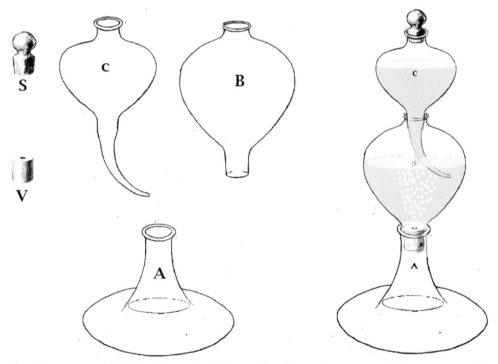

Nooth's apparatus. Marble chips and acid were placed in the botton vessel **A** and water in the middle vessel **B**. A one way valve prevented water flowing into **A**. Carbon dioxide bubbled through the water in **B** and, as the pressure built up, the carbonated water was pushed into the top vessel **C** which was closed by a glass stopper **S.**

Haygarth's design for carbonating water. The gas is generated in vessel E, and flows into the large container A, displacing air via a one way valve O. The gas can then be pumped into the water vessel W by using the attached bellows B.
(*From a contemporary engraving published by T. Cadell*)

Published as the Act directs Sept.ʳ 29. 1785 by T.Cadell in the Strand

taste. If he was to interest the Navy, he had to devise some way of making sparkling water in large quantities.

The problem was solved by Dr Falconer's colleague, Dr John Haygarth, physician to the Chester Infirmary who moved to Bath in his retirement. Haygarth's designs for a carbonation apparatus employed bellows in place of bladders and this was used by Thomas Henry in the large scale commercial production of carbonated mineral water for medicinal purposes. The business flourished and in 1804, Henry proposed opening further factories at Bath, Glasgow and Birmingham. He asked James Watt for assistance in fitting up the Birmingham factory, requesting that the project should be kept secret 'lest the enemy should steal a march on us'.

The 'enemy' in question was to become, and still is, one of the best known names in the soft drinks industry, Jacob Schweppe. Born in the German town of Witzenhausen in 1740, Schweppe moved to Geneva in 1765 where he established himself as a jeweller. Schweppe had read about Priestley's discoveries and set out to construct a pressurised apparatus which could provide a much higher level of aeration than had already been achieved, even higher than that of naturally effervescent water. As well as an inventor, Schweppe was an astute entrepreneur and as soon as he began producing high quality mineral waters, he offered free samples to doctors in Geneva for distribution to their poor patients. Within a short time, Schweppe was at the helm of a profitable business. In 1790, he invited Nicholas Paul, an engineer and Henry Gosse, a pharmacist to join him in partnership; both had previously dabbled with aerated water production, though with little success.

The partners were eager to expand their business internationally and an English physician living in Geneva, William Belcombe, was recruited to publicise the business in the UK by making contacts with the medical profession. Schweppe would oversee the development of a factory in London. After a rather shaky start, Schweppe's mineral waters rapidly achieved a reputation outshining most other manufacturers. Matthew Boulton, a Birmingham industrialist whose firm made Watt's first steam engine, was an enthusiastic imbiber and wrote in October 1794 that Schweppe's mineral waters were impregnated 'so highly with fixable air as to exceed in appearance Champagne and all other Bottled Liquors. He prepares it of 3 sorts: No.1 is for common drinking with your dinner, No. 2 for Nephritick patients, and No. 3. contains the most alkali and is given only in more violent cases'. The fact that Boulton continued to purchase his waters from London when Thomas Henry and sons were manufacturing their own brand on his doorstep shows what a hold Schweppe had on the market.

Meanwhile, Falconer was still trying to prove that the therapeutic power of the Bath thermal waters was in part due to the dissolved carbon dioxide. Not everyone was convinced. Philip Thicknesse, who had no medical qualification but commanded respect amongst the intelligentsia, pointed out that there was more carbon dioxide in common spring water. Sir George Smith Gibbes, another physician at the General Hospital, analysed the Bath mineral water in 1800 and found that, besides carbon dioxide, there were small amounts of oxygen and azotic gas (nitrogen). He dismissed these for what they were, the constituent gases of dissolved air, and was more in favour of the solid residues being the curative agents. William Saunders, a physician at Guy's Hospital. wrote in 1800 that 'it has been asserted by some writers that the fresh drawn water appears brisk and sparkling as if it were strongly impregnated with some gas which is certainly a mistake'.[14]

Despite their lack of effervescence, there have been various attempts to bottle Bath thermal waters. In the eighteenth century, Bath water was one of many varieties of bottled spa water available at the London Water Warehouse, an establishment in London's Temple Bar run by Henry Eyre who also owned a spa at the Wiltshire village of Holt. Eyre sold bottles of Bath water at seven shillings and six pence a dozen; good value when compared with Holt water at ten shillings a dozen and water from Pyrmont in Germany at fourteen shillings. Bottles of Bath water were sold locally for as little as three shillings and six pence a dozen. To ensure the water was genuine, bottles carried a seal imprinted with the arms of the city. This was fairly standard practice for most bottled spa water during the eighteenth century. Pyrmont water, which was effervescent, had an additional anti-fraud device. The cork was wired down, coated with cement and covered with a white leather cap.

Bottled Bath water was never going to be a major success because it lacked effervescence and some of its mineral constituent precipitated as a brown sediment in the bottom of the bottle. It was largely superseded in the nineteenth century by the growing popularity of artificially reconstituted and carbonated mineral waters. Large manufacturers like Schweppes concentrated on reproducing the more popular spa waters of Malvern, Seltzer and Pyrmont. There was also a proliferation of smaller local manufacturers producing carbonated water and other soft drinks. In Bath, Walter Edward Annely set up his Aerated Water Manufactory in Corn Street, which was subsequently taken over by an engineer, Jonathan Burdett Bowler and remained viable until its closure in 1969.[15] The spa water itself was carbonated and bottled for a brief period between the late-nineteenth and early-twentieth century by Fortt and Sons. It was marketed as *Sulis Water*. A local author writing in 1893 described it as crisp and pleasant in flavour, excelling all others 'as an admixture with wine and spirits for the invalid.[16]

As well as bottling mineral water at Bath, there was an attempt to produce artificial mineral water on draught. Around 1810, Dr Charles Hunnings Wilkinson (1763–1850) leased a suite of newly built baths on the south side of the Abbey which were known as the Kingston Baths, where he introduced the Russian method of vapour baths. Wilkinson had moved to Bath from London where he had worked as a surgeon and lecturer at St Bartholomew's hospital. A local writer described him as lively, garrulous, amiable, kindly natured gentleman, dogmatic and outspoken, but overall, very talented.[17] He was certainly something of a polymath with interests in geology, chemistry, electricity, soil analysis, gas lighting, and languages, as well as medicine. His expertise as a linguist did not prevent him from being duped by a woman who posed as a princess from an exotic land abroad. Wilkinson vouched for the authenticity of the woman, known as Princess Caraboo, who was in reality a cobbler's daughter from Devon.

Wilkinson arranged for the erection of a pump room adjoining the Kingston Baths where he offered four different kinds of mineral water on draught: natural Bath water, saline Bath water, Harrogate water and Cheltenham water. The latter two were made by 'conducting the Bath water over artificial strata, arranged of the same materials as constitute that of Harrogate and Cheltenham. It has been satisfactorily demonstrated by the most eminent practitioners and chemists that such water when scientifically prepared excel in virtues the

Charles Hunnings
Wilkinson
*(Wellcome Library,
London)*

produce of the native springs'.[18]

By the nineteenth century, there was an increasing number of doctors, both in Bath and beyond who doubted that the mineral content played any role in the external applications of the waters. They were convinced that the water's effect was purely due to the hydrostatic and temperature effects of immersion and advocated ingenious ways in which the water could be applied to patient's bodies.

3. Therapies on Trial

Some say, the Waters heat them; some, that they make them giddy: others talk of other effects from them: I can only say that I have no effect, which I know of, from drinking the Water but that it quenches my Thirst, which at present is an excellent Quality in it.

Rev. John Penrose 1767

Much of the enthusiasm for new methods of hydrotherapy came from a Bath surgeon, Henry William Freeman (1842–1897), who had visited various European spas. Most of the important spas in continental Europe modernized their facilities in the nineteenth century and could offer patients a vast and varied array of treatments, from sulphur bathing for skin affections to pine-flowing bathing for nerve diseases as well as various douches and sprays which could be combined with massage.

Freeman and his colleagues investigated the physiological effects of warm bathing. They measured changes in patients' heart rates and circulation during treatment. Such physiological studies provide the basis of modern hydrotherapy.[19] However, Freeman was not the first to investigate the physiological effects of water. In 1758, Dr J. N. Stevens observed how a patient's pulse rate increased after various intervals of immersion. He also weighed patients before and after immersion and found their weight had diminished. [20] This led both Stevens and Freeman to reject the old established view that substances can be absorbed through 'pores' in the skin and exert a therapeutic effect on underlying organs. In fact the skin is impermeable to water and other aqueous solutions; there are only a few substances which are directly absorbed through the skin and many of these are extremely toxic. However, Freeman still believed that the chemical constituents of vaporised mineral water could penetrate the skin. There seems to be no evidence to support this.

In 1887 Freeman travelled to America to visit the Saratoga springs where he met the American pioneer of physical medicine, Dr Simon Baruch. Baruch believed spa treatment was effective for acute fevers and tuberculosis as well as chronic disease; his enthusiasm for treating a large range of diseases probably influenced Freeman, who fell into the same trap as his predecessors. His list of diseases in which he considered the thermal waters beneficial is almost as long as those of authors writing two centuries earlier.

Hydrotherapy reached its zenith in the early twentieth century, a time when physicians could choose from a bigger selection of gadgetry than at any other time before or since. Needle baths, douches, hydro-mechanical and hydro-pneumatic contrivances, reclining baths, upright baths, vapour baths, and hydroelectric baths. As methods of administering the waters became more complex, the methods themselves began to adopt more importance than the media.

The twentieth century witnessed a gradual decline in the popularity of the traditional British spa. In 1945, Professor Stanley Davidson predicted that patients visiting spas would 'mainly be suffering from minor complaints and only require a holiday with freedom from worry and work, and a course of massage or baths'.[21] By the 1980s, the traditional treatment centres of every major spa town in the UK were defunct.

The reasons for this decline have been studied in some detail [22] but the dismissal of spa therapy by the orthodox medical profession had primarily resulted from a lack of scientific evidence to support the claims made by the former spa enthusiasts. Until the last two decades, very few randomised and controlled studies had been carried out to establish the worth of spa therapies. Even some of the more recent trials lack rigorous methodology. In 1998, Ernst and Pittler searched several databases for randomised studies on spa treatment and found only three in which two patient cohorts, one with and one without spa treatment, had been compared. In all three, the evidence indicated some additional benefit from spa treatment but they had to conclude that the data were neither sufficient to prove the benefit of spa treatment, nor were they adequate to disprove it.[23]

From the nineteenth century onwards, spas offered an increasing variety of physical treatments. The plumbing became more elaborate and spa water could be delivered at variable temperature and pressure. In addition, electrical treatments began to feature in many spas together with other forms of radiant energy: dry heat, light and radioactivity.

Bathing, or more accurately immersion up to the neck in mineral water, represents the most traditional of all the spa therapies still practised today. A number of studies have been carried out in recent years to examine the physiological effects of prolonged immersion, both in ordinary and mineral water. A study to compare the physiological effects of tap water and Bath water immersion was carried out in Bristol during the 1980s but no difference in effect was noticed, although the Bath water had to be reheated after transporting it twelve miles away from its source![24]

Most studies have been done in tap water maintained between 34 and 35°C, so-called thermo-neutral water, because it has no effect on raising or lowering the body temperature. Hydrotherapists describe four types of bath, according to temperature. Cold baths have a temperature of between 10 and 29°C. They are stimulating and immersion in the coldest temperature is often restricted to a few seconds. In the tepid bath, the temperature can range from 29 to 34°C. This is a comfortable temperature, neither too stimulating or too relaxing. Temperatures above 38°C, the so-called hot bath, promote sweating and are good for pain relief. In Japan, the traditional hot-spring bath is taken at temperatures as high as 47 °C. Prolonged immersion in hot baths is not possible owing to the risk of hyperthermia, three to fifteen minutes being the maximum, depending on temperature. Researchers in Japan demonstrated that, after three minutes immersion in a 47°C bath, the sublingual temperature is transiently increased by about 1.8°C, returning to the baseline level within sixty minutes. Change in clotting activity was apparent after five minutes and was significantly elevated at ten minutes. In contrast, there was no significant change in clotting factors in water at 42 °C.[25] As bathing in excessively hot water could theoretically increase the risk of thrombotic events, it might be best avoided by someone with a recent history of thrombosis.

Immersion in any type of water up to the neck evokes a marked urinary excretion of water and sodium. Urine volume increases more than threefold after one hour of immersion, and peaks during the second hour. There is over a twofold increase in urinary sodium excretion.[26] .

The relaxing effects of warm water bathing have also been studied and it has been suggested that immersion

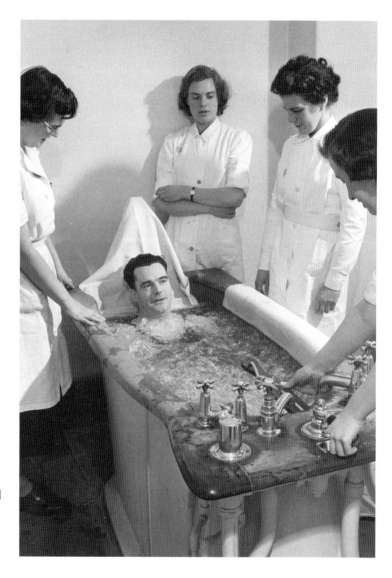

Patient taking a Nauheim effervescent bath under the watchful eyes of four physiotherapists. *(RNHRD collection)*

might cause release of beta-endorphin, the body's opiate-like hormone. One Japanese study suggested a transient rise in beta-endorphin may occur but the water used was much hotter (47 °C) than found in most spas, including Bath, and immersion was limited to a mere three minutes.[27] There is some evidence that relaxation therapies might be immune enhancing. A study on 50 volunteer college students using four different relaxation therapies, including massage, suggests that one component of the immune system, salivary immunoglobulin A, may be enhanced by such methods, though there was no comparative control group.[28]

There is also evidence that repeated immersion can enhance excretion of lead[29] which may explain the success of Bath spa during the seventeenth and eighteenth centuries when a large percentage of the population was suffering from various effects of plumbism, including saturnine gout, the Devonshire colic, the West Indies gripes and even subfertility.

The *effervescent spa bath* became popular in the nineteenth century. Named after the German spa of Bad Nauheim, it featured a standard shaped bathtub filled with naturally effervescent water. If a subterranean source of sparkling water was unavailable, as at Bath, a similar effect could be produced by blowing air or carbon dioxide through a perforated pipe under slats in the bottom of the bath. Modern variations in bath tub design are common and produce a similar effect. Ozone is sometimes used in place of carbon dioxide, but both these gases can be dangerous if the room is not well ventilated. Air is entirely safe and is probably effective through hydro-mechanical stimulation of the body.

The effervescent bath was traditionally used for treating circulatory disorders and in particular raised blood pressure. Patients treated at Bath spa during the twentieth century were immersed at a temperature of about 38°C, and the light percussion effect of the gases or air on the skin caused dilation of the capillaries, so producing a transient fall in blood pressure. Given at a lower temperature (about 32°C), this type of bath was considered useful for treating insomnia, neuralgia and rheumatic disorders. Nauheim baths were installed in the New Royal Baths from around 1880 but have not been used at Bath since the 1960s.

They are still employed in some continental European spas. There has been little comparative research on this method of treatment, but several observational studies have been performed, one of which was carried out in the spa town of Dudince on twenty-eight patients undergoing twenty minutes immersion in baths aerated by carbon dioxide[30]. Measurements were made on biochemical indicators of kidney function, and on heart rate and blood pressure and showed an overall favourable response, but the effects noted did not significantly differ from other studies where immersion took place in un-aerated water

Aromatic herbs and other substances were often added to water to provide the so-called *medicated bath*. Dr Samuel Johnson, who visited Dominicetti's eighteenth century bathing establishment in London where medicated baths were available, was unimpressed: 'Medicated baths can be no better than warm water; their only effect can be that of tepid moisture.' In the past, it was assumed that dissolved substances in water could pass through the skin and exert a therapeutic effect on deep seated ailments. Healthy skin is virtually impermeable to both water and its constituents, though the skin itself can absorb water if dehydrated. Over the years there has been a vogue for adding sulphur, borax, sodium bicarbonate, creosote, coal tar, resorcin, phenol, iodine, salicylic acid, linseed, oat bran and even marsh mallow; the list is endless.

The odour of herbs can certainly make the treatment a more pleasurable experience. Comparative studies are rare. Researchers in Vienna carried out a study to determine whether whirlpool baths with plain water or with water containing pine oil and valerian had a different influence on pain, disturbed sleep or the number of tender points found in patients with fibromyalgia.[31] They performed a randomised, comparative and investigator-blinded study on outpatients with generalised fibromyalgia. Ten baths were given three times a week. The researchers concluded that plain water baths modify pain intensity, whereas medicinal baths improve well-being and sleep. However, the number of patients studied was too small to be statistically significant.

Whirlpool and turbine baths were also developed during the nineteenth century. They relied on a propeller mounted in the base of the bath to agitate the water, causing increased pressure against the skin. This had a mechanical massaging effect on the parts of the body which were immersed and were employed to reduce tissue swelling due to oedema (fluid retention). In the early years of the twentieth century, patients with oedema of the arms following mastectomy were treated in British spas by immersing their swollen limbs in a bath in which the water was agitated either by a turbine or by compressed air, in

Patient undergoing treatment for arm lymphoedema in a turbine bath c1930. *(RNHRD collection)*

much the same way as a jacuzzi operates. Though massage by jets of water may produce some benefit, modern research suggests that a combination of treatments, including compression bandaging and the use of containment garments may be the best way of dealing with lymphoedema of the arms after mastectomy.[32]

Douches and sprays also became more sophisticated during the nineteenth century. Localised application of water to parts of the body probably originated in Roman times. Bathers could place themselves under a water chute, and irrigate an aching limb or painful spine. With the invention of the rubber hosepipe, a stream of water could be readily directed at parts of the body. Complex pieces of plumbing were installed in spas, allowing fine jets and sprays, at various pressures and temperatures, to rain upon the areas requiring treatment.

These methods were popular in the late nineteenth century and early twentieth century when there was a vogue for 'toning' treatments using contrasting temperatures which could be varied at the will of the hydrotherapist. Very little scientific studies have been carried out on these methods and their value is largely anecdotal. Some, like the Aix Douche and the Plombière Douche, were named after European spa towns.

The Plombière Douche was a polite way of referring to a spa water enema. The treatment involves the instillation of warm mineral water into the large bowel through a rubber enema tube. Two wash-outs were traditionally given, varying from one to three pints each, and the patient had to retain the fluid for about ten minutes before it was released from the bowel. (Colonic irrigation, still popular in some spas, is slightly different in that a two way tube is inserted into the rectum and a continuous flow of water is instilled.) Treatment by Plombière douche was usually followed by a reclining bath with an underwater douche spraying relatively hotter water onto the patient's abdomen to allay any colic induced by the former operation! Another douche treatment, the Douche Écossaise, involved hosing the patient with alternate jets of hot and cold water. Despite it's name it was invented by a French doctor, Charles-Humbert Antoine Despine (1777–1852), who was Director of the baths at Aix-les-Bains.[33] Despine had trained in Edinburgh where cold showers were de rigueur for treating certain disorders.

At the other end of the scale, *vapour baths* were a feature of many spas, and have been in use for centuries. The Romans called them *vaporaria* and they were used to induce sweating, as was the dry hot room or *calidarium*. The modern sauna is based on the same principal but is of Finnish or possibly Russian origin. Other ancient cultures also used vapour baths. Mexican Indians devised a primitive vapour bath called a Temezcalli. Some American Indian tribes used vapour baths to treat venereal disease[34]. Most European cities in the Middle Ages could offer sweating baths but many of them quickly degenerated into brothels and served merely as meeting places for libidinous characters. In London, these establishments were known as *stew houses* and became so notorious that they had to be outlawed. Virtually all of them had been closed by the mid-sixteenth century.

Vapour baths were reintroduced into Great Britain towards the end of the eighteenth century when an Indian

Steam Rooms, Thermae Bath Spa; the twenty-first century equivalent of the Roman vaporaria. *(Photo:Dave Saunders, courtesy of Themae Bath Spa)*

doctor called Sake Deen Mahomed started a bathing and massage establishment in Brighton and introduced the term 'shampoo' to the English vocabulary. About the same time the Italian quack called Dominicetti opened his suite of luxury medicated sweating baths in Cheyne Walk.

As well as sweating rooms, more localised treatment was given by enclosing a limb, or sometimes the whole body, in a sweating box or cabinet. At first these were constructed from wood but modern sweating cabinets are fabricated from plastic or metal. One popular type found in European spas is known as a Berthollet cabinet and looks rather like a large dustbin, with tubes projecting from the sides into which the patient can place arms and legs requiring a steaming – a sort of vapourised version of the village stocks.

It is not possible to remain in a steam room for long as the body temperature rises continuously because there is virtually no evaporation from the skin. It is usually followed by a cold plunge or shower.

Other gadgets were available at Bath to promote sweating. With the arrival of mains electricity in the Mineral Water Hospital at the turn of the twentieth century, patients could be baked as well as boiled. The Greville Electric Hot Air Bath was a popular model. It was theoretically possible

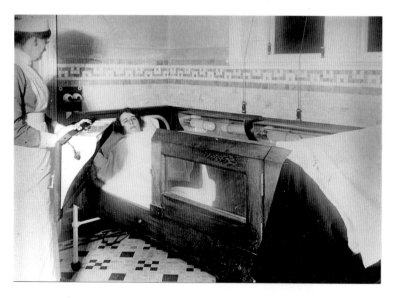

Electric light bath cabinet, early 20th century. The patient was bathed in both radiant heat and light *(Author's collection)*

to treat the whole body, though Dr Preston King recommended that it was probably better to treat only one or two joints at a time 'as exposure of the entire body to heat is naturally somewhat trying.' Temperatures often reached 300°F.[35]

Dr Percy Wilde, medical director of Bath's former Lansdown Hospital, was also keen on heating patients suffering from rheumatic disorders, although he did so from a homeopathic perspective, hypothesising that rheumatism was probably caused by chilling of the body and as the body's defences produced heat by initiating inflammation, elevating the body temperature would help combat the disease process. Wilde described how nurses at the hospital were taught to use an apparatus he invented in which a double skinned metal jacket filled with boiling water could be hinged in place over the patient's bed and left until sweat broke out on the patient's brow[36].

The obsession with heating patients in boxes seems to have started quite early in the history of the Mineral Water Hospital. In 1759, Jerry Peirce presented the hospital with a sweating box.[37] Described in one of the hospital's case books as a sweating chair, its employment as a method of treatment was not taken on lightly. In April 1760, a certain Michael Aberdeen, whose lumbago and shoulder pains failed to improve after the usual course of bathing, 'was ordered to try what effect the sweating chair might have on him' and accordingly was put into it one evening in the presence of a physician and two surgeons. He was incarcerated for one hour, during which time it was reported that he 'sweat pretty much, particularly in his face, in the pit of his stomach and down his back.... he bore the operation very well and was no ways fainty.' Despite some temporary improvement, the patient was ultimately discharged no better.

Both hot air and vapour bathing cause various transient cardiovascular and hormonal changes but vapour bathing is well tolerated by most healthy adults and children. It is safe for healthy women during uncomplicated pregnancies. Some studies have suggested that repeated sweating induced by steam room bathing can help lower blood pressure in patients with hypertension and improve the functioning of the left ventricle in patients with chronic congestive heart failure[38]. It may also improve vascular endothelial function in patients with coronary risk factors.[39] Transient improvements in pulmonary function may provide some relief to patients with asthma and chronic bronchitis, and steam room bathing may also alleviate pain and improve joint mobility in patients with musculo-skeletal disorders.

Patients with eczema sometimes find that sweating increases itching. Steam and hot air bathing, like hot water immersion therapy is best avoided by persons suffering from unstable angina pectoris or within six months of a coronary thrombosis. It is also dangerous for anyone with severe aortic stenosis. It is considered safe for most people with coronary heart disease with stable angina pectoris or who have had a coronary thrombosis more than six months before. Very few acute coronary events or sudden deaths have occurred in hot air baths, but alcohol consumption during sauna bathing increases the risk of hypotension, arrhythmia, and sudden death, and is best avoided.[40]

The use of *fango*, a volcanic mud product traditionally found in the north of Italy near Padua, dates from Roman times and was used in the ancient bath complex at Battaglia. Galen recommended mud taken from the banks of the Nile. Fango has a silky smooth consistency and is grey brown in colour and odourless. Bath had its own version of fango, made from a mixture of mineral water and fuller's earth mined on the hills to the south of the city. This was the basis of mud treatment in the spa from the nineteenth century to the mid-twentieth century onwards. Many European spas use their own variety of mud for treatment and these muds are generically known as *peloids*. Mud from Neydharting (Austria) is reputed to contain natural antibiotics as well as vitamins, minerals and trace elements. Clays are also used. A clay known as Bentonite is available in some health shops for use in the bath at home. Peat has also been used, especially at the former spas of Harrogate and Buxton. At Bath, locally mined fuller's earth was employed until the 1970s.

Fango or other suitable muds, warmed to between 35°C and 40°C and applied to painful osteoarthritic joints, can provide considerable relief. In some centres the fango is

applied at temperatures as high as 46°C. Peloid has a plastic
quality like modelling clay and moulds itself to the contour
of the body. It also retains its heat for a long time. It was
customary to leave it applied for between half an hour to an
hour and then wash it off with a spray of hot mineral water.
This was followed by a deep bath and towelling to promote
sweating and relaxation.

Hydrotherapists taking a break from applying mud packs. *(RNHRD*

A variation of mud treatment, known as parafango
comprised a mixture of dried mud mixed with soft paraffin
which was formed into bars rather like soap. Before use,
the parafango bars had to be melted, heated and then
applied to specific portions of the body. Heat retention was
better than with mud alone and the chief effect on the skin
was to promote increased blood flow, known technically as
hyperaemia.

Much of the 'hands on' treatment given in spas involves massage,
often combined with sprays and douches of mineral water. Several
specialised techniques have been popular since their introduction in
the nineteenth century. The Vichy spray massage is a particular
favourite of traditional spas, the patient lying prone on what looks

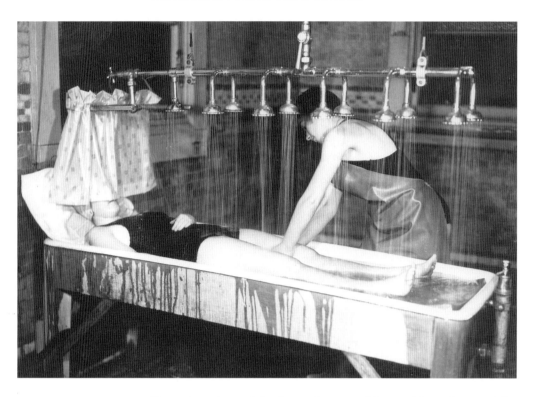

Vichy spray massage
(RNHRD collection)

like a butchers slab draped over with a rubber sheet whilst warm mineral water rains down from a line of douche heads and the masseuse works her way over the dorsal musculature. After the decline of the old Bath spa in the 1970s, British NHS hydrotherapists abandoned the Vichy massage though it continued to be widely used in continental spas. It has been reintroduced in the present Thermae Bath Spa.

Most research on the effects of massage has been carried out using conventional techniques where massage oil rather than jets of mineral water is employed, though studies on the physiological effects of hydro-massage given after vigorous exercise have been made in Poland.[41] There are several different techniques of massage which are commonly used. *Effleurage* involves gentle stroking along the length of a muscle, whereas with *petrissage* pressure is applied across the width of a muscle. Friction describes the sort of deep massage which is applied by circular motions of the thumbs or fingertips. Kneading involves squeezing across the width of a muscle and hacking is characterised by the therapist giving the patient a series of light slaps or even karate chops. Myofacial trigger point massage involves manual stimulation of localised painful zones or nodes in the muscles and is similar to Shiatzu therapy, although the latter is directed to the traditional acupuncture points and meridians. A modification of this technique, done in water, has been given the hybrid name of Watsu (water shiatzu).

Some of the beneficial effects of massage may result from changes in the patient's psychological state. Touch is a fundamental and primitive need for human beings. A research study demonstrated that a small group of patients undergoing hands-on therapy, when compared with a group in which the therapist used only a mechanical vibrating massager, developed greater empathy with their therapist.[42] Massage has been advocated to enhance the well-being of patients needing palliative care in terminal illnesses such as cancer. In a small study, massage was reported by patients undergoing treatment for malignant disease to be universally beneficial, assisting relaxation and reducing physical and emotional symptoms.[43] Another similar study showed benefit in both anxiety and pain control.[44] There

Right: Watsu therapist at work in the Old Royal Bath, Thermae Bath Spa (*Photo: Rob Slade, courtesy of Themae Bath Spa*)

Below: Masseuse using aromatic oils at Thermae Bath Spa (*photo: Rob Slade, courtesy of Themae Bath Spa*)

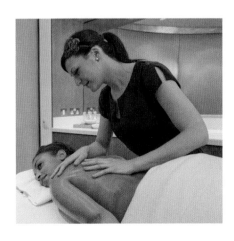

has been a suggestion that massage and spa therapy might cause this feeling of well being by increasing the serum levels of beta-endorphin but there is no evidence that this happens.[45] Curiously, Thermae Bath Spa currently advises people with cancer to avoid massage, and indeed any of the treatments on offer.

More controlled and randomised studies on the effects of massage are needed, especially as some practitioners make claims about the clinical effects of their treatments without any attempt to explain the basis upon which these claims are made. Some therapists rely on personal experience as a source of knowledge and then disseminate this as generalised wisdom. A lot of literature about massage contains inconsistencies such as different properties being given to the same oil and this casts doubt on the reliability of the knowledge base of such therapies.[46] Observational studies have sometimes failed to include a control group. One recent study demonstrated how a fifteen minute massage reduced the subjects blood pressure,[47] but there was no control group.

Mineral waters were not only used externally, and drinking was recommended as an adjunct to bathing. Many spa waters taste rather revolting and Bath is no exception. Charles Dickens described it as having the taste of warm flat irons. Traditionally spa waters were imbibed hot and fresh from the spring head but, if chilled, Bath spa water becomes very palatable. Some spas bottle their mineral waters and some, like Vichy and Evian water, have become internationally known. Bath's mineral water does not travel well, and bottling has never enjoyed much commercial success. As discussed earlier, it has been tried at various times during the spa's history. Of the traditional English spas, Buxton and Malvern water have enjoyed the greatest commercial success, although the latter ceased production in 2010.

Little research has been carried out on the effects of drinking the Bath waters, apart from the small study in the early twentieth century by Peskett and Raiment who concluded that there was no detectable difference between the physiological effects of Bath mineral water and plain tap water. However, the amounts of water imbibed by patients in the eighteenth and nineteenth centuries was considerable and often continued for several weeks and there have been no studies on the effects of prolonged mineral water drinking. A recent study determined the mineral content of several commercially available bottled waters. The variation in concentration was great. Among the bottled waters reviewed, magnesium content ranged from 0 to 126 mg per litre, sodium from 0 to 1200 mg per litre, and the calcium content from 0 to 546 mg per litre.[48] Theoretically, magnesium may reduce the frequency of sudden death, sodium contributes to the occurrence of hypertension, and calcium may help prevent osteoporosis, so the authors concluded that the ideal bottled water would be one rich in magnesium and calcium and have a low sodium content. There appear to be no studies to confirm this.

A questionnaire survey was carried out in 1998 on visitors to the Italian spa at Montecatini. The researchers concluded that drinking the spa's mineral water therapy caused a 'striking' short and medium-term improvement in their patients' clinical symptoms, reducing their annual consumption of gastrointestinal drugs and their number of working days missed. Like so many questionnaire surveys, this study lacked the rigorous method required to render reliable data.[49]

Though hydrotherapy has been the physical treatment *par excellence* at Bath, both in the spa and the hospital, it has not been the only non-pharmacological therapy to be used there. At the time the hospital opened in 1742, a Lay Clerk of Worcester Cathedral called Richard Lovett (1692–1780) was busy electrifying his fellow citizens. Lovett had no medical qualification but he realised the potential of using electricity therapeutically and his publication, *Subtil Medium*, which appeared in 1756, influenced others to adopt the novelty. Lovett claimed that electricity could bring relief for all violent pains, particularly toothache. It was also useful in wasted muscles and hysterical disorders where there was coldness of the feet. Unfortunately for Bath, it failed to cure rheumatism.

Perhaps it was the ethereal quality of electricity which rendered it attractive to ministers of religion. Whilst Lovett was pottering around Worcester cathedral dispensing shocks to his congregation, the Methodist John Wesley was busy in London offering to electrify his followers. Wesley's book on medical electricity appeared in 1759. Similar publications had already appeared on the continent. A German, Christian Kratzenstein (1723–1795) had, in 1745, advocated electricity in the treatment of paralytics.[50] It may have been one of these publications which influenced Dr Edward Harington to try the effects on some of the paralysed patients in the Bath General Hospital before his death in 1757, though he apparently had little success. Dr Charleton, writing in 1774, was also unconvinced of its worth[51] but in 1788 a London optical glass and scientific instrument maker called Edward Nairne (1726–1806) presented the hospital with 'an electrical machine and apparatus thereto belonging,'[52] though there is no information about its use. Nairne had patented several electrical machines, including an electrostatic generator for medicinal use. Several hospitals in London were using electrical machines at this time but Nairne's machine may have lain idle in the Bath Hospital since the hospital physicians had stated that many of their patients who received benefit from the Bath waters 'have, before their admission, had various experiments of electricity made upon them to no purpose.'[53]

The machines in use at this time were generators of static electricity, produced by friction between a revolving glass globe or cylinder and a small cushion of leather, a rod of amber, sulphur or sealing wax. The electric charge was collected in a Leiden jar. The patient had to stand on a glass legged platform so that his body was insulated from the ground. Treatment was effected by electrifying the patient and drawing sparks from the affected part, or administering shocks.

Jane Austen, in one of her letters to her sister, describes how her brother 'tried electricity' whilst at Bath in 1799[54] and a certain Mr G., a patient of Joseph Hume Spry 'went through a course of bathing and pumping, together with electricity for a considerable time without much benefit.'[55] Static electricity continued to be used into the twentieth century and the stream of sparks bombarding the skin provided pain-relief by so-called counter irritation. In 1905,

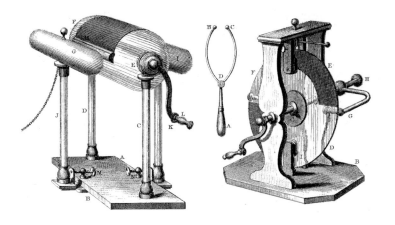

Two electrostatic generators and a hand-held electrode. The model on the left is a Nairne generator.

the hospital hired a Whimshurst machine.[56] Dr George Kersley recalled[57] how, in the 1930s when he was first appointed as a consultant to the hospital, patients were placed near such a machine from which they were subjected to a sort of miniature thunderstorm to get their muscles twitching vigorously. This was thought to break down adhesions which were considered to be the cause of fibrositis. Fortunately for today's patients, both fibrositis and Whimshurst's machines are out of fashion.

Other innovations in the realm of electro-therapeutics came with the invention of the battery in 1799. The application of current from a battery was known as galvanism. It was first adopted by fringe practitioners who brought it into disrepute trying to resuscitate hanged criminals and drowned men. The hospital purchased its first galvanic machine in 1821 for five pounds,[58] which was replaced in 1850 by a more powerful model.[59]

The vogue for the electric bath seems to have first become popular at this time, and a local druggist, Mr John Palmer Tylee, published his *Practical Observations on Galvanism, Electricity, and Electromagnetism as employed in the cure of disease with remarks on the advantages of their application through the medium of baths.*[60] His bath was part of an electrical circuit in which the patient sat, presumably somewhat nervously, despite the reassurance from Tylee that it did not produce 'violent shocks'. He recommended this method for treating 'muscular atrophy after continued fevers, gouty articular deposits, lead poisoning, and certain forms of paralysis'.[61]

Patients reported miraculous improvements after one session, perhaps because they were too scared of having to endure further electrification and electric baths soon became available in the New Royal Baths. As well as a druggist and electrotherapist, Tylee was one of the first practitioners in Bath to administer an anaesthetic.[62]

In the latter part of the nineteenth century a French physician, Jacques-Arsène D'Arsonval, had examined the physiological effects of electrical stimulation at various frequencies up to 10,000 cycles per seconds, producing increasingly strong muscular contractions. (Above this frequency, muscles stop contracting and there is no longer any sensory stimulation.) Meanwhile in America, Nikola Tesla suggested that physicians should experiment with the heating effects of radio waves. Both discoveries led to the development of electrotherapeutic gadgets which were

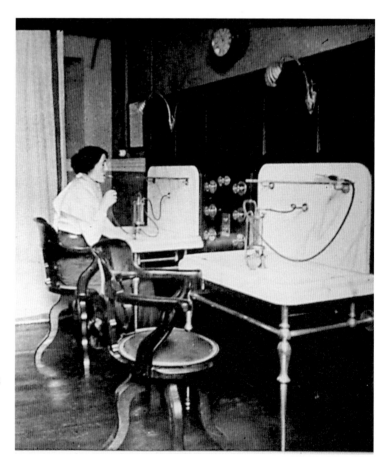

Patient inhaling radon in the Radium Inhalatorium.
(Bath and Wessex Medical History Group)

regularly used by physiotherapists on patients in the spa until the latter end of the twentieth century. The hospital opened a dedicated Electrical Department in 1913 and the New Royal Baths had an electrical room, complete with electric couch.

In 2000, the Dutch Health Council published a report on the efficacy of electrotherapy for musculoskeletal disorders. The assessment was based on a meta-analysis of a large number randomized clinical trials. Almost no conclusive clinically relevant effects were found.with the possible exception of electrotherapy used to treat osteoarthritis of the hip or knee.[63]

Even in the twentieth century, efforts continued to find an alternative explanation for the thermal water's curative effects. The discovery that some spa waters are radioactive rekindled ideas that they contained a labile curative principle and for a time radiation was believed to explain their beneficial effect. Radiation certainly had dramatic biological consequences which was more than could be said for the chemical components of the water. Such was the enthusiasm for radioactivity that a Bath baker offered 'radium bread' for sale [64]. However, the amount of radioactivity in the Bath springs is well below a hazardous level.

In a brochure, proudly entitled *The Radium Waters of Bath* which the city corporation published in the early 1920s , health seekers were exhorted to expose themselves to the highest levels of natural radiation possible by entering the *Radium Inhalatorium* - a room in the new Queen's Bath fitted out with apparatus for delivering radon evolved at the source of the spring.

As the twentieth century moved on and Bath embraced the age of nuclear energy, the pendulum swung strongly away from radioactive cures and the *Radium Inhalatorium* was demolished and its site became a gift shop for spa mementoes. In the 1960s, spa brochures failed to mention radioactivity even though the concentrations of radium and radon are not sufficient to pose any risk. There has even been some recent research suggesting that radioactive spa waters might exert a beneficial effect. A group of physicians at the German spa of Bad Elster observed that patients with rheumatoid arthritis who bathed in mildly radioactive water seemed to have a longer remission of pain and stiffness than those who bathed in ordinary water though no definite conclusions can be reached because the numbers studied were small. [65]

Curiosity about thermal springs has generated many theories about their supposedly curative nature. At various times, these have embraced virtually every facet of the water, from metaphysical considerations invoking spiritual and supernatural properties to more rational ideas like temperature, hydrostatic effect, mineral content, dissolved gases, radioactivity, the presence of elements in the form of free ions, electrical conductivity, the colloidal condition of the substances present, and the presence of rare metals in minute quantity. There were also those who thought there was nothing medically special about the water at all.

Until the last third of the twentieth century, survival of the spa had largely depended on obfuscation of arguments and bias of observation from those whose livelihood depended on the spa's reputation. Any attempt to diminish its success was vigorously countered. It is rather reminiscent of the plot of Ibsen's play, *An Enemy of the People*. In the play, Dr Stockman, whose brother is mayor of a spa town, discovers that the waters are contaminated by dangerous microbes. At first the doctor is seen as a saviour whose scientific observation will be able to avert a public health disaster but when the reality of the spa's closure and costly redevelopment dawns upon the town's worthies, they turn against him, branding him an enemy of the people and hound him and his family out of town.

Most sceptics were outsiders who had no vested interest in the survival of the spa. In 1769 William Cullen, the great Edinburgh clinician commented that those patients who could not afford to go to Bath need not despair as he had known cases where assiduous use of the common hot bath for a similar space of time had been equally serviceable. A decade later, William Heberden wrote 'It is by no means clear to me that the external use of the water is more beneficial than that of equally warm common tap water, or at all different from it'.[66] In a similar vein, William Saunders, a much respected London physician, wrote in 1800 that externally applied, the Bath Waters differed in no respect from common water heated to the same temperature since any active ingredients were too minute to exercise a stimulant effect on the skin[67].

The established Bath practitioners maintained there was a difference. William Falconer observed that sudden sweats and faintness which often came on after using a bath of common water of a considerable degree of heat rarely came on after use of the Bath waters; but the bathers were observed to be more alert and vigorous and to have a better appetite on the days of bathing than during the intervals. Yet in another passage Falconer demolishes his own side of the argument by stating that 'we should also consider that the patients are able to bear without faintness a greater degree of heat in an open bath than in one that is confined in a room'. Much of the supposed invigorating quality of Bath waters may have been determined by the fact that the main public baths were open to the elements.

Though the general knowledge of chemistry and physics continued to accumulate during the nineteenth century, physicians in Bath lost interest in analysing the waters after C. H. Wilkinson's publication in 1811.[68] There are several reasons for this. Doctors had failed to turn up any component with significant therapeutic effect. This in turn led to a growing scepticism amongst the local medical fraternity. More accurate chemical analyses had proved the traditional dogma totally fallacious. The water did not after all contain free sulphur and the amount of iron was far smaller than had been postulated by the earlier authors. Furthermore, until 1770, the established physicians in Bath were almost without exception graduates of Oxford or Cambridge. After this date the proportion of Oxbridge graduates fell dramatically and the Scottish Universities, particularly Edinburgh, were chiefly represented. These doctors were less accepting of traditional dogma and were trained to diagnose from observation.

Moreover, the physicians who were protagonists of Bath water treatment in the latter part of the eighteenth and early nineteenth century, Falconer, Gibbes and Wilkinson, were chemists. The main antagonist, physician Caleb Parry, was an experimental biologist. Parry was the most successful physician of his time in Bath and his opinions were no doubt held in high esteem by his professional colleagues. He was also acquainted with William Heberden. It is significant that the decline in publications on the water coincides with a definite upsurge in medical publications dealing with pathology and experimental physiology, and with the establishment of a scientific community in Bath in which medical practitioners played a significant part. As a result the spa sank into such decline that a medical writer in 1841 commented that his professional brethren in Bath had nearly forgotten the waters were in existence[69]. When the tide turned after a further twenty years, Bath medical men were eager to put spa therapy on a much more scientific footing.

However good for business, the reputation that the Bath thermal water had as a panacea did them great disservice in the eyes of the scientifically trained medical community of the nineteenth century. There was growing awareness that if Bath was to make a comeback as a spa, the treatment would need to be based on sound physiological principles and the theories of the old empirical era swept away. Even in 1800, Sir George Smith Gibbes warned that the Bath waters had been extolled for too many virtues which had caused them to be undervalued; a patient investigation of their real powers would have showed their true worth.

Scepticism over the water's efficacy which had begun in the eighteenth century gathered momentum in the twentieth. The comparative trial of the effects of drinking mineral water and tap water carried out by Drs Geoffrey Peskett and Percy Raiment in 1925 failed to show any difference in their effects on human physiology.[70] For the next generation of doctors, the comparative trial became the yardstick of evaluating therapeutic efficacy, though the methodology of such trials has raised criticism. Many of the newer pharmaceutical preparations passed through these trials with spectacular results when compared with placebos, eclipsing any improvements which could be made by more traditional treatments which were increasingly viewed as placebos themselves.

There was also a shift in attitude of doctors at the Mineral Water Hospital. As Dr George Kersley commented in 1969, the focus of interest had turned away from the

Portrait of Tobias Smollett. The novelist was a vociferous critic of the spa. *(Author's collection)*

concept of the spa to the study and relief of disease. This was reflected in the medical board's decision in 1935 to rename the hospital, omitting any mention of mineral water in its new title, the Royal National Hospital for Rheumatic Diseases. The doctors became known as rheumatologists and no longer specialised as 'medical hydrologists'. Their new remit was the investigation and treatment of rheumatic diseases. When it came to treatment, the Bath waters were no match for new drugs like corticosteroids though, as the rheumatologists themselves pointed out, the waters, unlike steroids, never harmed anyone. Unfortunately, they were to be proved wrong.

Some degree of danger had always attended bathing. Apart from a number of recorded drownings, including two doctor's children, hygiene left much to be desired. In the eighteenth century, John Wood commented that the walls of the baths were 'encrusted with dirt and nastiness' and the slips at the corners where the bathers descended into the water were like 'cells for the dead'. The water was changed once a day to protect bathers from Bath Mantle, a condition characterised by a rash of pimples on those affected. This may have been what is

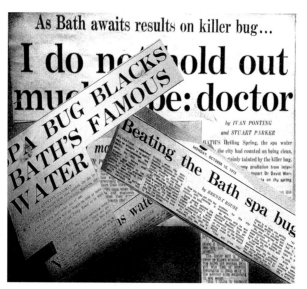

now termed swimming pool rash, caused by the bacterium Pseudomonas. Smollett, who practised briefly in Bath as a surgeon-apothecary, was particularly concerned about the risk of infection.

> *Two days ago I went into the King's Bath by the advice of our friend Charleton in order to clear the strainer of the skin for the benefit of free perspiration; and the first object that saluted my eye was a child, full of scrofulous ulcers, carried in the arms of one of the guides under the very noses of the bathers. I was so shocked at the sight that I retired with immediate disgust and indignation. Suppose the matter of those ulcers, floating in the water; comes into contact with my skin when the pores are all open, I would ask you what must be the consequence? Good heavens! The very thought makes my blood run cold! We know not what sores may be running into the waters while we are bathing and what sort of matter we may thus imbibe; the King's Evil, the scurvy, the cancer and the pox; and no doubt the heat will render the virus the more volatile and penetrating.* [71]

Risk of contamination also worried the surgeon, Archibald Cleland. In 1739 he wrote to the Mayor suggesting that serious accidents might arise when people with 'foul and catching diseases' mixed with others in the water. Cleland's opinions were largely ignored and the General Hospital authorities do not seem to have been unduly worried until 1852 when a patient complained that she, along with the majority of patients in her ward, had suffered from *the itch*. The infestation was attributed in part to the admission of a filthy patient onto the ward but also to 'indiscriminate use of bathing dresses and the foul state of the baths from leprous patients.'

Spa water bathing is certainly not without hazard: as well as contagious diseases like dysentery and poliomyelitis spreading from one person to another, the water has frequently been contaminated by the excrement of animals and birds. In 1956, the Medical Officer of Health for the city recommended that patients at the hospital should not be given the mineral water to drink as it had been found to be contaminated with an avian strain of bacteria, though this information was never made public for fear of adverse repercussions on spa treatment which was then still a going concern. It was not until 1978, when a young girl who had been bathing in one of the spa swimming baths died of a rare form of meningitis, that the public were informed that bathing was attended by serious risk. The water was contaminated by an amoeba called *Naegleria Fowleri* which had the potential to penetrate the lining of the bathers' brains if they happened to sniff spa water up their noses. On the advice of the public health department, all facilities using spa water were closed although the Spa Treatment Centre, as opposed to the leisure facilities, had closed two years before anyone knew anything about amoebae; closed on the advice of doctors who could see no reason to preserve a therapeutic anachronism.

Thirty years on, the water is free of infection and the new spa at Bath is thriving, but for primarily the pursuit of leisure rather than a means of treating disease. Spas in continental Europe, where there has only been a partial decline in their popularity, are moving away from the panacean attitudes which have prevailed in the past. The large variety of disorders which used to be treated at spas has been abandoned in favour of a relatively small number of medical conditions. There are still some dubious claims made and the word 'detoxifying' seems to be a popular concept in spa literature although nobody seems to agree what this is. However, most people who have visited a spa would agree that the experience is very enjoyable.

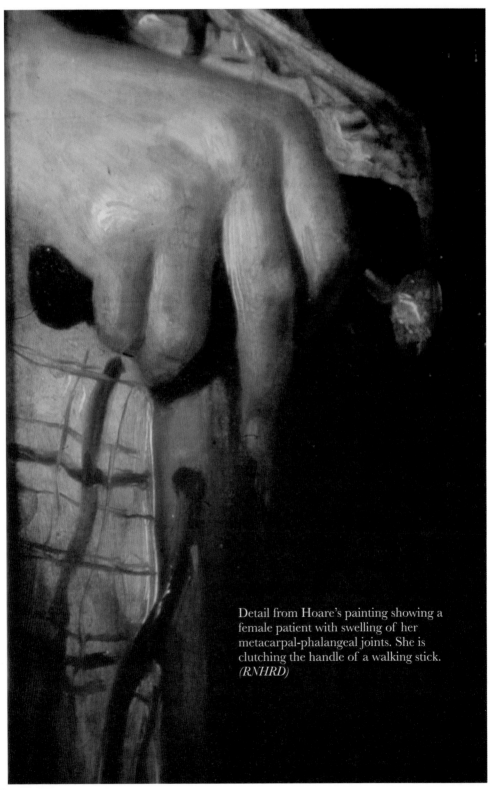

Detail from Hoare's painting showing a
female patient with swelling of her
metacarpal-phalangeal joints. She is
clutching the handle of a walking stick.
(RNHRD)

4. Aches, Pains and Rheumatism

Of all disorders of the body, rheumatic diseases are probably most closely associated with Bath. The term *rheumatism* is rarely used now but was in common medical parlance until the mid-twentieth century. Doctors used the terms *acute* and *chronic* rheumatism. The former was a sequel of infection by streptococci, the bacteria which can cause tonsillitis and scarlet fever. Acute rheumatism is now called rheumatic fever.

Chronic rheumatism referred to recurrent muscular pains, a symptom which may be caused by a large number of pathological processes. It was sometimes also applied to joint pain. The word *rheumatism* derives from the ancient word *rheum,* meaning flow or discharge of fluid. The word is still used in France to mean a nasal discharge or cold. Rheum and humour have etymological connections and rheumatic pains were traditionally ascribed to accumulation of phlegm in the affected organs. The idea of flowing humours also led to the notion of gout, a term derived from the Latin gutta, from which we get our word gutter and the French their words for drain, drop and taste. The swollen hot and painful joint of the gout sufferer was thought to be caused by drops of phlegm or, according to later theory, corrosive fluid wreaking havoc and corruption to its interior. The cold wet climate of the British Isles was thought to aggravate these rheumatic conditions.

Peirce's descriptions of patients visiting Bath in the seventeenth century were selected to demonstrate the efficacy of bathing in as wide a range of disorders as possible and thus promote the spa as a suitable place for treatment A few failures and deaths are included, though one suspects with some reluctance as Peirce remarks that 'the physician that doth not cure shall be sure to have the reputation of killing the patient that dies, be the disease or the patient never so much curable'. Nearly half his book is devoted to cases involving painful or weak limbs and swollen joints, what we would today term musculo-skeletal and locomotor disorders.

Sometimes the cause of the patient's problem is obvious, like an injury after falling from a horse or a war wound as was the case of Colonel Sackville Tufton whose hand had been shattered during a naval battle against the Dutch fleet. His muscles and tendons had been lacerated and bones broken and he required several surgical operations to remove the bone fragments, performed without the benefit of anaesthesia. At length, he arrived in Bath in the spring of 1674. His hand, or what remained of it, was useless and still extremely painful. Peirce notes that the pain was quickly relieved after bathing and pumping water on to the hand. He returned to Bath over several years for further treatment

Portrait of Col. Sackville Tufton (1644–1721) by Antonio Verrio. Tufton's left hand is obscured, but his right hand, the supposed site of injury, is prominently displayed and shows little sign of trauma.
(*Courtesy of Abbott Hall Art Gallery, Kendal*)

COL. THE HON^BLE SACKVILLE TUFTON,
BORN JUNE 11.ᵗʰ1644. OBᵗ MARCH 18.ᵗʰ1721.
ÆTAT 75.   VERIO. PINXᵗ

and 'at length even the forefinger and thumb became in some measure useful, though a whole joint of the latter is quite lost and the former remains very crooked - the whole hand is as serviceable to him as a maimed forefinger and thumb will permit'. [72]

Restoring adequate function following damage to muscles and joints is one of the main purposes of present day physiotherapy. Evidently the same aims applied to many people who visited Bath three centuries ago and who would have otherwise spent their lives hampered by contracted limbs and stiffened muscles. Many of these were casualties of the wars which raged in Europe, including the English civil war. In 1652, Parliament paid £1000 to send one hundred and eighty-six injured soldiers to the baths for treatment, and another two hundred and twenty were sent the following year.[73]

Unlike today, injuries, even when quite minor, resulted in serious infection. Peirce's book is full of examples of abscesses developing in injured joints and around muscles, resulting in severe disability or death. Mortality from infection was appalling and the long, slow and uncomfortable journeys to Bath which many patients undertook weakened them to the point where they were near to death as they passed through the city gates. Such was the state of Sir Thomas Mauleverer (1643–1687) who had injured his hip after falling from his horse whilst hunting. He arrived in Bath in June 1687 'very weak and ill as well as lame; swell'd from head to foot, especially on the lame side. He was stomachless [sic], nauseated everything they offer'd him to eat and what was forced down was usually returned again by vomit.' Despite being lowered several times into the King's Bath, he died a month after arrival. An autopsy showed he had formed a huge abscess around the upper end of his femur.[74] (He probably died from septicaemia.)

No amount of spa therapy could have cured such a dangerous condition. Others were more fortunate after injuries and seemed to benefit from a month or two of daily bathing.

Therapeutic bathing involved immersion up to the neck, but swimming was discouraged. Particular parts of the body could be treated by directing jets of water at them. In Elizabethan times, this form of treatment must have been a rather hit or miss procedure because buckets filled with water and with holes in their bases were held over the patient. Samuel Pepys described in his diary how he was bucketed and was obliged to wear a crownless large-brimmed hat to protect his face.

By the middle of the seventeenth century, the corporation installed hand pumps in and on the side of the baths. Physicians had to specify the number of pump strokes their patient was to receive, sometimes as many as several thousand. The poor fellow operating the pump must often have been in need of treatment himself after such exertion. By forcing the mineral water against the affected part, physicians imagined it was more likely to pass through the pores of the skin and act on the underlying tissues. There is no evidence that this happens.

Disabled patients were aided into the bath by attendants who also offered to work the pumps. The bath attendants also helped to stretch patients' contracted limbs whilst they were in the water and raise and lower them on specially constructed harnesses. In this respect, the treatment on offer in the seventeenth century was little different from the way patients are handled by today's hydrotherapists.

Locomotor disorders of one sort or another make up the bulk of cases collected in seventeenth century literature. In the early eighteenth century, Dr John Quinton published another collection[75] but the least biased and largest series of historical cases can be found in the bound book of transcribed referral letters which belonged to the Bath General Hospital. Often the letters gave detailed descriptions of the patient's illness which allowed the hospital's physicians a means of judging whether the case was suitable for Bath water treatment. The volume contains notes of over 1500 cases admitted between 1752 and 1758 and, together with the collection of cases already mentioned and cases published by Drs Oliver, Charleton and Falconer during the eighteenth century, it provides a wealth of historical clinical data about patients and their diseases during the heyday of the spa.

As with the seventeenth century publications, many disorders in the hospital letters book relate to musculo-skeletal conditions. Some of these are labelled as chronic rheumatism or sciatica (the terms osteoarthritis and rheumatoid arthritis were not in general usage until the nineteenth century). In an historical context, sciatica is an ill-defined term. It was sometimes applied to pain arising from a diseased hip-joint or femur and sometimes to pain due to irritation of the sciatic nerve. (In its modern sense, the word *sciatica* applies only to the latter.)

As well as providing clinical details, the letters book gives some idea of the social circumstances leading to the patient's admission to the hospital. For example, in 1754 an excise officer called Walter Flea who lived at Calne in Wiltshire paid a visit to a local soap maker. The business was carried out in a particularly damp and cold cellar and Mr Flea was obliged to stand there for some time, watching the man at work. It was an inspection the excise man was later to regret. During the next three years, his health took a downward turn. Severe pains and swelling began to afflict his limbs, flying from one joint to another. His legs became grossly swollen with fluid. Sometimes the pains abated, leaving him in a weakened state, only to return a few weeks later with equal vehemence. Whenever the pains were bad, he became feverish. By 1757, he had become a cripple, both feet distorted by severe contractures.

There was one feature of this man's disease on which all his medical advisers agreed: the illness had been caused by the damp chilling atmosphere in the soap maker's basement. Cold and damp were considered to be the principal causes of rheumatism, both acute and chronic. Doctors referring patients for treatment in Georgian times frequently allude to damp and cold precipitating the illness: cases like that of William Eason, a sawyer from Dorset whose rheumatism was supposed to have developed after 'taking a violent cold by sawing in rough, cold, turbulent weather,' or John Bowen from Monmouthshire whose weak back was 'occasioned by sitting on the ground when hot.'[76]

Dr William Falconer suggested that agricultural workers, miners, washerwomen and anyone employed in moist surroundings ran a high risk of contracting rheumatism because of their exposure to cold and damp.[77] He was so convinced of this dictum that he suggested the majority of rheumatic cases admitted to the hospital could have avoided their illness if only they had been more sensible in their habits.

A necessitous person may indeed suffer an attack of rheumatism from want of sufficient clothing, scarcity of fuel, by being obliged to labour in cold wet seasons or in moist ground, or in other employments exposed to the vicissitudes of heat and cold. But neither poverty, nor any duty a man owes to his employers, obliges him when heated by exercise to pull off what clothes he has and expose himself, when at rest, to a current of air, to plunge into cold water, to drink enormous draughts of cold liquors, or to lie down and even sleep on moist ground, and often in the autumnal season; all of which, and many similar incidences of rashness, are so common that I am convinced more than two thirds of the rheumatic and hip cases (admitted) might be traced to such causes.[78]

The idea that damp was the cause of rheumatism was still being debated in 1928 when a large assembly of physicians attended the Mineral Water Hospital for an international conference on rheumatic diseases. By this time, the nosology of rheumatic disease had become more logically based as much on its pathology as on its symptoms though, even today, the pathology of many rheumatological conditions remains enigmatic and provokes considerable controversy amongst doctors.

Of all the rheumatic diseases, none has been associated more with damp than rheumatic fever, (also known as acute rheumatism). Once exceedingly common, its incidence began to decline in Britain after the first world war and is now so rare in this country that most doctors entering practice since 1970 have never seen a case unless they have worked in the Third World. The earliest case description from Bath dates from 1665 when Dr Robert Peirce related how a young female patient of his had developed rheumatism as a result of lying on damp ground after an attack of scarlet fever.

Now that rheumatic fever has virtually vanished from English society, nobody gives much credence to damp any more. People still pull off their clothes and expose themselves to currents of air in a manner considered so reckless by Dr Falconer two centuries ago but they do not necessarily develop disease. Perhaps exposure to the inclemencies of the British climate posed more threat in the days when a large section of the population was malnourished and living in squalor. If nothing else was achieved by this theory, it was largely responsible for the improvement in the standard of housing during the nineteenth century and Dr Falconer, in preaching prevention, must take some of the credit for this.

Peirce's observation that his patient developed rheumatism after scarlet fever highlighted a relationship which was not fully appreciated for another two centuries when the world became aware of bacteriology. Physicians began to consider that rheumatic fever might be an infectious disease. At first it was thought that almost any micro-organism might provoke the disease if it attacked a suitable person, but from 1900 onwards, researchers increasingly believed the streptococcus to be the germ responsible. Ultimately, the exact nature of its pathology was worked out and revealed by

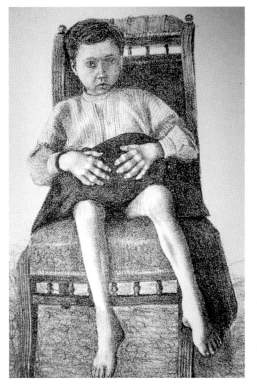

Child patient admitted to the Mineral Water Hospital in 1890 exhibiting swelling of the small joints of his hands. *(RNHRD collection)*

65

three doctors from the Rockefeller Institute who addressed an international conference on rheumatology at Bath in 1928. They presented a theory that the disease was due to an immune reaction associated with infection by streptococci, the germs which cause tonsillitis and scarlet fever.[79] Since that time, the study of immune reactions and the part they play in other rheumatic diseases has become one of the most important avenues of research in rheumatology.

Pain in the hip and leg was another so called rheumatic disorder treated at the hospital in the early days. 'If you enquire of these patients where their pain is situated,' wrote Dr Charleton in 1774, 'some will point to the groin, some to the great trochanter of the thigh bone and others to the junction of the *os innominatum* with the *os sacrum* (sacroiliac joint). Temporary pains are also often spoke of in the knee, the shin and ankle of the diseased limb. Many of these patients can bear to have the head of the thigh bone moved around in its socket without the least uneasiness. If the buttocks be examined, that of the diseased side will be found lower than that of the well side. The disorder is sometimes brought on by colds which have been caught by sitting on damp ground. Sometimes it is the consequence of external injuries – falls, leaping down from high places, etc, and very often no assignable reason can be given for it.'[80]

Between 1761 and 1773, there were 296 patients admitted to the hospital with this sort of history.[81] They were diagnosed as suffering from sciatica or hip-gout, and were more generally classified as *hip cases*. Many were cured but some developed swellings in their thighs, became feverish and then died. Unless the swellings spontaneously burst as an abscess, one of the surgeons would have to apply his lancet to encourage the flow of 'laudable pus'. Either way, abscesses nearly always heralded the patient's demise; 'the flux of the matter is usually more than his strength can support and he sinks under the discharge.'

Pains in the hip and leg still cause diagnostic confusion though the 'flux of matter,' a consequence of bone infection or osteomyelitis, is seldom seen today. The condition was frequently encountered by physicians in Bath, even in the days before the hospital was established. 'It is not so easily palliated or cured,' wrote Dr Peirce in the seventeenth century, 'because affluent sharp humours lie deeper upon the bone and thick and large muscles intervene, and therefore no outward application can so easily reach it as in a less fleshy part. The matter, being long imprisoned there, corrupts more, grows more acrimonious and becomes at length corrosive.... which in the process of time penetrates the bone itself.'

During the seventeenth century, the cause of death was sometimes established from a post-mortem examination. These autopsies were usually carried out by surgeons with physicians and relatives in attendance. Dr Peirce mentions at least three in his book, including the case of Sir Thomas Mauleverer.

Oliver and Charleton were happy to treat sciatica as long as their patients were young and healthy. The affected buttock was usually cupped before a course of bathing. Cupping entailed applying the mouth of a glass hemisphere to the skin overlying the painful area after the air inside the glass had been heated by a piece of burning tow. As the air cooled the skin would be sucked into the cupping glass by the partial vacuum created. Irritation of the skin in this way may have helped by reducing pain sensation. In the same way, lime poultices were sometimes used to irritate the skin[82] or Spanish fly used to raise blisters.

The number of post-mortem examinations done in Bath hospitals before the mid-nineteenth century is unknown but, despite the absence of records, such examinations were certainly performed. The Bath United Hospital, built in 1826, had a mortuary in its basement which communicated with an adjacent room for postmortem examinations (right) and there may have been a similar arrangement for the Mineral Water Hospital. It was usual for autopsies in hospitals to be carried out by one of the surgeons, with the medical staff in attendance. An autopsy was carried out on a patient called John Stillman, a Trowbridge man, who had been referred to the Mineral Water Hospital for treatment of severe headache and vomiting. He died two months after his admission. Ten fluid ounces of liquor was extracted from his brain. The first inquest on a patient at the Mineral Water Hospital took place in 1847. A verdict of death from apoplexy was returned.

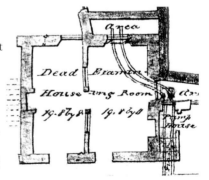

Counter-irritation, as this type of therapy became known, remained the favourite method for treating sciatica well into the twentieth century. Only the irritants have changed. Spanish fly, or cantharides as it is more correctly termed, was once ordered by the General Hospital's pharmacy in large quantities but was ultimately banned after it achieved notoriety because of its dangerous misuse as an aphrodisiac. Towards the end of the nineteenth century acupuncture was the principal method in use. Three, four, five or even more needles, about two and a half inches long, were plunged into the patient's thigh along the course of the sciatic nerve. Hugh Lane, who treated patients at the Mineral Water Hospital with this method, wrote:

Patients, after two or three experiences of acupuncture needles, have begged for a repetition of their use with the result that they have at length derived that immunity from pain which they day after day craved for. [83]

Fifty years on, needles had given way to cautery and Dr George Kersley found that a line of small burns on the skin over the sciatic nerve produced effective relief. In the last few years, acupuncture has become popular again and some physiotherapists at the hospital are using the technique.

Some cases of sciatica were the result of compression of nerve roots in the back. In the eighteenth century, tuberculosis often affected the vertebrae causing collapse of the spine, so-called Pott's caries. There were many such cases admitted, though the cure rate was certainly not spectacular. Often the physicians simply played for time. Matthew Ball, a twenty-eight-year-old Gloucestershire man, was 'seized with a defluxion on the lungs which continued two or three years with great weakness.' He went on to develop a considerable distortion of his spine and he lost so much weight that 'a consumption was thought inevitable.' Five months before his admission, he began to experience numbness and weakness in his hips, thighs and legs. He was in the General Hospital for four hundred and four days before being discharged in 1755, much better. He was lucky. Others died, or were discharged as *improper* because they developed a prolonged high temperature known as a hectic fever, often a symptom of TB or osteomyelitis.

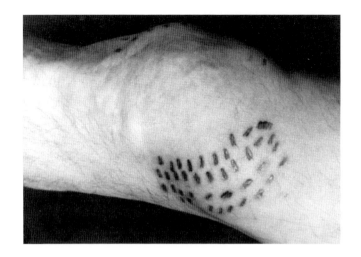

Knee showing multiple burns from an electro-cautery instrument. Cautery was originally done with an intrument similar to a branding iron but in the 1950s when this photograph was taken, doctors used electrocautery *(RNHRD collection)*

With the decline of spinal osteomyelitis, the commonest cause of nerve root compression is now the slipped disc. In 1934 two American surgeons, William J. Mixter and Joseph Barr, discovered that intervertebral discs could rupture and cause sciatica by pressing on the spinal nerve roots. They demonstrated how it was possible to relieve the compression by an operation known as laminectomy. Within months of their discovery, two patients with sciatica at the Mineral Water Hospital were the first to receive this revolutionary surgical treatment in Great Britain, performed by Bath surgeon Charles Kindersley.[84]

The operation was carried out at the Bath and Wessex Orthopaedic Hospital. Apart from a temporary operating room fitted out during the last war, the Mineral Water Hospital had no proper operating theatre until 1965; indeed operative surgery was a notably absent feature of the hospital's early days. In the first century and a half, only one major operation is recorded and this was such a significant event that the Governors had to give their permission. In November 1807, the house apothecary reported that Philip Harding, a patient in the hospital, was 'in such a state as to require an amputation of the leg above the knee."

There may have been more operations carried out, but no other is mentioned in the Minute Books. According to the rules agreed by the 1739 Act of Parliament, 'When any surgeon has any considerable operation to perform he shall acquaint the physicians and surgeons of the House when it is to be performed that they may be present if they please.'

Minor surgery seems to have been carried out as much by the resident apothecaries as the surgeons themselves. Certainly bleeding and cupping, traditionally the province of surgeons in hospital, was carried out by the eighteenth century apothecaries.

The surgical procedures carried out in the hospital at this time were of a minor nature. They included:

> Bleeding
> Excision of tophi (uric acid deposits)
> Cupping
> Catheterisation
> Blistering
> Issues
> Clysters (Medicated enemas)
> Plastering
> Cauterisation

Such procedures were probably carried out in a room set aside for the purpose. John Wood's proposed plan shows a surgeons' room on the ground floor, as well as the apothecary's and physicians' rooms. In 1750, the hospital Minutes record that a dozen cupping glasses and a lamp were required in the surgery. In 1829, the surgeons' room and adjacent matron's room were knocked into one to form a new Committee Room. The matron's apartments were moved to the west wing and, on a plan of the hospital drawn in 1857, all trace of a surgeons' room has vanished. This probably indicates that there had been so few considerable operations performed that the surgery was no longer thought necessary. Furthermore, a proper operating theatre, complete with tiered auditorium,[85] became available to Bath surgeons in 1826 at the newly erected United Hospital in Beau Street and any patients requiring major operations could theoretically be admitted there. After 1844, surgeons and physicians were able to hold honorary appointments at both hospitals which facilitated transfer of surgical patients between the two institutions. Even today, major orthopaedic procedures are transferred to the Royal United Hospital at Combe Park.

The greatest challenge for early surgeons was the treatment of patients with contracted limbs. When a limb becomes immovable from injury, paralysis, or from joint disease, the affected muscles slowly contract to pull the joints into a permanently flexed position. The early hospital records frequently refer to patients with contractures and their treatment in the baths. Straightening was accomplished by immersing the patients and stretching their contorted limbs in the hot water. Progress was painstakingly slow and, even with regular treatment, it often took a year to effect any significant change. Mechanical contrivances were also used: in 1795, the Governors bought a Lobb's machine, a sort of traction apparatus for stretching contracted limbs.

Simple stretching was both slow and uncomfortable. The discomfort was even greater when the problem was due to arthritic joints, but the advent of anaesthesia in the mid-nineteenth century opened the door to a much quicker and effective means of releasing contracted limbs, though the first mention of anaesthesia in the hospital records does not appear until 1885. Four years later, Thomas Pagan Lowe, a surgeon at the hospital, published his experiences in treating arthritis by forcible movements.[86] Publications by the honorary surgeons of this time demonstrate their interest in orthopaedics but they were essentially generalists. Charles Kindersley, appointed in 1932, was the first surgeon to be officially designated orthopaedic.[87] Kindersley pioneered the use of plaster splints to immobilise acutely inflamed joints and to treat contractures. Despite his specialist interest, he was still a general surgeon. Only since the second world war have the consultant surgeons at the hospital confined themselves entirely to orthopaedic practice. During this time, surgery has come to play an increasingly important part in the treatment of arthritis and the replacement of diseased joints by artificial ones has revolutionised the outlook for crippled patients who would otherwise be consigned to wheelchairs.

The technique has now reached such a stage of perfection that over ninety percent of patients whose hip joints are replaced can expect to be relieved of their pain and stiffness. The hope amongst rheumatologists now is that the understanding of the disease processes responsible for arthritis will increase to the point where it will soon be possible to prevent and control rheumatic diseases, so obviating the need for the large volume of repair work with which the present day surgeons are burdened. The Bath

Patient with
contracted legs being
supported around the
torso by another man.
Detail from a painting
by Humphrey Repton.
1784.
(Victoria Art Gallery,
Bath and North East
Somerset Council)

Mineral Water Hospital has played an increasing role in
unravelling the mysteries of those disease processes, a role
which began three quarters of a century ago.

Despite Bath's magnetic attraction for arthritic patients,
no descriptions of rheumatoid arthritis were published by
any of the hospital's physicians until 1888[88]. This is all the
more remarkable considering the large number of so-called
rheumatic cases admitted to the hospital over this period.
One possibility strongly debated amongst rheumatologists,
is that this particular form of arthritis was rare in the
eighteenth century and was only recognised later because its
incidence suddenly rose in the nineteenth century. This
theory is born out by analysing the hospitals case referrals
for 1752–56. Out of a series of seven hundred and eight-

five cases admitted, joint symptoms are only specifically mentioned in fifty-six of the referral letters, and of these only twenty-five refer to swelling in more than one joint. Very few descriptions in the series match the clinical picture of what we now call rheumatoid arthritis, though there are some which suggest the diagnosis. Forty-year-old Martha Smith from Chedworth in Gloucestershire, who was admitted in July 1755, was described by her own doctor thus:

> *Always of tender habit of body, she has had several children, one about three months ago. She hath been much afflicted with rheumatic pains these eighteen months past. Her hands, feet and legs swelled and the tendons of her hands and feet are contracted and the joints have become large. In the last few months she has become quite lame and helpless in her hands and feet.*[89]

Another case, a young woman from Devon, was described as 'labouring under great weakness and relaxation of her wrists and ankles' and with weakness in her dorsal spine. Her doctor mentioned nodes in the joints of her fingers and swellings and pains in her knees and diagnosed her condition as 'scorbutic rheumatism.'[90] Were these cases examples of rheumatoid arthritis?

William Falconer had made some attempt to describe a series of eight hundred and ninety-five cases of rheumatic disease admitted between 1785 and 1793.[91] He regarded acute and chronic rheumatism as different stages of the same disease, distinguished from gout in as much as the joint pain was bearable and the joints themselves were never red. Falconer regarded rheumatism primarily as a muscular disorder though he accepted that the joints were commonly affected, even to the point of becoming ankylosed (fixed). Very few cases of gout are recorded in Falconer's series though he does mention a small number of patients suffering from 'gout conjoined with rheumatism.' True gout was unlikely to occur in hospital patients of this time simply because their poverty precluded the sort of meat-rich diet necessary for the disease to manifest itself.

Unfortunately there is no way of deciding what Falconer meant by 'gout conjoined with rheumatism,' though the term rheumatic gout was later used by some doctors to describe rheumatoid arthritis. The nomenclature of the various forms of arthritis remained in a state of total confusion for most of the nineteenth century. It was not until 1876 that Sir Alfred Garrod (1819–1907), professor of medicine at University College Hospital, London, first used the term *Rheumatoid Arthritis* to describe the distinctive form of joint disease that we recognise by this term today. Was this the same disease as that identified by the French physician Landré Beauvais in 1800, and subsequently by William Heberden, John Haygarth and several others over the next half century? Nobody really knows. Haygarth may have been describing a variation of osteoarthritis rather than rheumatoid disease. Even when we have reasonably detailed descriptions of patients' cases, as we do with the case of Martha Smith mentioned above, retrospective diagnosis is pure guesswork. Before the mid-nineteenth century, medical terminology was beset by ambiguity and confusion and even after Garrod coined the term rheumatoid arthritis, the confusion remained: John Kent Spender (c1830–1916), who was the first Bath doctor to publish an accurate description of the disease in 1888,[92] at first referred to it as osteoarthritis, a term now reserved for an entirely different kind of joint disease.

Spender's description of rheumatoid arthritis is easily recognised as the disease which doctors still deal with at the hospital in modern times, though it seems to have been a more aggressive illness in Spender's time with a profound anaemia and often with curious pigmented spots appearing on the skin. These brown patches were subsequently known as Spender's Spots. They are rarely seen now.

It is perhaps strange, in view of the opportunities for research offered by the large concentration of rheumatic cases under one roof, that the hospital contributed so little to the advancing knowledge of chronic rheumatic disease in the first two thirds of the nineteenth century. Spender himself acknowledged these opportunities when, on his retirement, he wrote: 'Nowhere else in the kingdom could I have prosecuted those researches which helped to prove the clinical identity of rheumatoid arthritis.'[93]

Within a decade of Spender's retirement, a spate of observations on patients at the hospital with rheumatoid arthritis appeared in print. In 1890, Hugh Lane and Charles Griffiths, reviewing hospital cases, published the first clear differentiation of rheumatoid arthritis, chronic rheumatic arthritis and osteoarthritis. Hugh, whose brother Sir William Arbuthnot Lane achieved eminence as an orthopaedic surgeon by using plates and screws to treat fractures, was appointed honorary surgeon to the Mineral Water Hospital in 1891.[94]

The calibre of the resident medical officer, or resident apothecary as he was formerly known, may have been the decisive factor in determining what, if any, research was done during the early history of the hospital. Evidence from the minute book suggests that much of the data collected for William Falconer's publication in 1795 was the result of meticulous recording by William Balne Farnell, who was then the long-suffering and dedicated house apothecary. A half-century later, James Tunstall analysed records he kept while he was resident apothecary so that, at the end of his term of office, he was able to publish a book about the sort of diseases which were most benefitted by spa treatment.[95] By the final decade of the nineteenth century, the quality of applicants for the resident medical officer's post had improved to such an extent that the Governors were able to appoint candidates in possession of higher medical degrees.

Rheumatological research was now in full flow and the resident medical officers contributed a large part to it. One of these was a young doctor called Arthur Stanley Wohlman (d1944) who graduated with honours from Guy's Hospital in 1891 and obtained his MD degree in the following year.

Perhaps the most promising development in the work of the hospital since the last war has been the expansion of laboratory investigation into the nature and treatment of rheumatoid disease. In 1975, the Bath Institute of Rheumatic Diseases (BIRD) was established by the hospital and Bath University to provide research laboratories which are housed in a building opposite the hospital known as the Bath Arthritis Research Centre.[96] But rheumatological research had not always been viewed enthusiastically in Bath. For many years, the concept of a research laboratory was alien to the hospital's board of Governors.

Dr Wohlman was eager to develop his interest in the fashionable scientific pursuit of bacteriology. Year by year

Dr A.S. Wohlman was engaged in rheumatological research at Bath before emigrating to New Zealand where he became Government Balneologist. His book, 'The Hot Springs of New Zealand' was published in 1914 under a pseudonym, Arthur Herbert.

From an illustration in the *New Zealand Illustrated Magazine, 1 Oct 1904, p4*

since the mid-nineteenth century, diseases hitherto attributed to obscure physiological imbalances, genetic defects or adverse climates were proving to be caused by micro-organisms. In 1882, the famous German bacteriologist, Robert Koch, had demonstrated bacilli in tuberculous joints and a year later others found gonococci in cases of gonorrhoeal arthritis. Might not rheumatoid arthritis, the disease which Spender claimed was 'merely one sign of a profound nerve disorder,' also be caused by bacteria? Dr Wohlman, together with a newly appointed honorary physician called Gilbert Bannatyne were convinced that it was.

> *For some time, Dr Wohlman and I, looking at the clinical nature of the disease and at the course of the symptoms, had practically made up our minds that the disease was microbic in character. The absence of post-mortem material complicated the case, but we decided to obtain what specimens we could from the living subjects. In this way, we were led to aspirate affected joints and examine the fluids so obtained microscopically and by cultivation. On staining we were readily successful in determining a micro-organism was present, but at the same time were troubled with the difficulty of staining it properly and getting it free of precipitate. Our first culture attempts utterly failed, but by degrees we got fair results. Having arrived at this stage and feeling the utter inadequacy of our apparatus, I felt compelled to call to our assistance more skilled aid.[97]*

They enlisted the help of Dr Frank Blaxall (1867–1930), a bacteriologist at the Westminster hospital[98], who agreed to examine more samples of synovial fluid collected from the joints of patients at Bath. With some difficulty, Blaxall confirmed the presence of small bacteria in the specimens sent to him. [99] Even though Bannatyne and his colleagues believed they had discovered the causative agents of rheumatoid arthritis, others remained sceptical. They were probably nothing more than contaminants.

What is most remarkable about this project is that it ever happened at all. Facilities for this kind of research were woefully lacking in the hospital. The only scientific equipment which the hospital possessed at this time was a microscope and apparatus for analysing urine. Pathological research was regarded as having no place in the hospital's constitution and the only permissible studies were on the efficacy of the Bath mineral water. Medical staff who wished to observe other aspects of the cases under their care were expected to satisfy their intellectual curiosity in their own homes at their own expense. Pathological research was certainly not something to be financed out of the charitable funds of the hospital.

It took an outsider to change this attitude. In 1905, a professor of pathology at Cambridge University with the somewhat curious name of Dr Thomas Strangeways Pigg Strangeways (1866–1927), had set up a small clinical research hospital in Cambridge to study patients with rheumatoid arthritis. One of Dr Strangeways' proteges was a young medical graduate called James Lindsay who in 1906 was elected resident medical officer to the Bath Mineral Water Hospital. Dr Strangeways was eager to investigate a possible link between rheumatoid arthritis and the presence of infection elsewhere in the body. He encouraged Dr Lindsay to make such a study of patients at Bath. One hundred and seventy two hospital cases were analysed and Lindsay's findings were published by Dr Strangeways in 1907. At first sight it looked as though vaginal infections and gum disease had some link with rheumatoid disease because Lindsay found well over a third of his female cases were suffering from these complaints.[100]

In October 1908, Dr Strangeways wrote to the Governors of the Mineral Water Hospital seeking their permission to send a research pathologist to carry out further bacteriological studies on patients. The pathologist would require a laboratory but if the hospital could provide a room with gas and water on tap, Cambridge University would fit it up with the necessary apparatus.[101] The Committee, happy that the project would not involve the hospital in any expense, agreed to provide a room next to the mortuary.[102] The research pathologist, Dr Emily Morris, moved in just before Christmas and became the first woman doctor to work in the hospital. She stayed four and a half months, collecting numerous vaginal swabs from patients with rheumatoid disease. She probably had a hard time for she concluded in her report that 'the investigation was unsatisfactory because the vagina only was examined, the circumstances under which it was carried out did not permit an examination of the cervix."[103] It must have been virtually impossible to perform satisfactory vaginal examinations in the gloom of the gas-lit night wards.

These early investigations tended to support the notion that rheumatoid arthritis was linked to foci of infection elsewhere in the patient's body and led doctors to adopt an obsessional preoccupation with tooth extraction and the surgical removal of other offending organs, such as tonsils and gall bladders, where occult infections might be smouldering. The theory of an infectious aetiology was also responsible for maintaining the time-honoured ritual for flushing out the bowel, performed in the nicest possible way at Bath with mineral water enemata, so that the bacterial flora suspected of inducing the patient's arthritis could be safely swilled away. A dental chair and a Plombière Douche became prominent amongst the hospital's therapeutic armamentaria, and the Governors felt it expedient in 1906 to appoint an honorary dental surgeon to the hospital. Just how many teeth were drawn in the hope of curing patients' joint disease must, like the teeth themselves, remain buried in obscurity. (Recently, rheumatoid arthritis has again been linked to dental infection, but mediated via an immune reaction to a type of bacteria found in diseased gums.)[104]

After Dr Strangeways and his colleagues had completed their programme of research, they offered the apparatus in the laboratory to the hospital for twenty-five pounds. The Committee refused to buy it and the medical staff had to raise the money amongst themselves. The hospital's microscope was so antiquated that Dr Bannatyne lent his own instrument. So the Governors rather reluctantly took up the cause of laboratory medicine and invited Dr Lindsay to become the hospital's first honorary pathologist[105]. Despite the medical staff's enthusiasm, the Committee were resolute that no money could be granted from hospital funds towards the new laboratory.[106]

By 1913, the Committee's attitude to pathology had undergone a dramatic turn about. When Dr Bannatyne retired and removed his microscope from the laboratory, the Committee agreed unhesitatingly to buy a replacement.

The hospital management seem to have woken up to the realisation that they were in the twentieth century. Pressure was put on the three honorary physicians, now rather long in the tooth, to resign and make way for new blood. They were replaced by Frederick Thomson, Richard Llewellyn, Rupert Waterhouse and Gilbert King Martyn. James Lindsay was also made an honorary physician, thereby relinquishing his post as pathologist. Where he had been content to work in a tiny box-room laboratory, his replacement required a laboratory with more room. Two new pathologists were appointed: John Munro, a doctor of science, and George Almond, a medical graduate who was later killed in action on the Western Front in the closing months of the first world war. Together, the new medical team stood poised to forge the hospital into a nationally and internationally recognised centre for rheumatology.

The large number of cases of gout, rheumatism and allied conditions which pass yearly through the wards offer a wide field for collective clinical observation and research, and carefully compiled statistics with regard to etiology, cause and effect of treatment in a large number of these cases should prove distinct value towards elucidating the many obscure points which still exist in connection with these diseases.[107]

The new laboratory was fitted out in a house in the hospital's garden, previously used as a nurses home (and the site of an inn known as the Sedan Chair). Annexed to the laboratory was a medical museum for pathological specimens relating to bone and joints, and a small medical library. The latter was started by Sir William Osler who was invited to Bath to open the new facilities in June 1914 and donated ten pounds, a not inconsiderable sum in those days, for the purchase of books. By the end of the year, the library contained over five hundred volumes[108]. Within a few months of the new laboratory's opening, the wards of the hospital were full of wounded soldiers returning in droves from the front lines; the 'requirements' of a country at war precluded any further ideas of expanding research until the decade ended.

By 1920, with the last of the soldiers discharged, the hospital had returned to its more usual role as a treatment centre for rheumatic diseases. The medical staff resumed their aspirations to create a rheumatological centre of excellence with national and international reputation.

The first postgraduate course in rheumatology to be held at the hospital (1920) attracted a large number of physicians from all over Britain and provided much needed publicity about the work of the hospital amongst the medical profession. The mood amongst the medical staff was one of optimism and a desire for expansion. The closure of the Blue Coat School meant a sizeable premises next to the hospital became vacant and the medical staff encouraged the Committee to make an offer for its purchase to provide accommodation for research work and surgical facilities. A research fund was started and the Medical Research Council approached to help finance the project.

In June 1921, the hospital bought the old school building for twelve hundred pounds but there was insufficient money in the Research Fund to do anything, so the building was temporarily let to a firm of estate agents in the hope that the finances would soon improve. The Committee was hoping to raise money by admitting patients of 'moderate means' and charging them fees, but this was such a dire departure from the original intentions of the hospital's founders that the charity commissioners continually stalled on their approval of the scheme. The Medical Research Council were also stalling and after three years of procrastination on all sides, the hospital management were obliged to return the Blue Coat School to the market where it was sold to the city council.

Despite the disappointment over the Blue Coat School, research continued at the hospital during these years. In 1913, the hospital's pathologist, Dr John M.H. Munro, was paid four hundred pounds a year to pursue 'a certain series of pathological, bacteriological and biochemical investigations' and a local printer and publisher, Cedric Chivers, offered to pay the salary of a biochemical assistant. Some of the money was used to finance the study by Peskett and Raiment, the two Oxford biochemists, into the biochemical effects of drinking Bath mineral water. Four male beds were lent to admit non-rheumatic patients on which to carry out the investigations.

Munro's research focused on the effects of hydrotherapy on normal individuals, and biochemical and metabolic investigation of various types of arthritis. He also studied the way in which antibodies react with bacteria involving a substance called *complement*. Munro and his colleagues hoped to fund their research with a grant from the Medical Research Council but this august metropolitan body was unmoved by the enthusiasm of provincial researchers. For one thing, the laboratory facilities were Dickensian. The laboratory building was adjacent to the local newspaper's print shop and vibration from the presses was so bad that it was impossible for the pathologists to accurately weigh anything on their balances. Until 1927, there was neither electric power nor electric light in the building. Progress in rheumatological research could hardly be expected in such an environment, but the medical staff were still quite pleased with their achievements. In 1921, Dr F. G. Thompson wrote:

During the last eight years investigations have been carried out in the Pathological Department of the hospital in an attempt to elucidate some of the problems connected with the pathology of arthritis. These investigations afford strong evidence of the presence of infective processes in a large proportion of patients, though in many cases the precise location and determination of the infective agent may be quite impossible, and remain a matter of inference. The chronic infective processes associated with arthritis are found with extreme frequency among the community in general, and only a certain proportion of those affected develop joint change. In other words, certain persons appear to be more susceptible to arthritis than others under the same conditions. The personal factors which predispose the individual to the onset of arthritis are at present an unknown quantity, and biochemical investigations into this aspect of the question are urgently needed.[109]

Dr Thompson's words were prophetic. It was indeed to be a long and difficult business but, seventy years later, the technology of biochemical investigation had advanced sufficiently to prove the link between the patient's genetic constitution and their susceptibility to arthritis. Today's research scientists can work out the molecular structure of patient's genes in order to discover which particular bits are associated with rheumatic diseases.

Throughout the thirties, appeals for money to fund research and rebuild the hospital went hand in hand. Though most members of the hospital management committee now appreciated the need to improve the facilities for research, not all were convinced. Dr Preston King, one of the old guard of physicians who stepped down from office after the Great War, complained that the hospital was being diverted from its proper use as a mineral water treatment centre and was fast becoming 'an institution for the study of disease.' Pathological research and biochemical work carried out in the laboratory was, in Preston King's view, both costly and unnecessary.[110] The younger physicians, like Vincent Coates (1889–1934), an internationally respected rheumatologist who was tragically killed in a train accident, inevitably took the opposite view and were concerned that the hospital was already losing ground in its efforts to keep up to date.

In 1934, a large donation was offered by one of the Governors, Sidney Robinson, to fund the full-time research worker for whom the medical staff had been canvassing for so long. Robinson's daughter, Violet Prince, suffered from rheumatoid arthritis and both she and her father were major benefactors of the hospital in the years between the two wars. The Medical Research Council were also adopting a more positive approach to providing research funds, having been encouraged by news of the Governors' proposals to rebuild the hospital on a new site. With sufficient funds now at their disposal, they appointed a Jewish refugee, Dr Walter Levinthal (1886–1963), as a full-time research pathologist. Dr Levinthal had been assistant professor of pathology in Berlin before fleeing Nazi Germany. During his sojourn at the hospital, he became interested in the possibility that rheumatoid arthritis was caused by an abnormal response of the body's immune system. A series of observations on blood and joint fluid led him to conclude that persons subject to rheumatic diseases had fewer antibodies in their blood but their tissues were much more immunologically sensitive.[111] This rather simplistic theory marks the commencement of the hospital's continuing interest in the immunological basis of rheumatic disease, a line of research which is still being investigated in its laboratories at the Bath Institute of Rheumatic Diseases.

Part of Levinthal's work involved animal experimentation. Despite assurances that no vivisection was going on, voluminous correspondence from concerned readers began to appear in the local press. Amid protests, the work continued, carried out in a refitted laboratory in the Sedan Chair building, and by 1938 at the International Rheumatology Congress taking place in the city, the hospital was acknowledged as the most progressive rheumatology unit in the world despite its building being declared by Lord Horder as 'only fit for rats to live in.'[112] Plans were put in place to raise funds for a new hospital with two hundred and fifty beds to be built on a site near the river. With a substantial sum collected, the Queen was invited to lay the foundation stone on 11th September 1939. Eight days before the ceremony was due to take place, Britain found herself at war and the building scheme had to be postponed. Money for medical research dried up and Dr Levinthal was laid off in 1941. The ultimate blow literally came when the laboratory was wrecked by a bomb blast which destroyed much of the hospital's west wing during one of the Nazi Baedecker raids on Bath. With half the medical staff called up for military duties, research came to all but a standstill.

It was to be largely the enthusiasm and dedication of one man that resurrected it after the war was over. George Durant Kersley was born at Bath in 1906, the same year that James Lindsay, then a young resident medical officer at the hospital, was busy conducting his research on arthritis. Unbeknown to either of them at the time, they would eventually practice medicine together. Years later, when Kersley was himself a young doctor at St Bartholomew's Hospital, he received an invitation from Dr Lindsay to join his practice at Bath. Dr Kersley had already become particularly interested in rheumatology and Lindsay's offer presented a chance not only to work in his native town but also become honorary physician to the foremost rheumatology centre in the country, a post to which he was elected in 1935 and held for a further thirty eight years.

After the war, the damaged Sedan Chair building was refurbished and named the Sidney Robinson Laboratory after its main benefactor. Dr Kersley was particularly keen to revitalise rheumatological research at the hospital and, in 1947, he facilitated the creation of a research fellowship under the auspices of Bristol University and funded by the remainder of the Robinson money. The first fellow was a Mauritian doctor called Max Desmarais whom Dr Kersley discovered in a middle-eastern convalescent depot during the war and who arrived at the hospital in 1945 to become its first medical registrar. In 1948, fifty of the hospital beds were appropriated for clinical research to form a new Rheumatism Research Unit.

Useful research papers began to flow from the unit and over the years, there has been a prodigious output of publications from the various doctors, including many from abroad, who have worked there. Working conditions were still very primitive in the first few years and Dr Kersley recalls how he sometimes had to carry on his medical research at home in his own kitchen. During the early postwar years, the hospital led the field in rheumatological research. Pioneer work on the microscopic appearance of tissues affected by rheumatoid disease was carried out by the hospital's pathologist, Hubert Gibson. Research in those days was not for the faint hearted. George Kersley had to inject some of his own muscles with irritants and then cut bits of them out so that Dr Gibson could examine them beneath his microscope to compare the appearance of diseased and healthy tissue.

Since that time, the laboratory accommodation has steadily improved. After 1965, when the war damage was finally repaired, the extra storey added to the West Wing provided much-needed new accommodation for research. The considerable cost of equipping the new Princess Marina Research Laboratory was assisted in part by a grant from the Medical Research Council, but largely from the public appeal in the early sixties which raised twenty thousand pounds in two years. In subsequent years, the main financial support has come from the Arthritis and Rheumatism Council. The laboratory included an infrared thermal imaging unit, directed by Francis Ring, which gained international recognition for its work on the temperature measurement of diseased tissues. Professor

Site for a new RNHRD photographed in 1939. The building of the hospital was interupted by the war and abandoned afterwards. The Bath Technical College was later developed on the site. *(Author's collection)*

Ring was able to develop this technique to accurately measure the degree of inflammation in a joint, providing researchers with an objective way of assessing the effects of anti-arthritic medications. Most of the anti-inflammatory drugs in use today were assessed in clinical trials at the hospital using this method. In the early days of corticosteroids, when they were first hailed as a miracle cure for painful joints, the hospital's infrared imaging equipment was used to measure the effectiveness of all the new and developing forms of steroids, working in collaboration with the Bath University Department of Pharmacology. Pioneering work on arthroscopy, the technique of looking inside the knee joint, was also done in the hospital's laboratory.

In 1975, the hospital's regular pathological service was transferred to a central laboratory at Combe Park which served all the hospitals in the Bath district. The former laboratory at the Mineral Water Hospital was given over to immunological research. With the opening of the Bath Arthritis Research Centre opposite the hospital in 1981, more laboratory space became available and most of the microscopic work is now performed in this building. In 1985, Bath University set up a Postgraduate School of Medicine and Dr Peter Maddison was appointed first Glaxo Wellcome Professor of Bone and Joint Medicine and Dean of the Faculty. The faculty has since closed.[113]

The investigations carried out into the pathology of bone and joint disease, together with clinical enquiries, immunological, genetic and epidemiological studies, and research into the technology of relieving physical handicap, has made the hospital a leading centre for research into the nature and relief of crippling disease[114]. It continues to attract postgraduate students and in the last half century many of the world's leading specialists in musculoskeletal medicine have trained in its wards and out patient clinics.

Does the spa still have any role in today's approach to rheumatic disease? Bath became renowned for the treatment of rheumatoid arthritis in the late nineteenth and twentieth centuries. Although there have been a number of research studies demonstrating beneficial effects of spa therapies on the outcome of both rheumatoid and osteoarthritis, hard evidence is still lacking. A systematic review published in the Cochrane Database in 2000 examined ten trials with over six hundred patients, most of which reported positive findings. It concluded: 'One cannot ignore the positive findings reported in most trials. However the scientific evidence is weak because of the poor methodological quality, the absence of an adequate statistical analysis, and the absence, for the patient, of most essential outcome measures (pain, quality of life), Therefore, the noted 'positive findings' should be viewed with caution. Because of the methodological flaws a confident answer about the efficacy of balneotherapy in treating rheumatoid arthritis cannot be provided at this time.[115] All that can be said is that large numbers of patients suffering from this condition who were treated at the Bath spa treatment centre before its closure in 1975 gave anecdotal testimony to its efficacy.

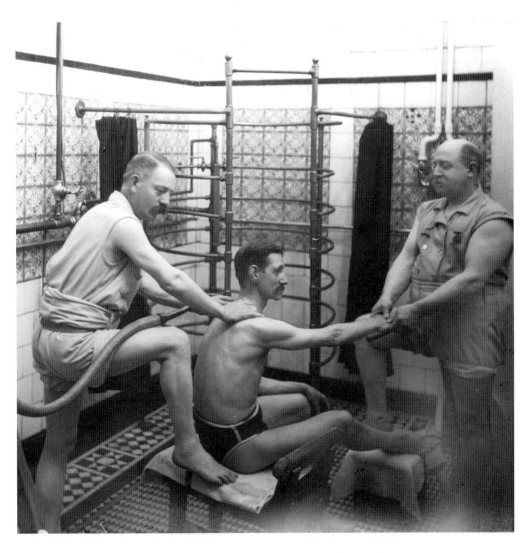

Therapists mobilising a shoulder using the Aix douche. Note the needle
bath in the background.
(RNHRD collection)

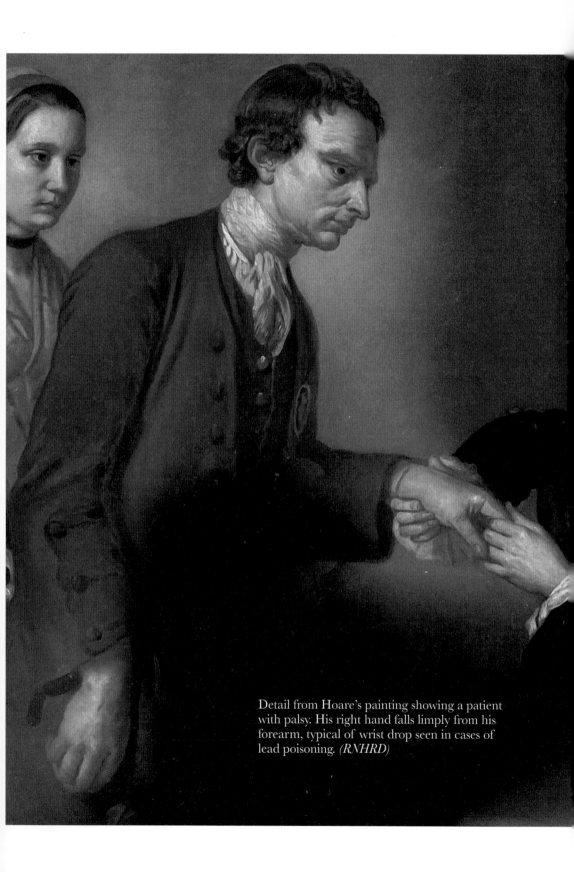

Detail from Hoare's painting showing a patient with palsy. His right hand falls limply from his forearm, typical of wrist drop seen in cases of lead poisoning. *(RNHRD)*

5. The Palsy

Rheumatic disorders were not the only illnesses associated with Bath. Any disease that was thought to benefit from mineral water therapy was considered appropriate for treatment. Palsies, skin disease, gynaecological disorders and disease of the digestive tract were given as much consideration as rheumatism and, in the eighteenth century, these non-rheumatic diseases comprise the bulk of the cases recorded in the Bath General Hospital records. It was only during the nineteenth century that rheumatic diseases began to form the majority of admissions.

Despite the wealth of data in early publications and hospital records, imprecise usage of diagnostic terms makes it difficult to perform any retrospective analysis of the incidence or types of diseases as we now define them. There is however one condition that stands out in all these series of case descriptions, both from the seventeenth and eighteenth century sources. Robert Peirce described it as the 'Palsie after the cholick' and wrote how he had found 'no one distemper more frequent among my adversaria,' nor had any single condition had 'so many eminent recoveries of persons thus disabled after assistance of the Bath and the Bath waters.'

Sir John Gell, a sixty-eight-year-old retired Parliamentary army officer who was a patient of Peirce, regularly visited Bath in the seventeenth century to take the waters in the hope that this would ward off the palsy. He liked to have his bare head pumped with mineral water, starting with eight hundred strokes on the first day, and gradually increasing to a daily maximum of two thousand strokes. His early symptoms were a feeling of dullness and stupor in the head and clumsiness and creeping feeling in the arms or legs.

89

These symptoms always vanished after a few weeks in the Queen's Bath and his pumping routines. Gell owned lead mines in Derbyshire and may have suffered from a mild degree of lead poisoning though he lived until the relatively great age of seventy eight. He returned annually to Bath during subsequent years until he became too old to sustain the journeys. He died in London from a 'scorbutical dropsie'.

Peirce was not the only physician at Bath to note the outstanding success of spa therapy in this particular disorder. Half a century later, Rice Charleton, one of the doctors appointed to the Bath General Hospital, published an analysis of all cases of palsy admitted to the wards between 1751 and 1764. He noticed that many of the paralysed patients who suffered from colic were regular cider drinkers. When it came to success in treatment, these patients' cure rate was impressive – ninety-two percent recovered. Only palsies caused by mineral fumes had a better outcome at ninety-five percent. The cider colic, as it was known, was a common disorder in the western counties of England, particularly in Devon. In 1724, there had been a particularly severe outbreak in that county which was described by a Plymouth physician, John Huxham. He called it Devonshire Colic and wrote about it first in Latin and later in English. The recommended treatment was to give emetics and purges.[116]

A typical case concerned a farm labourer called William Bishop from Dunster in Somerset whose case is recorded in Charleton's book[117]. Like most country labourers, Bishop and his companions spent long hard hours bringing in the harvest and haymaking. They were paid very poorly so farmers offered free cider to attract the extra labour needed at this time. On hot days the cider flowed freely. A man could consume several gallons in a day, though his usual allowance was two quarts.

Dr Charleton described how his patient's hands 'fell pendulous from the wrists, the power of raising them being gone.' The patient in Hoare's picture appears to be suffering from this condition and Jeremiah Peirce, who is examining him, is probably demonstrating the limpness of his wrist rather than feeling the man's pulse.

Dr Rice Charleton.
Portrait painting by
Thos. Gainsborough.
(© *The Holburne
Museum of Art, Bath*).

A similar case, but diagnosed as the West Indian Dry
Gripes, involved a young sailor called Allen Lane. He had
been working on a boat which had berthed in the West
Indies. Rum was cheap and plentiful and Lane was
determined to enjoy himself but, shortly after his arrival
there, he became acutely ill and suffered griping belly ache
and repeated fits. Nearly twelve months passed before he
was well enough to return to England and pursue a course
of treatment in the hospital. On admission, 'his arms hung
like flails from his body; his fingers were drawn into the

palms of his hands, the backs of which were covered with large hard swellings and his legs were contracted close to his buttocks and so fixt there that no external force could displace them.'[118] The contraction made it impossible for him to put his feet to the ground so that he had to move around by crawling on his knees and his elbows. His whole body was reduced to little more than a skeleton clothed in flesh and he was frequently tormented with violent stomach pains.

Lane stayed in the hospital for six hundred and twenty-two days with no other treatment than mild laxative medicines, a simple diet and frequent immersions in the hot waters of the King's Bath. By the end of his sojourn, the contraction in his legs was entirely removed, his muscles had regained their proper proportions and he could walk unaided, though his arms were still weak and wasted.

Though common in the seventeenth century, paralysis seems to have reached epidemic proportions by the eighteenth century. The Bath General Hospital was full of young men dragging themselves around the wards, their arms hanging limply at their sides. Dr Charleton was particularly struck by the youthfulness of the patients affected, remarking that the palsy, formerly the attendant of worn-out nature, had now become the 'miserable

Table from Rice Charleton's *Three Tracts on the Bath Water* in which he analyses the outcome of various forms of palsy. Bath treatment was particularly efficacious for paralysis from cyder and bilious colic.

A State of the Paralytic Patients admitted into the		Bath Hospital, from *May* 1751, to *May* 1764.								
Total Number admitted.——1053. viz.		Cured and Benefited.	No better.	Dead.	In-proper.	Discharged for Misbehaviour.	Discharged at their own Request.	Eloped.	Total.
45	General Palsies	28	12	2	1		2		45
283	Hemeplegias	204	41	12	20	1	4	1	283
144	Palsies of the Lower Limbs	92	21	10	18	1	2		144
3	Dead Palsies	3							3
5	Shaking Palsies	1	3		1				5
237	Palsies from Cyder and Bilious Cholics	218	5	9	4		1		237
40	Palsies from Mineral Effluvia	38	1	1					40
17	Fevers	13	2		2				17
27	Rheumatisms	22	3	1	1				27
9	Nervous Affections	6	2		1				9
2	Suppression of the Menses	2							2
1	Miscarriage	1							1
1	Lying-in	1							1
19	External Accidents	16	2	1					19
2	Scrophula	1	1						2
24	Extreme Cold	19	2		1		1	1	24
11	Palsies without any assignable Cause	9	2						11
183	Whose Cases were not properly described.	139	16	7	12	3	5	1	183
		813	113	43	61	5	15	3	1053

Cured and Benefited - - - - 813.
Not Benefited - - - - 240.

companion of youth.'[119] Most of his cases were aged between twenty and forty. Over a thousand paralytics were admitted to the wards between 1751 and 1764, which means that almost half the patients in the hospital were suffering from this sort of disorder.

Not all had wrist drop. Some were admitted with hemiplegia, the name given to paralysis of one half of the body with or without disturbance of speech. Analysis of the Letters Book records reveals a relatively older group of patients with this type of paralysis, with a preponderance of male cases in the fifth and sixth decades. In this respect, the pattern resembles present day experience though many patients were young by modern standards: we do not expect to find many strokes in thirty and forty-year-olds now. Many of these strokes occurred after fevers, particularly puerperal fever due to infection of the womb after childbirth. Such fever is usually caused by streptococcal infection and, with the high probability of damaged heart valves from previous rheumatic fever, lying-in women were particularly susceptible to strokes from emboli flowing from the heart to the brain, either blocking the arteries there or producing brain abscesses. Sometimes children were admitted with strokes after contracting smallpox or meningitis, both of which may have caused cerebral haemorrhages.

Paralysed limbs also resulted from accidents. Dislocation of the shoulder with resulting weakness or paralysis of the arm was a common injury seen at the hospital. Back strains accounted for some cases of nerve damage, just as they do today, leading to paralysis of the leg muscles through pressure on the spinal nerve roots from a damaged intervertebral disc.

Paralysis, like rheumatism, was often attributed to damp. In one of the hospital referring letters, a doctor thought his patient's paralysed legs had resulted from wearing a damp waist-coat. Indeed, for most eighteenth century patients, the cause of their affliction remained a matter for the theories of their medical advisers like that of a Dorset surgeon called Mr North who referred a paralysed carpenter to the hospital in 1752. The carpenter had been to the nearby town of Glastonbury where he had mentioned to some residents that he was suffering from corns. They persuaded

Glaziers were successfully treated at the Bath General Hospital for symptoms of lead poisoning. *(Author's collection)*

him to try the effects of the newly discovered Glastonbury mineral spring by filling his boots with the water and then riding home, a distance of thirty miles, with it sloshing about around his ankles. We do not learn whether the carpenter was cured of his corns but his palsy, coming on soon afterwards, was imputed to have been caused by this reckless treatment!

Painters, refiners, plumbers and glass workers were frequent residents in the hospital's wards and even the earliest physicians to the hospital were aware that these particular trades exposed their artisans to the pernicious effects of lead. In 1753, a patient called Samuel Butts arrived from London. Like the man from Dunster and the sailor from the West Indies, Butts suffered from violent colics which gave way to weakness of his arms and legs. The symptoms progressed until he was unable to feed or dress himself. Butts did not drink cider and he did not follow any hazardous trade but his house had been freshly painted just before he was taken ill.

Dr Charleton was convinced Butts had been affected by lead in the paint fumes. 'It shows,' he wrote, 'that a very small quantity of that noxious mineral, lead, is capable of producing the most pernicious effects. Happy it would be if some other pigment could be discovered which might supply its place, for even the very effluvia which arise from newly painted houses have sometimes proved as hurtful to the inhabitants as mixing the colours and laying them on commonly proves to the painters themselves.'[120]

Could the cider colic have also been caused by very small quantities of lead dissolved in the drink? Certainly this idea does not seem to have occurred to Dr William Oliver, even though he must have seen many cases when he was practising in Plymouth during the 1724 outbreak of Devonshire colic. He was probably satisfied with the explanation of his fellow Plymouth physician, John Huxham who assumed the disease was caused by drinking improperly fermented cider. 'Crude juice,' wrote Huxham, 'ferments vehemently in the stomach and intestines and hence distends them greatly with wind and racks and gripes them.' As for the palsy, this was caused by 'sharp coagulated matter' being thrown into the blood so that instead of 'an exceeding soft lymph to moisten the nerves,' a 'corrosive ichor' created havoc on the patient's neurological system.

Such an explanation seemed very plausible to the eighteenth century mind until another Devonshire physician dispelled this fanciful theory. Sir George Baker, a Devonian by birth but successful as a London practitioner, was convinced that cider colic was none other than lead poisoning and set out by chemical analysis to prove that the beverage was contaminated with small but significant amounts of the noxious element.

His work was published in 1768, and came to the notice of Rice Charleton in Bath who commented: 'In a very ingenious pamphlet lately published by Dr Baker, the Devonshire colic is attributed to lead, dissolved by the juice of the apples in the manufacture of cider. Lead we know is remarkably productive of this complaint. The sugar of lead, when either given internally, or externally applied, is found

POUND-HOUSE—THE MILL AND PRESS.—FILLING "THE MOCK"

Cider press. From the *London Illustrated News.*

to bring on the disease. The same effect is produced by correcting acid wines with sugar of lead and a similar instance fell under my own knowledge of six persons who became at the same time paralytic by drinking cider brought to them while at harvest work in a new earthenware pitcher, whose inside was glazed; which glazing is chiefly made of lead, and was undoubtedly dissolved by the cider as appeared not only from those unhappy effects which drinking it produced, but also from its having given that astringent sweetish taste to the liquor by which solutions of this mineral are peculiarly distinguished. But whatever be the cause whence cider derives this deleterious quality, this however is certain, that all such paralytics come to our hospital from Devon, Somerset, Gloucester and Cornwall. It is very remarkable that during the 13 years to which my inquiry extends, there has been only one such patient sent to us from Herefordshire and not one from Worcestershire'

Cider colic did occur in the latter two counties, though on a much smaller scale. It is always possible that patients from these counties did not present themselves at Bath because of difficulty of access due to the appalling state of the roads. This theory is supported by finding that less than 1% of all admissions to the hospital between 1752 and 1756 came from Herefordshire and Worcestershire, compared with 47% from Somerset, Gloucester and Wiltshire.

Baker's theory supposed that the cider produced from the apples in the presses of Herefordshire and Worcestershire was relatively free of lead, unlike most of that produced in the south-western counties. Baker's findings, though based on experimental evidence, were not universally accepted and during this period West Country cider continued to be liable to contamination from dissolved lead. Devonians did not want to see their cider industry ruined and preferred to listen to other West Country physicians who condemned Baker's opinions. Commercial interests were sufficiently strong to obscure the truth. Ultimately the truth did prevail after James Hardy, a physician at Barnstable added further evidence that cider could easily be contaminated by lead simply by allowing it to stand in glazed earthenware jugs. The acetic acid in rough cider leached out the lead in the glaze.

The Bath waters appeared to be remarkably effective in curing lead palsy. Baker had acquired the figures for cure rates for Devonshire colic at both the Exeter and Bath hospitals between 1762 and 1767. Of the two hundred and eighty-five patients admitted to the Exeter Infirmary, only 73% were cured or improved compared with 92.5% (out of two hundred and eighty-one) at Bath. The outcome of all patients' admissions was published in the local newspapers so it was obviously in the hospital's interest to demonstrate a high cure rate to would-be subscribers. For this reason, a certain amount of scepticism is necessary when judging the efficacy of treatments. Furthermore, patients were often admitted for a very lengthy stay, sufficient in most instances for an improvement to be seen if the disorder commonly resolved naturally. Those who had failed to improve in Exeter and were subsequently sent to Bath had even more time in which to make a recovery.

Even allowing for such bias, the evidence obtained from analysing the outcome of the lead-related paralytic cases admitted between 1752 and 1758 demonstrates a remarkable success rate in the treatment of this disorder compared with other types of paralyses. An aggregate of paralytic case outcomes over the years 1799 to 1828 is equally impressive.

Did the mineral water treatment in some way help rid these patients of their lead? This intriguing possibility was investigated in the 1986 by Drs Audrey Heywood and Paul O'Hare who studied the effects of prolonged immersion on reducing the lead levels of industrial workers exposed to the metal. Their results suggest that immersion in deep baths is of benefit and may explain why so many of the eighteenth century paralytic cases did particularly well at Bath.[29] Together with copious and frequent draughts of mineral

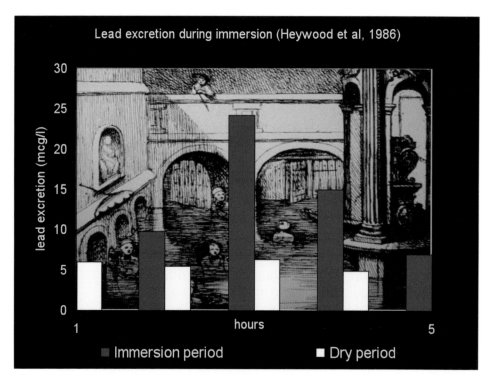

Heywood and O'Hare recruited people who worked at a lead shot tower in Bristol to take part in an immersion study. All of them had a raised level of lead, though not sufficient to produce symptoms. Their urinary lead levels were measured over a five hour period and the results compared with a similar period of time spent resting out of the water. At two hours, there was an almost 5-fold increase in lead excretion in the immersed group, compared with the control group.

water, and the hospital's tough policy towards patients' sorties into the town's public houses, a sojourn of three to six months at Bath probably effected a virtual elimination of lead from most of these patients and thereby cured their symptoms.

Though one can only confidently attribute lead poisoning to those eighteenth century cases where there is a clear description of colic preceding palsy, or where a palsy occurred in a patient whose trade involved high risks of lead exposure, such cases are possibly only the tip of an iceberg of plumbism which affected much of the population at this time. Muscular soreness and stiffness (i.e. symptoms of rheumatism) often precede the paralytic phase, and constipation, a frequent complaint in patients' case descriptions at this time, was the natural consequence of the bowel spasm which accompanies chronic lead toxicity. Close examination of the cases in the 1752-58 Letters Book reveals patients successfully recovered from symptoms such as convulsions, blindness, vomiting, and tremors, all of which could be caused by poisoning by lead or other heavy metals.

Until the hazard of lead toxicity was recognised, its ubiquitous and insidious presence in the environment of pre-Victorian society left few people unaffected at some stage in their lives, either manifesting as gout and muscular aching and weakness, or actual paralyses of hands and feet accompanied by constipation and abdominal colics. Add to this a few other effects, for example infertility and miscarriage, and it becomes clear that regular bathing and water drinking, both of which aid elimination of lead from an affected person, could effect impressive cures and assure the reputation of spa therapy, at least until the incidence of lead poisoning declined from the mid-nineteenth century onwards.

6. The Gout

Let the Gouty Person, after the excess either in meat or drink, swill down as much fair water as his stomach will bear, before he go to bed; whereby he'll reap advantages: First, either the contents of the stomach will be thrown upwards, and he freed from a great part of the load. Or, secondly, both meat and drink will be much diluted; and the labour and expense of spirits in digestion much saved. And thirdly, the gouty salts will thereby be dissolved and distanced from one another; and so be more readily carry'd off by the free perspiration, sweating and urine.

George Cheyne. *An Essay on Gout.* 1721

The reputation Bath had for alleviating gout depended as much on its physicians' advice on living a more healthy lifestyle as it did on taking the waters. It was recognised quite early on that bathing could bring on an attack of gout but that, by persisting, the gouty matter would be eventually washed out of the body. It was important not to effect the release of too much gouty matter into the circulation by staying in the bath too long or becoming overheated. Patients were recommended to temporarily stop bathing if they became feverish. This would indicate that gouty matter was not being eliminated from the blood. Elimination was evident by turbidity of the urine and foetid sweat. It could be enhanced by giving the patient emetics and purges, of which there were plenty of medicines from which to choose in the eighteenth century pharmacopoeia.

Both George Cheyne and William Oliver identified that intemperance exacerbated the condition and Oliver suggested patients too fond of the bottle should be given their favourite tipple with some ipecacuanha added. Syrup of ipecacuanha, derived from a South American plant, has a long history of use as an emetic and is still used to induce vomiting in patients with acute poisoning.

Opposite: Patient with gout, attended by doctors. Detail from Rowlandson's 'Comforts of Bath' (*Private collection*)

If the patient is used to drinking too much wine, I choose he should promote the vomitings with that sort that he likes best, because it gives him an aversion to it for some days afterwards, and he is more easily induced to submit to the restraint his physician ought to lay upon him in the article of drinking.. Three or four full pukes are sufficient.[121]

Although gout can be related to drinking excessive amounts of alcohol and eating a diet rich in meat, it can also be precipitated by lead poisoning because of the toxic effect on the kidneys which leads to the retention of uric acid. Traditionally, gout was associated with port drinking and it has been suggested that fortified wines in the eighteenth century were heavily contaminated with lead. A chemical analysis carried out on some very old bottles of port and madeira have proved this to be so.[122] Rum from the West Indies was another potent source of lead and was undoubtedly the cause of the West Indies Colic.

Though gout was extremely common in the eighteenth century, there are remarkably few cases mentioned in the hospital records at that time. William Oliver who suffered from the disease himself, remarked that gout was 'not a very common distemper amongst the poor'.[123] There are a few recorded cases in tradesmen, mostly those whose work exposed them to lead. Philip Tuckey, a painter and decorator from London who enjoyed 'a very free way of life,' had a particularly severe attack after painting a newly built house 'which threw the gout all over him and the head, stomach and bowels did not escape without their share'. [124]At the time he was admitted to the Bath Hospital in 1752 his knees were almost immoveable, his hamstring tendons contracted, he had no appetite and his bowels were disordered. After a month of bathing and drinking large draughts of mineral water, he 'could walk two miles with only a single stick.'

Gout was primarily a disease of the affluent and well-fed who were in the daily habit of consuming large quantities of meat, the principle source of uric acid. Some of the more celebrated visitors to Bath came for relief of their gout. The eminent Elizabethans, Lord Burghley and his son Robert Cecil, Earl of Salisbury, both visited Bath suffering from this condition and spent their last days in the city.

Queen Anne visited the spa to relieve her gout. This could also have been caused by lead poisoning. There are two possible sources to which the queen might have been unwittingly exposed. Between 1645 and 1715, the quality of German and French wines suffered from the ravages of atrocious weather and the Thirty Years War, encouraging widespread adulteration of wines with litharge to improve their flavour.[125] One can assume from her girth that Anne was probably as much a wine swilling gourmand as her husband and possibly preferred sweeter wines which would have been more highly contaminated. Furthermore, she covered up her poor complexion with cosmetics which were quite likely to have been compounded from lead salts.

The treatment of gout has been attended by the most successful progress in the field of drug research, much of which was carried out in the Mineral Water Hospital. As a result, victims can now effectively prevent attacks by taking a drug called allopurinol which prevents the formation of uric acid in their bodies. Like the effect of warm bathing, there is an increased risk of precipitating an acute attack during the first few weeks of treatment with allopurinol. It coincides with the period during which serum uric acid levels are diminishing and crystals in the joint become unstable. Once the level has stabilised at a lower level, attacks of gout are unlikely.

The first drug which had any appreciable effect on treating an acute attack of gout, colchicum, was introduced into the hospital practice by Dr Edward Barlow (1785–1848) in the 1820s. The drug is derived from meadow saffron, a plant used in medicine in ancient times by Arabian physicians as a remedy for gout and rheumatism. Because of its reputation as a deadly poison (the seeds were powdered down and added to the victim's alcoholic drink), it was not favoured by English physicians who omitted it from the London Pharmacopoeia until 1788, though King James I is said to have been prescribed the herb by his physician who mixed small portions of the root with the powder of unburied skulls.[14] In tiny doses the herb causes diarrhoea and mild sedation. Anything more has the effect of gradually paralysing the central nervous system so that the victim slowly asphyxiates or has a heart attack because the root also contains a cardiac poison, veratrine. In the second half of the eighteenth century, it became increasingly popular as a remedy for gout after a Swabian physician, Dr Anton Stoerk (1731–1803) described a safer way of extracting the drug from the plant.

Barlow treated his gouty patients in the hospital with an alcoholic solution of colchicum seeds. He described the action:

> *Colchicum purges, abates pain, and lowers the pulse. Its sedative powers, though sensibly connected with its evacuant action, are not however wholly dependent on them. The motions are copious, frequent and watery. I have known even twenty motions occasioned by a dose of colchicum – the patient not complaining of the least debility. These circumstances will guide our employment as a remedy for gout. By means of the treatment now prescribed, a paroxysm of gout is capable of being effectually relieved, the constitution re-established, the powers of the affected limb preserved and the gouty disposition diminished.*[126]

Certainly the drug produced great benefit to 47-year-old John Kenny, admitted to the Mineral Water Hospital in April 1821. The patient had suffered from intermittent attacks of gout for fifteen years and at the time of his admission, 'his locomotive powers were so much diminished that he had not been able to walk for fourteen months.'[127] He was treated with colchicum and bathing, and was discharged in the August 'greatly improved and able to walk short distances. He was so sensible of the benefit which he had derived from colchicum under the paroxysm that he solicited copies of his prescriptions in order to resort to them under any future attack.'[128]

Colchicum, and later its alkaloid, colchicine, continued to be used in treating the acute attacks of gout. Colchicine still has a place in its management, though safer drugs are now available.

Gout is caused by an excessive amount of uric acid accumulating in joints and other tissues, so any treatment which prevents this build up will serve as an effective prophyllaxis against the disease. The earliest drug to produce any appreciable reduction in uric acid levels of gouty patients was first used for this purpose in 1908. Called Cinchophen, it was a chemical derivative of cinchoninic acid, a substance extracted from the bark of the cinchona tree. Cinchona bark, variously known as Peruvian Bark and Jesuits' Powder, was widely used in the eighteenth century as a treatment for fever. Cinchona bark is a potent source of the anti-malarial drug, quinine. The supposedly specific action of the bark in a disorder known as the ague has led to the idea that this ancient ailment was malaria. More likely, ague was a term used to describe any feverish illness of an intermitting nature, and the bark worked because it contained drugs, including quinine, which reduced the patient's fever. Substances which act in this way are known as antipyretics. Many modern anti-rheumatic drugs have this property.

The increasing cost of imported drugs encouraged physicians to find homegrown alternatives to cinchona bark. Daniel Lysons, physician to the Bath General Hospital between 1781 and 1800, experimented with elm bark as a treatment for skin disease[129]. In 1798, William White who was apothecary to the Bath City Infirmary and Dispensary, demonstrated how the bark of the English broad-leaved willow was just as effective in the treatment of fever as the more expensive cinchona.[130] Willow was originally advocated in the belief that diseases common in damp environments would probably be cured by plants growing in a similar situation, a piece of pseudo logic known as the doctrine of

Portrait of Dr Daniel Lysons by Tilly Kettle. (© *The Samuel Courtauld Trust, The Courtauld Gallery, London*)

signatures. However, in the case of willow, its efficacy was later proved to be founded on more scientific principles for it contains salicylic acid, a compound from which several modern anti-rheumatic drugs have been derived including the best known drug of all, aspirin.

Despite its widespread use by the 1930s, aspirin does not seem to have been used very much by the physicians at the Mineral Water Hospital at this time. Coates and Delicati's book, *Rheumatoid Arthritis*, makes very little mention of drugs at all.[131] Even with gout, the treatment was largely dietary, with abundant swilling of Bath waters, low protein and high carbohydrate intake.[132] One of the reasons for the reluctance to use drugs at this time was their considerable toxicity. Cinchophen may have effectively cured patients with gout but it probably killed quite a number.[133]

The saga of cinchona bark and its derivatives did not finish there. People had noticed that sufferers of rheumatoid arthritis sometimes improved when they travelled abroad and took anti-malaria tablets. In 1952, Drs Mandel and Kersley tried the effect of two anti-malaria drugs, plaquenil and camoquin, on a series of patients with the disease. Although the patients enjoyed a suppression of their disease, the high doses necessary to produce an improvement were accompanied by serious side effects.

Many other drugs have been tried out on hospital patients in the last forty years, including early trials with steroids and gold compounds. Great care is taken to monitor the bad effects as well as the good. Though there is now a large number of anti-rheumatic drugs from which to choose, none of them are entirely free from adverse effects, particularly irritation of the stomach from the so-called non-steroidal anti-inflammatory drugs. By looking directly into the patients' stomachs with a flexible endoscope, physicians at the hospital have recently become aware of the extent of this problem. It is to be hoped that the next generation of drugs will prove safer and more efficacious.

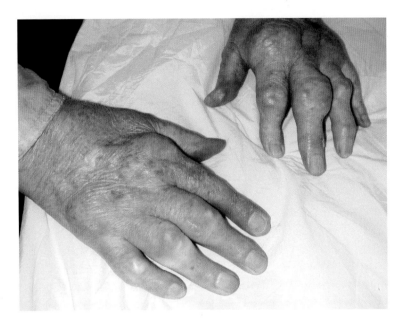

Hands showing the swollen joints typical of untreated gout. Uric acid crystals accumulate under the skin forming chalky deposits known as tophi.
(*Author's photo*)

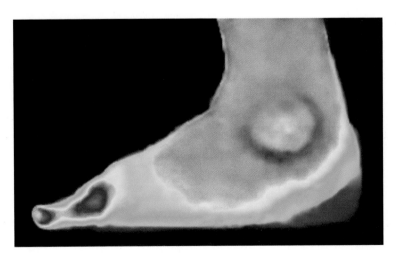

Thermograph showing inflammation (red) in a gouty big toe. Thermal imaging is used to assess the effectiveness of anti-inflammatory drugs (*F. Ring*)

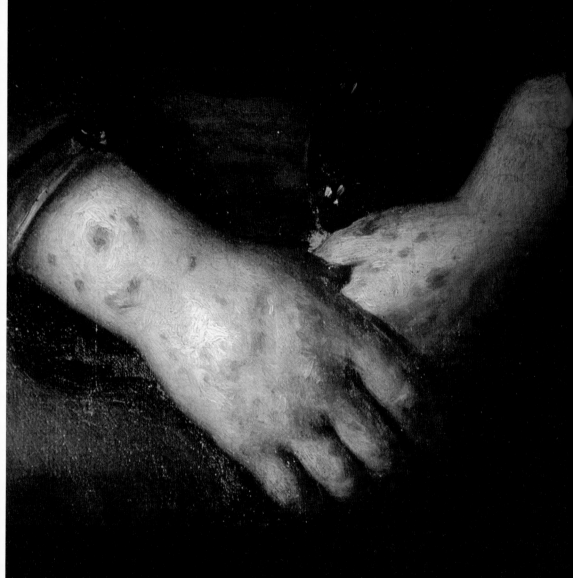

Detail from Hoares's painting of
boy's hands, showing a skin rash.
(Clive Quinnell/*RNHRD*)

7. Scabbes, Scurf and Lepers

The third patient in Hoare's picture is a boy, clearly suffering from some sort of skin rash on his hands and his right hand appears swollen. The description attached to the picture describes this as leprosy. The term *leprosy* as used in the seventeenth and eighteenth centuries is not synonymous with the modern term and referred to chronic skin disorders characterised by severe scaling or thickening of the skin, a common example being psoriasis. True leprosy (Hansen's disease) had been endemic in this country until the late fourteenth century and many leper hospitals were founded during the Middle Ages, including one in Bath which was first mentioned in 1212 in the will of the Bishop of Lincoln[134]. It was situated in Holloway on the southern slopes leading away from the city and was dedicated to St Mary Magdalen. Only the chapel remains although there is a small house of much later date a little further down the hill which is marked as a leper hospital by a small plaque on its wall. The site of the original hospital buildings was almost certainly further up the hill, near the chapel and on the site of the present Magdalen Avenue.

In most of these institutions, the emphasis was on residential care and segregation from the rest of the community rather than treatment. However, bathing was recognized as a form of therapy and there is evidence that some medieval institutions had bathing facilities available for their afflicted inmates as well as offering medical and surgical treatments.[135]

At Bath, the tradition of the waters for healing leprosy forms the basis of the Bladud story. Prince Bladud was the legendary founder of Bath after discovering the curative properties of the hot springs whilst observing how the scabby coats of some pigs he was tending improved in

The chapel of St Mary Magdalen in Holloway in the 19th century. There is no trace of the mediaeval leper house which was probably on the site of present day Magdalen Avenue. A small house further downhill is sometimes mistaken for the leper hospital but was used from the 18th century as accommodation for children with severe learning difficulty. (from *Engravings of Bath & Bristol. 1829*)

appearance when the animals wallowed in the hot muddy pools around the springs. The origins of the story are obscure but it does connect the spa waters with the treatment of skin disease and there is plenty of evidence that the waters were advocated as a means of treating dermatological disorders.

John Leland, on his visit to the city in c.1540, remarked that the Cross Bath was 'much frequentid of people deseasid with lepre, pokkes, scabbes and great aches" and that 'many be holp by this bathe of scabbes and aches.'[136] William Turner advised that 'leprous' patients should use a separate bath and such a bath was finally constructed towards the end of the sixteenth century and became known as the Lepers Bath. It was annexed to the west side of the Hot Bath and measured about twelve feet square. A seventeenth century plan of this bath shows a small hospital in proximity to it, suggesting that this building lodged leprous persons. The building is attributed to John de Feckenham, the last Abbot of Westminster.

In 1576 Feckenham purchased three tons of timber and four hundred laths to build a house for the poor by the Hot Bath. On close inspection, the building appears to have a small bath, supplied with water from a conduit and situated

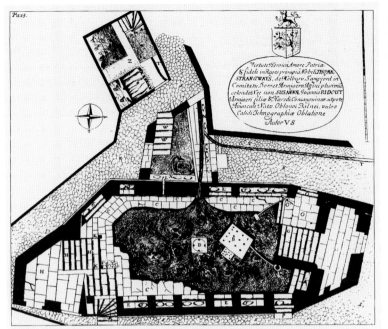

The Hot Bath, Leper Bath and Feckenham's Hospital. *From T. Guidott 'De Thermis Brtiannicis' 1691*

at the foot of a flight of steps. Three people are lying side by side along its length, an unusual position to adopt as bathing was traditionally done semi-recumbent or sitting. This may have been because the depth of the bath was limited or, alternatively, that this was a mud bath. Though there are references to the use of mud as cataplasms (poultices) in contemporary literature, both Dr Edward Jorden and Thomas Johnson claim that very little use was made of it. Robert Peirce, writing at the end of the century, commented that 'leprous, scabby and scurfy persons' might have been sooner cured if they had bathed in mud and water together, but that the 'nicety of his age' was satisfied with nothing but fresh baths.

Three other figures are depicted lying in what appears to be straw and this is supported by an account of one of Robert Peirce's cases in which he described a poor man from Coleshill, Warwickshire, who came to Bath in 1684 suffering from a leprous skin disorder. He was accommodated in 'a covert' close to the Lepers Bath 'where they lye upon straw'. Peirce adds that, unlike patients in Bellotts hospital, residents of the covert had no maintenance allowance save what the charity of well-disposed people gave them. It is therefore curious to account for the other two figures

Detail of Feckenham's Hospital showing two patients in a bed with linen sheets and pillows whilst others appear to have to make do with straw! Steps lead down to what appears to be a bath supplied by a conduit.
From T. Guidott 'De Thermis Brtiannicis' 1691

depicted in the southeast corner of the building where they are lying in a large bed adequately provided with pillows and bedclothes.

Feckenham's leper hospital was given a boost in 1712 when Miss Strode[137] of Downside endowed it with five pounds a year.[138] The money was paid over annually to the representatives of the leper hospital until, in 1786, the building was destroyed. Whether it was pulled down or simply fell down is uncertain but Miss Strode's endowment lay fallow for the next thirty-nine years until some observant Governor of the General Hospital remarked that as the hospital admitted cases of leprosy, it could rightly claim the endowment.

Patients with skin diseases represent between 10% and 15% of admissions to the Bath General Hospital during the eighteenth and early nineteenth century. Between 1752 and 1764, two hundred and forty-one 'lepers' were admitted of whom one hundred and twenty-two were 'perfectly cleansed' and eighty-five 'much benefitted.' Only sixteen received no benefit, and four of these died in hospital.[139] The remainder were discharged because they misbehaved or were unable to take the waters. One of the most florid cases that Dr Oliver and his colleagues had ever seen was a young woman from Bicester called Mary Tompkins. Born in the same year the hospital opened, she developed a rash on the skin when she was five years old. At first it was mild and was diagnosed by the local apothecary (William Hicks) as being due to a surfeit. It was a common belief at this time that drinking large quantities (i.e. a surfeit) of cold liquid, particularly if the body was heated, was the cause of such rashes. As Mary grew older, her rash got worse so that by the age of twelve, she was confirmed as having leprosy. Every part of her body, including her face and head, was affected. At the age of fifteen, she was sent to St Bartholomew's Hospital in London where a variety of medicines was tried, including mercury. All treatment failed miserably and she was discharged as incurable. Back in Bicester, Mary's disfigurement was so appalling that nobody was prepared to have her in their house.

In 1763, Mary was sent to Bath and was admitted to the hospital on New Year's Eve under Dr Oliver's care. He wrote:

> *I never saw so bad a leprous case. The girl's skin was almost universally covered with large, thick, hard. dry scabs, of a dark brown colour. These brown scabs were specked with white shining silver scales which gave her countenance a very shocking appearance. The clefts between the scabs were wide and deep so that her skin resembled the bark of a tree.*

Apart from the state of her skin, she was in good health and Oliver ordered her to be bled and purged and then to embark upon the usual Bath water regimen of drinking and twice weekly bathing. Bathing was discontinued after a month and she was prescribed an ointment made from a mixture of tar (Ung. e Pice) and oil obtained from the hooves of oxen. Neat's foot oil, as the latter preparation is known, was used quite widely in the Bath Hospital during the eighteenth century, not only for dermatological cases but as an application to crackling joints on the supposition that it could traverse the skin and thereby lubricate the offending organ. The ointment was applied twice daily for three weeks, and then bathing resumed. It must have been a very sticky business. In 1851, the Hospital Minutes record that twelve new flock mattresses were needed to replace those soiled by ointment.

Mary Tompkins drank a pint of mineral water each day, together with a medicine containing mercury, antimony and sarsaparilla. By alternating periods of water treatment with

113

application of ointment, her condition steadily improved and she was able to leave hospital on 8th August 1763, 'perfectly cleansed.'[32] Patients like this were sometimes resident in the hospital for more than a year. The diagnoses in modern terms can be no more than pure conjecture: psoriasis, eczema, tuberculosis of the skin, fungal infections, impetigo, syphilis, arsenic poisoning; all these have probably been treated at some time in the hospital. The eighteenth century descriptions are for the most part lacking in the necessary detail to allow accurate identification, though sometimes one can be fairly confident of the diagnosis. Henry Robjohn, a poor eight-year-old lad admitted in 1745 whose grazed elbows became scabby and crusted and failed to heal, was almost certainly suffering from impetigo. Dr Oliver's explanation was simply that the graze caused an impairment of circulation through the skin and 'corrosive particles', which were normally dispersed and harmlessly diluted by the fluid parts of the body, accumulated at the site of injury and began 'eating away the adjacent parts, exciting intolerable itchings and covering the skin with foul scabs'.

After the installation of baths at the hospital in 1830, many patients with skin disease were immersed in a foul-smelling concoction of potassium sulphide and mineral water, the so-called sulphur bath. Vapour baths were installed in the hospital in 1863. By now the term 'leprosy' no longer appears in the admission records. As with the arthritic cases in the hospital, the medical staff made virtually no attempt to distinguish the various cutaneous disorders which were referred to them. Dr James Tunstall, writing in 1850, was convinced that 'such distinctions, however useful to the student, are of no practical avail to the practitioner of medicine.' He held that the different types of cutaneous eruptions were merely examples of the same disease modified by the patient's habit, temperament and constitution. For example, an error of diet might in one patient lead to impetigo while in another, the same dietary indiscretion could manifest as eczema. All such skin disorders were considered to be caused by want of cleanliness, errors of diet, cold air, hereditary disposition and various trades.

Dr A. Beaufort Brabazon, reviewing the success of spa treatment in skin disease in 1878, was at least able to separate eczema from other dermatological conditions; 28% of his patients with eczema were deemed 'cured' and 52% were 'much better'.[140]

Recent research at a spa on the Dead Sea has demonstrated successful outcome for psoriasis. The results are remarkably similar to the outcome of skin cases treated at the General Hospital two and a half centuries before. There are compelling reasons to explain this success. Psoriasis improves with exposure to ultraviolet light and in the eighteenth century bathing was carried out in the open air, so there would have been plenty of opportunity for long exposure to sunlight. In an age when people were less bothered to maintain personal cleanliness, regular immersion in the warm mineral water would have both cleansed and hydrated the skin. This would have helped ameliorate scaly diseases like psoriasis and infected sores might have benefited from adequate lavage. Physicians at the hospital did not rely exclusively on the Bath waters. They applied tar ointment and Neate's foot oil (nowadays used for softening leather) to the patient's skin. This probably had more effect than any minerals in the water because the total mineral content is low, about two grams per litre. The constituents are principally calcium and sodium sulphate, chloride and bicarbonate. There is no free sulphur and virtually no selenium. There is a low level of radioactivity, mostly from radon and radium. Some German researchers have suggested that low levels of radioactivity in spa water may in some way benefit inflammatory disorders, but the numbers studied are too small to be statistically significant. Mud and scum were applied to the skin from the seventeenth century onwards and are a potent source of various minerals. In the nineteenth century. minerals, particularly sulphur, were added to some spa baths, but this practice did not occur until the nineteenth century.

Dr Anthony Beaufort Brabazon, MD (1820–1896). Hon Physician to the Bath Mineral Water Hospital, and Medical Officer of Health for Bath.
(Author's Collection)

Mary of Modena, wife of King James II, who conceived after bathing in the Cross Bath. Portrait by William Wissing. (*National Portrait Gallery, London*)

8. Fecundity and Fatigue

Thermal springs enjoyed a reputation for promoting conception and fecundity and this was given a fillip at Bath in 1687 with the arrival of Mary of Modena, wife of King James II. She bathed for some time in the Cross Bath and had the satisfaction to find herself pregnant, giving birth in 1688 to a son who was to be denied enthronement as a result of the Glorious Revolution in the same year. Robert Peirce gives several instances of women who had failed to conceive for a number of years before taking the water at Bath and conceiving shortly after. Was this more than a happy coincidence? A few of these instances may, as is discussed earlier, have been a result of reducing lead toxicity. Probably most of the women who benefited from a few weeks regular immersion in the Cross or King's Bath did so because they were suffering from chronic vaginal infections which may have improved from the hygienic effects of bathing. Peirce recommended that women used a syringe to douche their vagina with mineral water, a technique that was euphemistically termed the *douche ascendante* during the nineteenth century.

However an old Italian proverb, giving advice to husbands, hints at the most cogent explanation for the success of bathing in matters of fertility: 'If you want your wife to conceive, send her to the baths and stay at home yourself'. An Italian scholar, Gian Francesco Poggio Bracciolini (1380–1459), visiting a German spa in 1416 commented:

> *I believe there are no baths in the world more efficacious in promoting the propagation of the human species. This may indeed be in some measure accounted for by the following circumstance. An innumerable multitude of persons of all ranks repair to this place*

from the distance of two hundred miles; not with a view of recruiting their health, but of enjoying life. These baths are the general resort of lovers and their mistresses, of all, in short, who are fond of pleasure. Many ladies pretend to be sick, merely with a view of being sent for cure to this watering place. You consequently see here a great number of handsome females without their husbands, and not protected by any male relations, but attended by a couple of maids and a man servant, or some elderly cousin, who is very easily imposed upon. And they come adorned with such costly apparel, that you would suppose they were coming to a wedding, rather than to a watering place. Here we find Vestal, or to speak more correctly, Floral virgins. Here we meet with abbots, monks, friars, and priests, who live with greater license than the rest of the company. These ecclesiastics, forgetting the gravity of their profession, sometimes bathe with the ladies, and adorn their hair with silken ribbons. For all people here concur in banishing sorrow, and courting mirth. Their objects is, not to divide that which is common, but to communicate that which is appropriated. It is an astonishing circumstance, that in so great a multitude (nearly a thousand persons) of various dispositions, and so much given to riot, no discord or dissension ever arises. The husbands see their wives gallanted, and even attended tête-à-tête by strangers, and yet they are not disturbed or rendered uneasy.

Hence it happens, that the name of jealousy, that plague, which is elsewhere productive of so much misery, is here unknown. How unlike are the manners of these people to ours, who always see things on the dark side, and who are so much given to censoriousness, that in our minds the slightest suspicion instantly grows into full proof of guilt. I often envy the apathy of these Germans, and I execrate our perversity, who are always wishing for what we have not, and are continually exposed to present calamity by our dread of the future. But these people, content with little, enjoy their day of life in mirth and merriment; they do not hanker after wealth; they are not anxious for the morrow; and they bear adversity with patience. Thus are they rich by the mere disposition of their minds. Their motto is, 'live while you live.' But of this enough – it is not my object to extol my new friends at the expense of my countrymen. I wish my epistle to consist of unqualified good humour, that I may impart to you a portion of the pleasure I derived from the baths of Baden.[141]

Nearly three centuries later very little had changed. Ned Ward, visiting Bath, remarked :

Here is perform'd all the wanton dalliances imaginable; celebrated beauties, panting breasts and curious shapes, almost expos'd to publick view; languishing eyes, darting killing glances, tempting amorous postures, attended by soft musick, enough to provoke a vestal to forbidden pleasure, captivate a saint and charm a Jove.... The vigorous sparks presenting [the ladies] with several antick postures, as sailing on their backs, then embracing the element, sink in rapture and by accidental design thrust a stretch'd arm... but where the water concealed, so ought my pen.... The spectators in the galleries please their roving fancies with this lady's face, another's eyes, a third's heavy breasts and profound air.

Even in 1825 another Bath visitor, Bernard Blackmantle witnessed much the same voyeuristic spectacle.

On entering the King's Bath, to our great amusement and delight, we found ourselves surrounded by many a sportive nymph whose beauteous form was partially hidden by the loose flannel gown, it is true; but now and then the action of the water produced by the continued movements of a number of persons all bathing at the same time, discovered charms which to have caught a glimpse of in any other situation might have proved of dangerous consequences for the fair possessors[142]

The intimately physical nature of spa treatments in which the therapist provides a pleasurable tactile experience for the recipient may move dangerously close to that of a sexual encounter. In the seventeenth century, mixed-sex bathing appears to have been popular as is depicted in Thomas Johnson's view of the King's Bath. Complaints of promiscuous behaviour are mentioned by several authors writing at the end of the eighteenth century and rules controlling the behaviour of bathers, which dictated an expected level of dress and decorum whilst bathing, were introduced to prevent the spa degrading into a den for licentious and libidinous lechery. The resulting seminudity could, as Ned Ward and Bernard Blackmantle discovered, excite the passions to an even higher degree.

The Victorians disapproved strongly of mixed bathing but were quite relaxed about massage. After the mid twentieth century, physiotherapists were reluctant to carry on this particular type of therapy as massage became overtly associated with prostitution, and the appearance of the street massage parlours in the 1970s. Therapeutic massage was continued by some complementary therapists in this country and was still available in continental spas. With the reopening of Bath spa, water based massage is again available, but anyone hoping for any sex will be disappointed.

Another disorder which seems to have affected only women and appears in several treatises on the waters was known as the *Green Sickness* or *Chlorosis*. There has been considerable debate about the nature of this rather mysterious disorder. It was first described by a German physician Johannes Lange in 1554 who recognised it as a disease affecting virgins and young unmarried girls and advised sufferers to 'live with men and copulate; if they conceive, they will recover.'

The disorder was characterised by weakness, fatigue, weight loss, dietary disturbances, irregularity or lack of menstruation and most significantly, a greenish tinge to the colour of the skin. Various cures were proposed including bloodletting, diet, iron supplementation, exercise, and marriage. Not surprisingly, Bath physicians were convinced they could ameliorate the problem with spa therapy.

Robert Peirce is the earliest author to describe a case treated in Bath. Elizabeth Eyles was sixteen when she travelled from Devizes to consult him in 1657. Peirce described Miss Eyles as 'pale, thin and stomachless, faint and tyrie upon the least stirring and very often hysterical'. She stayed in the doctor's house for six weeks, bathing and drinking the Bath Waters and apparently made a full recovery, regaining a 'fresh colour and a good stomach' and a return of menstruation.

Although common in the seventeenth century and eighteenth century, chlorosis reached almost epidemic proportions in the latter half of the nineteenth century. In 1820, the *Invalids Companion to Bath* described the condition as 'a genuine Bath Water case' for which spa therapy held out a safe and almost certain remedy. To insure success the treatment had to be administered at an early period of the disease, and persevered in both externally and internally, under proper directions for a considerable time.[143]

Some cases of chlorosis may have been due to iron deficiency associated with chronic debilitating diseases such as tuberculosis and peptic ulcer. Since chlorosis was generally confined to adolescent girls, many physicians thought it was due to a nervous weakness and greater sensitivity of females in comparison with males. In 1887 Dr A. Clark, a physician at the London Hospital, explained chlorosis as an 'imperfect development of the heart and large arteries, associated with an original weakness of the blood cells'. Because of this weakness, the female was not able to meet the demands made by the advent of menstruation and the accompanying growth of the body. He mentioned other causes such as 'imperfect and improper food; deficient air, exercise and light; overwork, especially of the brain; the dissipation of society; solicitude and the absence of healthy amusement; disappointment and sorrows, secret impurity; digestive and nervous disorder.' Thus the long history of its classification as an hysterical condition was not completely rejected. Modern theories suggest that most cases of chlorosis were either examples of nutritional anaemia or anorexia nervosa, or both.

Cessation of monthly periods was another female complaint which gave spa physicians a chance to intervene with a water cure. Once pregnancy had been excluded as a diagnosis, doctors assumed that periods stopped because of something obstructing the flow of blood from the uterus. The blood might be too thick and require thinning by blood letting. By the same rationale, mineral water was to be taken both internally and externally by immersion of the body up to the neck. Cessation of menstruation is rarely, if ever, caused by obstruction and apart from pregnancy, it usually relates to a change in female hormones. The menstrual cycle often resumes spontaneously after a lapse of some months, so a successful outcome after spa treatment in this condition might have been purely coincidental.

Detail ftrom Thomas Johnson's view of the King's Bath *(© Trustees of the British Museum, London)*

9. Children at the Spa

We daily see them brought here so weak from relaxation of their limbs
that they appear to be in danger of being cripples as long as they live
[yet are] restored to strength and vigour by moderate warm bathing.

Dr William Oliver. Bath. 1716.

We tend to think only of adults when considering the visitors who frequented the spa in former centuries, but children often came for treatment and might stay in the city for several months. Wealthier families often entrusted their children to the care of a nurse or servant who accompanied the child on their journey to the spa. In July 1666, a nurse employed by the Powell family arrived from Oxford accompanying their child of six who had developed palsy after suffering from epileptic fits. He bathed three or four times a week but made little progress before returning home. Another young patient, the ten year old son of Sir Thomas Skipwith, was sent from London suffering from rickets. He had 'great crookedness in his lower limbs so that he went very oddly, throwing out his legs with his knees striking one against the other by reason of their looseness.' His shin bones were crooked, 'bending outwards like a bow, or rather wreathed and twisted'. His physician at Bath, Dr Robert Peirce, suggested he should learn to swim, which he did. Ten years later, whilst returning to Bath to see his sister Lady Williams who was then a patient of Peirce, his posture was so much better that the doctor failed to recognise him.

Rickets, due to a deficiency of vitamin D, was a common condition in British children of former times. The long winters with little sunlight and the absence of large windows in houses, particularly those of the poor, meant that children had relatively little exposure to ultraviolet light which promotes synthesis of Vitamin D in the skin. Their diet was also unlikely to be rich in the vitamin unless they lived close to the sea where fish was readily available.

The baths were open to the sky and children usually bathed naked, so their exposure to sunlight provided an effective remedy to rickets. The success of spa treatment in this condition is well illustrated by the case of Gershom Carmichael. This six year old boy arrived from Scotland with his mother, Christine, in September 1678. Gershom's limbs were distorted and crooked. He had been under the care of so-called body-menders to try to straighten his limbs and was supported in iron braces. He visited the spa over the next three or four summers where he regularly bathed in the King's and Queen's baths and was eventually able to leave off his iron braces and was settled at a school[144]. As an adult he became Regent of Glasgow University and was later appointed Professor of Moral Philosophy. Carmichael's work fundamentally contributed to shaping the agenda of instruction in moral philosophy in eighteenth-century Scotland.

Braces and other gadgets which might help to straighten limbs are mentioned several times in Peirce's *Memoirs*. He also describes a swing from which children with spinal deformities could be suspended, thereby exerting downward traction on the vertebral column. James, the seven year old son of Sir Joseph Ashe, was brought to Bath by his mother, Lady Mary Ashe 'in a very weak condition, both inwardly and outwardly in body and limbs.' She had consulted a Sherborne physician, Nathaniel Highmore, who often accompanied his more wealthy patients to Bath. Highmore diagnosed hectic fever and advised that bathing would probably kill the child and that he should be speedily removed from the town. She was about to leave when she happened to call upon Mr Chapman, a Bath apothecary in order to settle his bill for some medicines she had bought from his shop. On hearing of the reason for her departure, Chapman suggested she seek an opinion from Dr Peirce. He found the child 'consumptive, thin, pale and hectical' and suffering from diarrhoea. His joints were 'relaxed' so that his body had grown asymmetrically to one side and his legs were crooked. The child had been fitted with iron braces which looked like some bizarre suit of armour. His feet were placed into half boots with iron springs to keep his ankles from turning out and he had similar devices fitted to his knee braces to stop them knocking together. The ironwork was held in place by broad leather straps which could be laced tightly to keep the limbs as straight as the child could bear. He was scarcely able to walk with these contraptions on, but was totally immobile without them.

In the midst of general pessimism about the wisdom of spa treatment for the child, Peirce recommended that he should spend six weeks bathing, at first for only short periods each day in tepid water, then gradually increasing the time of immersion and the temperature of the water. Miraculously, the boy gained strength and continued to improve after leaving Bath before the start of winter. He

Portrait of Dr Nathaniel Highmore, by an unknown artist. circa 1660–1665 (© *National Portrait Gallery, London*)

returned to resume treatment over the following three or four years and Peirce met him again in 1694 when he was on a social visit to Bath from Norfolk and found him 'an indifferently well grown man'. His mother seems to have been less impressed and regarded him as a very feeble son. Although the young man married and they had a child together, his wife left him after a short time because of his philandering which enraged her so much that she 'never bedded with him' again.[145]

Medical treatment in the seventeenth century and eighteenth century could be a very frightening experience for children but life was much tougher in those days. In 1681 Lady Colchester arrived in Bath with her only daughter, aged thirteen, who was nearly comatose. She had been under the care of Dr Edmund Borlase at Chester and a London physician, Dr Berwick. One doctor proposed using a bath tub at home whilst the other, who never once set eyes on the patient, recommended *testaceous powders* (made from crushed shells) and bitter infusion. Her mother felt that her daughter had been 'cloyed with physic to no purpose' and was not keen for her to take any more medicaments. In Bath, she was advised that blood letting was needed but the girl was afraid of being cut with the lancet and her mother would not consent to it. An apothecary was called to apply leeches over her jugular veins. They quickly engorged themselves then dropped off. The wounds were encouraged to continue bleeding by applying sponges dipped in warm water to her neck. After the veins had been kept open for some hours, the bleeding orifices were dressed with plasters and the girl put to bed. In the middle of the night, the nurse who was looking after her was shocked to find the pillows covered in blood. The family was awakened and the apothecary sent for. They wanted to call Dr Peirce out but with the arrival of the apothecary, they decided not to disturb him. Despite the massive blood loss, she did not feel faint or sweaty and according to Peirce, she began to recover from that time on, only to die some years later from smallpox.

Infectious diseases, particularly epidemic infections, were the greatest cause of mortality in children before the twentieth century and it has been estimated that at least half the children born never reached their fifth birthday.

Infections affected all classes and the wealthy could no more protect themselves from the tragedy of infant mortality than the poor. In the seventeenth century, plague, measles, smallpox, typhus, dysentery and influenza were the ubiquitous agents of the grim reaper, relentlessly scything babes and toddlers whilst the medical practitioners were ignorant of any effective treatment. These acute diseases were not suitable for spa treatment, which was limited to selected chronic disorders.

There was, however, one acute infection which led to paralysis and for which the spa was able to provide remedial treatment. Poliomyelitis, formerly known as infantile paralysis, occurred sporadically until the twentieth century when it reached epidemic proportions. At its peak in the 1940s and 1950s, paralytic polio affected over half a million people worldwide every year. Large numbers of children were rehabilitated in the spa's baths at this time.

The long duration of spa treatment meant that some provision had to be made for children to be educated and there is evidence that as early as the seventeenth century some children were boarded at school in Bath, possibly at King Edward's which had been founded a century earlier. More wealthy families would send a tutor with the child. There was little provision for children of very poor families until the mid eighteenth century when the General Hospital was established.

The care of children in hospital has moved on a long way in the last half century and even more so since the eighteenth century. Climbing the short flight of steps to the front door of the Bath General Hospital, children must have wondered what terrible deformities and disfigurements they were about to witness within. Compared with today's patients, the scene on the wards would have presented a lurid spectacle. Skin disease was much more florid in its appearance and the term 'leprosy' was an understandable description for the disfiguringly severe skin disorders then prevalent. Jemima Scott, a young girl from Essex, was admitted in 1754 with a 'scurfy humour all over her body' while nine year old Ann Gunstone from Bathford came in with scald-head, a disease due to staphylococcal infection which caused the hair to fall out and the skin to swell into a mass of red blisters, hence the name.

About five percent of admissions to the General Hospital in 1752 were under ten years old.[146] Like the adults, they often had to stay in the hospital for several months. Eight-year-old Alex Knapman from Crediton in Devon stayed for three months after injuring his spine. Seven year-old Sarah Sandford from Exeter was admitted for seven months and four-year-old John Sartain from Trowbridge stayed even longer. Children were accommodated on the women's wards. In an age when the young were treated at best like adults-in-miniature and at worst like animals, life in the women's wards may have been a pleasant release from the drudgery, harshness and poverty of outside. A century passed before child patients received regular education during their admission. Even then tuition was sporadic, probably because there were seldom more than a handful of children in the hospital and it was not felt worthwhile engaging an infant teacher as a permanent member of staff. Sometimes, female patients took it upon themselves to teach the children. In 1857, the chaplain suggested that the committee reward such women with six pence a week and engage the infant teacher of St Michael's parish to attend regularly on Saturdays.

It was not until the advent of paediatric wards in the late nineteenth century that any special provision for accommodating children occurred[147]. Despite this, the needs of children with regard their care and education was recognised in earlier times.

Designed & Engraved by I.ᵗ Eginton, Birm.ᵐ

10. Spa Doctors

During the seventeenth and eighteenth century, the number of medical practitioners in Bath steadily increased in line with the rise in the number of ailing visitors. Whereas in 1737, there were nineteen apothecaries living in the city, twenty years later the number had increased to 'above thirty, who constantly live there, many of whom make fortunes without dealing in the waters. These may be thought comfortable considerations for the sick who need not fear the want of any other physical aid in case the waters should fail at Bath or their sources be exhausted.'[148]

In a study on occupations of Bath citizens in the reign of James I, Elizabeth Holland discovered one midwife, one bonesetter, two apothecaries, two surgeons and about a dozen physicians practising in the city.[149] The hallmark of the latter group was a university degree, either Bachelor of Medicine or the higher degree of Doctor of Medicine. Of the two universities in this country, neither Oxford or Cambridge enjoyed a good reputation for teaching the subject in the sixteenth century, though Oxford rapidly improved its image during the first half of the seventeenth century.

A far more enlightened approach to medical teaching was available in continental Europe. Bologna, Ferrara, Padua, Paris and Rheims all provided excellent tuition and as previously discussed, some graduates of the two English universities opted to further their education abroad. William Harvey, whose observations on the circulation of blood made him the most celebrated doctor of his time, studied at both Cambridge and Padua. It should perhaps help to put the level of medical science in Stuart society into perspective when we consider how, until Harvey's publication in 1628, even the most enlightened doctors

Opposite: Doctor examining the pulse of his patient. from *New Bath Guide. 1788.*

131

were convinced that blood, lymph and other bodily fluids ebbed and flowed like the tides; and like those reciprocating marine gyrations, they were also susceptible to celestial influences and particularly to the those of the moon.

So we find medical writings of this period, even as late as the Restoration, preoccupied with lunar cosmology. Treatments, or even impassioned behaviour, which might be inclined to push humours or fluids up to the brain were best avoided during full moons lest fits of apoplexy or madness should result (hence the term lunacy). As a contemporary author commented, 'Physic without astrology is like a lamp without oil.' Thomas Guidott warns his readers of the danger of bathing during a full moon lest the natural heat of the bath sends too much humour to the head. Medical theory, as taught by the universities of Oxford and Cambridge, was firmly based on age-old paradigms which were so strongly rooted that many physicians continued to ignore the emergent body of new knowledge which was emanating from the experiments and observations of seventeenth century natural philosophers. Foreign universities seem to have taught a more pragmatic approach to medicine with greater emphasis on clinical observation.

Bath attracted pragmatists rather than theoreticians and there was a relatively large proportion of foreign trained doctors practising in the city during the early seventeenth century. Amongst these, Dr John Sherwood (1542–1620), who treated Lord Burghley on his visit to Bath in 1604, was a student at Rheims. Padua University spawned another two, Dr William Hatten (d.1634) and Dr Edward Jorden (1569–1632). Dr John Ostendorph, who published a treatise on the Bath waters in 1639, was a graduate of Leiden University. Dr Samuel Bave, the eldest of several generations of Bath medical practitioners, was a graduate of Paris. He removed to Bath from Gloucester at the advanced age of fifty-two. Guidott called him 'an able physician, well versed in high Dutch, low Dutch and French but, above all, eminent in Latin.' During his stay in Paris, Bave acted as tutor to the son of Sir Thomas Edmonds, English ambassador to France; no doubt the ambassador's allowance helped maintain Bave in his medical studies there.

English physicians of this period represented a spectrum of seventeenth century society though, as a rule, medicine was not a gentlemen's profession, the upper echelons preferring law. It is often assumed that the physician, as opposed to the other two branches of the profession, enjoyed an elevated status in English society but this has been erroneously extrapolated from the experience of the profession in the early twentieth century. Nevertheless, the Stuart physician often believed his skills alone merited an elevation of his social status, regardless of a lowly birth, thereby providing an entree into the upper strata of society in which he sought fraternisation. More often, this was achieved by playing on the vanities of society's upper cruSt

There appears to be a considerable preoccupation with status in the writing of Thomas Guidott. Ralph Bayley is described as 'a proper comely person" and John Dauntsey is styled a 'gentleman of good extraction', whilst John Maplet, the son of a London shoemaker, is described as a 'man well accomplished as a gentleman and a scholar'. Many practitioners at this time came from medical families. Ralph Bayley was nephew of Walter Bayley, Regius Professor of Medicine at Oxford while his son, Thomas, was a physician at Newbury. Bayley's wife was related to the mother of Robert Peirce, born in 1622 and who became the best known Bath physician of the seventeenth century.

Until the mid-eighteenth century many physicians only practised in Bath during the bathing season. This seems to have been necessary because of the seasonal influx of visitors to the city. Presumably there was not enough work to support most physicians during the winter months. Edward Baynard and Thomas Guidott moved between London and Bath. Both were rather brusque and outspoken personalities who had a number of acrimonious and stormy relations with other physicians. Peirce had little regard for Guidott but was happy to consult with Baynard, and with John Mayow, a bright young physician from Oxford who practised in Bath during the summer season. Tobias Venner moved between Bath and Bridgewater, renting accommodation near the Hot Bath during the summer.

Important families often travelled to Bath with their own medical attendants. Nathaniel Highmore had an extensive practice at Sherborne but frequently accompanied his patients to Bath. When Charles II and his wife came in 1663 to stay in the Abbey House, they were accompanied by Sir Charles Scarborough and Sir Alexander Fraizer. Fraizer, who was the queen's physician, had not previously visited the city and Peirce had to explain to him how the waters were used and enlighten him on their chemical composition. He maintained a correspondence with Peirce for some time afterwards. Realising that the composition of the Bath waters was very similar to the waters of the French spa at Bourbon where he had recommended many of his patients to travel, he resolved in future to send patients needing spa treatment to Bath, 'saving them the expense and hazard of a voyage by sea and a long journey afterwards by land'. He also decided that the English climate was more suitable for English bodies.

Physicians were not the only source for medical advice and treatment. There were apothecaries, surgeons, midwives, quack doctors and bone setters as well as wise women who employed a common sense approach to minor aliments. There were also a number of self-help books and the more educated families might keep a commonplace book in which recipes for medicaments and other tips on health would be recorded.

Unlike many of the physicians, the Bath apothecaries were usually resident in the city. Several were part of medical dynasties. The Gibbes family provides a good example. Gibbes is a name which frequently turns up in Bath and Bristol medical circles. A Bath apothecary, George Gibbes, is mentioned in the Abbey Registers as having died in 1607 and left five pounds to the Abbey in his will. He may have been the father of another George Gibbes who was an apothecary-surgeon in the city in 1634. Thomas Johnson, a well-known London apothecary who can claim fame for introducing bananas into England, visited Bath in that year with a party of botanically minded friends. Johnson wrote about his travels in a publication entitled *Mercurius Botanicus* in which he described Gibbes' garden and gives a list of one hundred and seventeen exotic plants which he saw growing there. Evidently Gibbes had collected some of the plants during a visit to America and another botanist of this period, John Parkinson, attributes the introduction of the Virginian Aster to Gibbes, whom he addresses as a 'chirurgion of Bath.' The terms *surgeon* and *apothecary* are often interchanged when referring to the same man and this habit led, in the eighteenth century, to the combination term *surgeon-apothecary* meaning a general practitioner.

The site of Gibbes' garden has not been determined though Holland suggests it may have been on land behind houses on the north side of Cheap Street belonging to the Perman family, related to Gibbes by marriage. The list of plants in Gibbes' garden contains some medicinal herbs, for example absinth, garlic, autumn crocus, liquorice, hyssop and rue, and it is possible that Gibbes ran a wholesale materia medica business beside his medical practice.

Knowledge of the activities of seventeenth century surgeons in Bath is a good deal more obscure than for the other two branches of the profession. The term was often used to denote a general practitioner and has little distinction from apothecary. Surgeons in the city were licensed to practice by the diocese of Bath and Wells and there are instances of offenders being reprimanded. In 1623, Rudolf Ewens was accused of practising surgery without a licence and in the same year Symon Bynion and Edward Bonnie were made diocesan licentiates. The Abbey Registers mention several surgeons, including John Hilmer (Elmer), who died in 1608, and Nevill Unwin who died in 1656. Peirce mentions surgeons in his book Bath Memoirs, in particular Henry Dyer who operated on the gouty swellings of Lord Digby's servant. Surgeons, like apothecaries, learnt their skills by apprenticeship. Major surgery was rarely carried out and their main concerns lay with dressings, blood letting, cupping, making issues, cauterising and making and applying medicinal plasters.

Besides the fees earned from medical work, it was not unusual for members of all three branches of the profession in Bath to enjoy a second income gained either directly or indirectly from property. Several lodging houses were owned or tenanted by medical men who ran them as

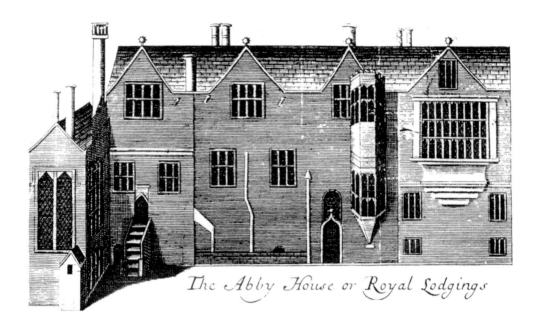

The Abby House or Royal Lodgings

Engraving of Abbey
House taken from
*Gilmore's Map of Bath
1694*

nursing homes. The grandest and most palatial was the
Abbey House. The building appears on Gilmore's map,
both in the plan and amongst the lodgings depicted around
the margin. It was demolished shortly before 1755 when
Charles Lucas made the first excavations of Roman baths
on the site. It appears to have been occupied by several
medical men during the fifteenth and sixteenth centuries.

Lady Rutland lodged there in 1605 when she came for
treatment. At that time it was in the possession of Dr John
Sherwood who charged Lady Rutland a total of thirty
pounds which included fees for medical advice and the cost
of lodgings. In 1653, Abbey House passed to Dr Robert
Peirce who used it as his private nursing home for nearly
half a century. During this time, King Charles II and
Catherine of Braganza were amongst the visitors.

Given that the majority of treatments in the seventeenth
and eighteenth centuries were useless or even dangerous, it
is not surprising to find the medical profession was at times
the subject of ridicule and satirical commentary. An
extreme example appeared in print in 1737, the year before
the Bath General Hospital was founded. In a long poem
entitled *The Diseases of Bath*[150] the anonymous author[151]

savages all three branches of the medical profession in the city, particularly the five physicians who were involved with the foundation of the General Hospital.

> But lo, a long Procession nigh -- make room:
> Five bred Physicians! Bred to fix our doom.
> Sad Evils these for one poor Town to bear:
> Five Plagues than Egypt's seven far more severe.
> Say, florid Florifer, if you can tell:
> How many Patients you've dispatch'd to Hell?
> Say Harrington of not inferior skill!
> How many Church-yards thy Prescriptions fill?
> Procus has laid his thousands on the Floor;
> And modest Bostick his ten thousands more.
> Big blust'ring Cheyne, not the last in fame,
> Tho' the Muse lead up in the rear his Name,
> Has sent such Colonies to Pluto's land;
> The God was forc'd to beg he'd stop his hand.

The doctor referred to as florid Florifer is thought to be William Oliver (1695-1764). He has since become a household name, not on account of any significant contribution to the advancement of medical science, but through having invented a biscuit, much appreciated by lovers of cheese and wine. There was an earlier Dr William Oliver (c1658-1716) who moved between Bath and London, where he mainly practised. This first Dr Oliver was the son of the vicar of Launceston in Cornwall. His medical studies had been interrupted by his decision to join the Duke of Monmouth's rebellion. After the defeat, he escaped and took refuge in various European countries, returning to England in the army of William of Orange, who rewarded him for his service. His main contribution to Bath medicine was his literary effort in publishing a dissertation on the hot waters which ran to five editions. [152]

The second and better known Dr Oliver was born near Penzance on the 4th August, 1695, being the second son of John and Mary Oliver of Trevarnoe, a house in the parish of Sithney, Cornwall. At the age of nineteen, he entered Pembroke College, Cambridge, graduating M.B. in 1720. In that same year he went to the University of Leiden, which

137

was then the principal resort of ambitious postgraduate medical students from England. After some years abroad he returned to England and took his M.D. at Cambridge in 1725. He was elected a Fellow of the Royal Society in 1729. Oliver had established himself as a physician in Plymouth and had introduced the relatively new practice of smallpox inoculation there. This technique, which involved pricking material from the pocks of a smallpox sufferer into the skin of a person requiring immunisation, was widely used in the eighteenth century until Edward Jenner pioneered the safer technique of cowpox inoculation, or vaccination, at the end of the century.

The idea of inoculating to produce smallpox immunity seems to have originated in Turkey and was first described in this country by Emanuel Timoni, who communicated his observations to the Royal Society in 1713, but nobody took much notice of him. Eight years later Lady Mary Wortley Montague, who had also been travelling in Turkey, popularised the technique in London.

By this time, the young Oliver had graduated in medicine from Cambridge and was attending a course of lectures at Leiden University given by Dr Herman Boerhaave, who was reputed to be the greatest medical teacher of his time anywhere in Europe. Boerhaave broke with the traditional medical teaching of the sort experienced at Oxford and Cambridge. These two universities, then the only centres of medical education in England, taught medicine purely as a theoretical subject. During his six years at Cambridge, Oliver would have studied little other than the classical texts and attended lectures purely with theoretical concepts of disease and its treatment. It was hardly surprising that physicians had a reputation for diagnosing, prognosticating and prescribing without as much as a glance at their patients. Indeed, they often relied only on a description of the case conveyed to them second hand by the patient's surgeon or apothecary. Those physicians who were fortunate enough to have been pupils of Boerhaave were imbued with the idea of bedside diagnosis, for the great man taught his students by demonstrating patients to them. This concept was a complete innovation in the history of medical education.

Although Plymouth was geographically remote from London's Royal Society, Oliver, like so many inquisitive gentlemen philosophers scattered around the provinces, maintained contact with the Society's affairs and a friendship with some of its members.

In 1723, he communicated a case description to the Royal Society of a patient from Fowey who had a malformation of his genitalia. By curious coincidence, the case was described by another Plymouth physician, John Huxham, and appears in the same edition of the *Philosophical Transactions*. Even more remarkable is the fact that the two doctors' descriptions are substantially different. Subsequently, the surgeon who attended the patient wrote to the journal accusing Oliver of gross carelessness and inaccuracy in his case description. Such a rejoinder must have been an embarrassment to Oliver and it is curious he did not try to vindicate himself with a published reply. Indeed the whole episode is puzzling. Huxham, despite being regarded highly as an author, had a notorious reputation in Plymouth where it was rumoured he was a liar and a cheat. It is therefore not inconceivable that Huxham, wanting to get rid of his rival physician, hatched up an embarrassment which ended in the two contradictory case reports being published. Whatever the explanation, Huxham's rival soon moved off to a more successful career in Bath.

He was thirty-three when he arrived at Bath in 1728 with his Cornish cousin, the Reverend William Borlase. Oliver rented a house in Westgate Street but as he became more successful he acquired a grand house set back on the west side of Queen Square. The house was later demolished and the site is now occupied by The Bath Royal Literary and Scientific Institution. The present building was designed in the Greek Revival style by John Pinch, the younger. During his time in Bath, Oliver purchased several other properties including a farm house at Bathford which he called Trevarnoe and land in Weston, a village on the western outskirts of Bath where he is buried.

Dr Oliver became friendly with Ralph Allen, a fellow Cornishman who had amassed considerable wealth from developing a postal service and subsequently from Bath

Dr William Oliver.
Detail from
Hoare's painting
in RNHRD (*Clive
Quinnell/RNHRD.*)

stone mining. The doctor was introduced to the coterie of
Allen's friends which included Alexander Pope, Beau Nash
and Oliver Goldsmith. He quickly built up a flourishing
private practice which probably owed as much to his
influential friendships as his medical skill. Certainly one of
his patients, Mrs Anne Pitt was impressed by his clinical

ability.[153]   Oliver published several medical tracts, none which could be said to advance the knowledge of scientific medicine, but then he lived at a time which narrowly antedated the arrival of evidence based therapeutics. The embryonic inspiration for modern medicine did not gather momentum until the last quarter of the eighteenth century. He contributed brief papers to the *Philosophical Transactions*, one noted previously and another on dropsy.[154]   He published a *Practical Essay on the Use and Abuse of Warm Water Bathing in Gouty Cases* (1751), a disease from which he himself suffered and *Cases of the Persons Admitted into the Infirmary at Bath under the Care of Doctor Oliver* (1760). His literary output was not confined to medical works and he published a short biographical sketch of his friend Beau Nash.

His most memorable claim to fame was his invention of the Bath Oliver, a low calorie biscuit which he recommended to his overfed and overweight patients. The doctor is reputed to have entrusted the recipe to his coachman, Mr Atkins who, with the aid of one hundred pounds and a supply of flour donated by his employer, opened a shop in Green Street and amassed a large fortune selling the biscuits. Unfortunately the documents relating to the biscuit's origin were lost in 1941 when the premises of its manufacturers, Fortt and Son of Bath, were bombed. The biscuits are still made today.

Oliver was one of the founding members of the General Hospital and in 1737 he offered a plot of land for its site, but the build eventually took place elsewhere. In 1739 he was made deputy president of the hospital and in the following year he and Jeremiah Peirce were elected as the institution's first physician and surgeon. These were honorary appointments and required attendance on patients for only a few hours each week. However both men played a major role in the hospital's administration until they resigned in 1761. Oliver managed to attend over six hundred meetings of the management committee which met weekly.

Jerry Peirce was born in 1697 at Ludgate Hill in the City of London. His father, also Jeremiah, was a lace dealer and member of the Merchant Taylors' Company who had married his mother, Mary Sarah Bishop. Peirce had at least one sister, Sarah (b.1692) who married a Capt John Burnett in 1721. At some point, Jerry Peirce moved to Bath and was made an honorary freeman of the city in March 1731 (along with Dr Alex Rayner, who was appointed a physician to the General Hospital). By 1738, Peirce was well established as a surgeon in Bath. According to the author of *Diseases of Bath*, Peirce was less of a butcher than some of his colleagues.

> *Pierce is humane, and, tho' a surgeon bred,*
> *Is much too honest to enhance his trade:*
> *Deals but against his grain in blood and steel;*
> *And can the pain, he gives to patients, feel.*
> *Not of that base, amphibious Fry of Men,*
> *Whose bare Approach wou'd make a Wound gangrene.*
> *Proof against gold; friend to his species; -He*
> *Hates Mischief's hand, tho' It present a fee.*
> *Oh! wou'd that cannibal, man-mangling Brood*
> *Learn from thee, Pierce, not to delight in blood!*

Though Peirce might have reluctantly wielded the scalpel, he did engage in some major surgery. In 1737 a report appeared in the Philosophical Transactions of the Royal Society describing a large bony tumour of the knee. The patient, a Somersetshire farmer called William Hedges, had the affected leg amputated above the knee by Peirce.[155]

He owned a tiny villa on the end of Lansdown, designed by John Wood and called Lilliput Castle. It has since been extensively enlarged and called Battlefields. Shortly after it was built, the roof was destroyed by a chimney conflagration which, according to John Wood,[156] was owing to Mr Peirce's hospitable nature; it appears that he was in the habit of over-stoking the kitchen fire for the benefit of his guests. Some sketches by Thomas Robbins in the Victoria and Albert museum show picturesque gardens complete with follies which were part of the small estate surrounding the property.[157] He also rented a house in Bath at 9 Gay Street and three stables in John Street.

Peirce died in 1768 and has a memorial plaque in St Swithin's Church, Walcot, where he is interred. After his death, the

Jerry Peirce, surgeon.
Detail from Hoare's
painting in RNHRD
(*C. Quinnell./RNHRD*)

stables in John Street were let to his widow, Ann until 1776.
Rental of the stables then passed to his nephew, Jerry
Peirce Crane, who also inherited Lilliput Castle. J. P.
Crane was born in January 1752 and was the son of Mary
and Stafford Crane, a London surgeon, who lived at
Salisbury Court in Fleet Street. J.P. Crane eloped with
Penelope Blathwayt who lived at Dyrham Park, but he ran
into debt and had to sell Lilliput Castle. Their son, William
Crane subsequently changed his name to Blathwayt so that
he could inherit the Dyrham estate.

Several other contemporaries of Oliver are mentioned in
the *Diseases of Bath*. Dr George Cheyne (blust'ring Cheyne)
was certainly a popular physician in his time, though as
much for his wit as his medical expertise[158]. On his arrival

in Bath, he weighed over thirty-two stone but this did not deter him from publishing *An Essay on Health and Long Life*, warning against excesses of food and drink. Samuel Johnson, John Wesley, Alexander Pope, David Hume, Catherine Walpole and Samuel Richardson all consulted him at one time or another. He was also Beau Nash's doctor though Bath's famous Master of Ceremonies held a cynical view of Cheyne's treatment. When Cheyne asked Nash if he had followed his prescriptions, he replied that if he had he would have surely broken his neck because he threw them out of an upstairs window.

Although Cheyne was active in establishing the General Hospital, he was never appointed as an honorary physician to the institution. Its first physicians were William Oliver (Florid Florifer), Richard Bostock (Bostick), Edward Harington (Harrington) and Alexander Rayner (possibly Procus). All were in their early forties when they were appointed and all had submitted theses to their universities to obtain MD degrees, Oliver to Cambridge and the others to Oxford. More important, all were established Bath practitioners and had made social connections with persons involved in raising funds during the years leading up to the hospital's foundation, though none more so than William Oliver.

The Bath General Hospital appears to have been a bastion of Oxbridge medical graduates until the latter part of the eighteenth century. This led to much bad feeling from the graduates of other universities who were eager to be elected honorary physicians to the hospital, an appointment which added to their reputations and enhanced their private practice. Many of the hospital's physicians were wealthy men. Oliver owned several properties in and around Bath, including the house in Queen Square and a farm at Bathford, three miles from the centre. Rice Charleton (elected physician in 1757) and Abel Moysey (elected in 1747) both commissioned Gainsborough to paint their portraits. Moysey was Gainsborough's personal physician until he upset the artist by telling him his daughter had hereditary mental disease, a diagnosis which was subsequently proved to be correct.[159] According to the Rev. Richard Warner, who was an outspoken rector of Bath

Abbey, Dr Moysey's methods of earning a living were not always beyond reproach.

Warner intimated that the doctor had an arrangement with a London physician to refer wealthy old ladies to him on the pretext that they needed some spa treatment. On one occasion, a lady arrived at Bath with a letter and Moysey was summoned to her lodging. The doctor read the letter and put it in his pocket. Having taken the patient's history and examined her pulse, he pronounced his opinion, recovered his fee and left the room. As he left, he pulled a handkerchief from his pocket and failed to notice the letter slip to the floor. The old lady, being of a curious nature, read the contents:

Portrait of Dr A. Moysey by Thomas Gainsborough
(© *The Holburne Museum, on long-term loan from a private collection)*

Dear Doctor, I send you herewith an old fat goose whom I have long been in the habit of plucking. One wing I reserve for myself, the other is at the service of my friends.

The following morning, the doctor revisited his patient and was about to take her pulse when she 'thanked him for his kind intention to strip her of her remaining feathers but observed that though she might be an old goose, she was not so far advanced in her dotage as to suffer such harpies.....to prey longer on her unfortunate carcass.'[160]

Satirical jibes at the medical profession were at least veiled by the use of pseudonyms (Warner disguised Dr Moysey as Dr Fleecem). The doctors themselves were less obtuse with their sneers. In 1757, William Oliver's public row with the Irish physician Charles Lucas, who had taken issue with Oliver over his analysis of the Bath waters, led to heated correspondence between the two men; the letters, liberally sprinkled with phrases like *scurrilous mouth, rancorous heart* and *infidel in physic* were subsequently published.[161]

Establishing a practice in Georgian Bath could be a daunting business for a freshly arrived physician, and even those who managed it could later fall on hard times. The Rev. Warner, who delighted in satirising Bath society when he was not preaching to his congregation, epitomised the plight of the failed physician in his character Dr Borecat. The satirist's character, believed to be based on a real Bath doctor called Burkitt, bemoans his predicament:

A thousand times have I cursed that foolish ambition which induced me to leave my pretty business in the country, go to the expense of £15 for an Aberdeen Diploma and settle at Bath as a physician. You will hardly believe I should be so mad as to quit a practice that cleared me about £200 per annum (all lying within the circumference of sixty miles) and come here upon speculation... When I have reflected upon this dangerous situation and compared with my present one – chance half guinea fees and half my time no fees at all – the sneers of my more fortunate brethren and jealousy of those who are upon the same lay as myself; ... I have more than once resolved to put my parchment in the fire, quit my present character and abode and go back to my old sign of the pestle and mortar in the village of Rattleguts.[162]

Buying medical degrees may seem a dubious business but towards the end of the eighteenth century, several of the newly founded Scottish universities were happy to confer M.D. degrees on established surgeons and apothecaries, provided they were sponsored by another medical graduate and were able to pay the fee. Though this was open to abuse, and provided graduates of the two ancient English universities with ammunition for cynicism, it should be remembered that surgeon-apothecaries were often more experienced and able as doctors than theoretically trained physicians. One of the most celebrated doctors of the time, Edward Jenner, purchased his M.D. from St Andrew's University in this way.

The honorary staff of the General Hospital were elected by a ballot amongst the Committee of Governors. For most of its history, the number was restricted to three physicians and three surgeons. In the early years, vacancies were announced on broadsides posted in the Pump Room. By the end of the eighteenth century, the posts were advertised in the local press. The successful applicant was usually a medical man already established in practice in the city. Abel Moysey moved to Bath in 1743, having previously practised in Sherborne, and was elected honorary physician after the short period of four years practice in the city. He was still a relatively young man of thirty-one, and it was more usual to elect physicians in their forties and fifties, after they had been established in a Bath practice for at least ten years. Surgeons appear to have been selected by similar criteria for age and experience.

Social connections were important in determining the selection of the eighteenth century medical staff. Many of the Governors who lived locally were members of the city council and might therefore be expected to show a preference for medical men with a similar involvement. As in the previous century one finds a significant number of the medical staff amongst the list of mayors for the city. Henry Wright, elected surgeon in 1742, was mayor on two occasions. Each of six successive surgeons elected at the end of the Georgian era were mayors. Physicians also played a part in the civic role, though more so in the nineteenth century. The most recent Bath physician to have

Portrait of Henry Wright, Bath surgeon. *(RNHRD/ Clive Quinnell)*

been elected mayor was George Kersley, but nowadays only a few local medical practitioners concern themselves with local politics.

Family connections were also helpful. Philip Ditcher, elected surgeon to the General Hospital in 1744, was a friend of James Leake, a well known bookseller in Bath who was one of the earliest Governors. Leake introduced Ditcher to his cousin, daughter of Samuel Richardson, the celebrated novelist and publisher. Ditcher subsequently married the girl after much wrangling over the dowry.[163] Another early surgeon, Joseph Phillott, elected to the hospital in 1797, was able to mobilise the influence of his three brothers. One was a Bath banker and the other two were immediate neighbours of the hospital; to its right, Henry Phillott was landlord of the Bear Inn and to its left, Rev. James Phillott was the incumbent of Rectory House (later to become the site of the hospital's west wing).

The local connection is far more evident with surgeons and apothecaries. This is probably a reflection of the way they were trained. Several had been apprentices of their seniors. For instance, Thomas Palmer, the son of a Wiltshire clerk, was apprenticed to Jerry Peirce, the senior surgeon. Palmer was subsequently elected surgeon to the General Hospital in 1742. In the same way, Joseph Phillott had been apprenticed to his more senior hospital colleague, Henry Wright.[164]

Hospital appointments, whether as honorary physicians and surgeons or as poorly paid resident apothecaries, were extremely sought after. For the former, it provided a subtle way of advertising ones excellence and for the latter it was a useful means of a younger man gaining experience and building up a practice in a very competitive field. Even allowing for the rise in population in the city during the first third of the nineteenth century, the increase in the number of medical practitioners at this time was astronomical.

The rise in numbers appears most prevalent amongst the surgeon-apothecaries. As in previous centuries, this group represent a considerable cross-section of practitioners, both socially and intellectually. Many of them came from local families. It is not unusual to find several generations perpetuating a practice. The Goldstone family was a good example. Charles Goldstone appears in the list of apothecaries for 1777. By 1819, there were two Goldstone's practising, both members of the Royal College of Surgeons and by 1830 there were four. The Spry's were also well represented as medical practitioners. Joseph H. Spry, his

Characature of Morgan Nichols (1740–1815), Bath surgeon-apothecary, by J Nixon. *(Victoria Art Gallery, Bath and North East Somerset Council)*

149

brother James, his nephew George and his father Joseph, who attended Lord Nelson, were all general practitioners. Nelson also consulted Morgan Nicholls, another Bath surgeon-apothecary. Other medical families of this time included Haviland, Anderdon, Horton, Crooke and Kitson.

Physicians on the other hand were not predominantly from local families, although there are some notable exceptions where sons and even grandsons of Bath physicians returned to practice in their native city. This applied particularly to the General Hospital were family names reappear in the list of physicians and surgeons. Edward Harington, elected physician in 1740, was the uncle of Henry Harington who became honorary physician to the hospital in 1780. The Harington family, well-known in Georgian Bath, was descended from the celebrated Sir John Harington of Kelston who distinguished himself as the inventor of the water-closet, some three centuries before its Victorian rediscovery.[165] Kelston Hall had to be sold in 1759 when the Harington then in residence, the brother of physician Edward, fell into debt. Dr Henry Harington (1727–1816), formerly a physician at Wells in Somerset, moved to Bath in 1757. Prolific in literary and musical creativity, Harington was a man of sharp wit and famed as a raconteur.

Claims that the selection of the hospital's medical staff was corrupted by nepotism may have been well founded. William Baylies, the aggrieved Bath physician who failed to get elected to an honorary post, learned that William Oliver's son would have been elected physician in 1758 had it not been for the objection of one of the Governors who said 'Call it no longer the Bath, but Oliver's Hospital.'[166]

Similarly, the names of two Falconers and two Parrys feature amongst the list of physicians. William Falconer was born at Chester in 1744, and commenced practice at Bath at the age of twenty-six on the advice of his friend and fellow physician, John Fothergill. He was a man of great literary distinction, publishing many books and papers on diverse subjects. He was appointed physician to the Mineral Water Hospital at the age of forty and, in 1797, he attended Horatio Nelson during his stay in the city, charging him a guinea for his services. William Falconer had one son,

Dr Henry Harington (1727–1816). Engraving from a painting by Thomas Beach. *(Wellcome Library, London)*

Thomas, who turned from medicine to the church and, though never a physician to the hospital, was a governor for some years. Thomas's son, Randle Wilbraham Falconer, also took a medical degree and returned to practise in Bath where he followed in his grandfather's footsteps by being elected honorary physician to the Mineral Water Hospital in 1856. R.W. Falconer wrote the first history of the hospital and his image is perpetuated in a rather sombre bust.

Caleb Hillier Parry, appointed physician to the hospital in 1799, had four sons. The eldest, Charles, took a medical degree at Edinburgh and then travelled to Germany with the poet Samuel Taylor Coleridge to study at Göttingen University. He eventually returned to Bath and was elected physician to the hospital in 1818. Charles youngest brother, William, achieved both knighthood and fame as an Arctic explorer.

As in the earlier centuries, physicians as a group were more mobile than the surgeons and apothecaries. Moves could be in both directions. Andrew Bain (c1755–1827) started practice in Bath but moved to London between 1801 and 1804, finally retiring to Dorset in 1820. Thomas Cogan (1736–1818), built up a successful obstetric practice in London during which time he helped to set up the Royal Humane Society. He retired to Bath at the age of 70 where he continued a small practice and founded a local humane society dedicated to rescuing and resuscitating persons who had drowned in the river or canal.

Other physicians retiring to Bath at this time included Matthew Dobson (Liverpool) and P. Elliot (Reading, London and Swansea). William Fraser (c1780–1807), physician extraordinary to the Prince of Wales, began practice in Southampton, moved to Bath for eight years from 1791, then moved to London and finally died at Shornbrook in Bedfordshire. These short-stay practitioners appear to swell the total numbers recorded in the Bath Directories, though they may have only maintained a miniscule practice in the city. Another group who swelled the numbers and were more eager to establish themselves in a larger way were practitioners, both physicians and surgeon-apothecaries, disbanded from the army and navy.

Besides established practitioners, there were a number of medical students in the city. Most would have been apprenticed to surgeons and apothecaries but some of the physicians with hospital or dispensary appointments took pupils. In 1758, the bodies of two criminals executed at Taunton were sent to Thomas Palmer, a surgeon at the General Hospital, for instruction of his pupil.[167]

Apprenticeships are mentioned in the lists of freemen and in the minutes of the corporation, though no complete list of medical apprentices exists. Apprenticeship lasted seven years and the starting age appears to have been about sixteen, though there is considerable variation. Charles Crook (1843) completed his apprenticeship in 1778, indicating that he started at the age of fourteen. Joseph Hume Spry commenced his apprenticeship at about seventeen and George Kitson at sixteen or thereabouts.

Apothecaries' apprentices seem to have been a recognisable element in the city's population. A theatre critic observed in 1816 that they 'hissed and attempted to kick up a riot' during a performance of a play called *Who's Who* which was performed at the theatre and in which there was an apothecary character.[168]

A good deal of medical education was carried out in Bath at this time, although no medical school was established. Students were allowed to attend patients in hospital. According to the rules of the Bath United Hospital which was established in 1823 after amalgamating the old Casualty Hospital and the City Infirmary and Dispensary, the Trustees and Committee reserved the power to reprimand or expel any pupil or apprentice behaving improperly either to patients, the apothecary, matron or nurses, or not conforming to the established rules[169]. There may have been a school of anatomy in the city, probably attached to the hospital but there is no definitive evidence for this. [170] In 1893 the Government's Inspector of Anatomy recorded that Bath had three bodies available for dissection. In the early nineteenth century at least one Bath surgeon carried out post mortem examinations on their own premises. John Cottle Spender (1801–1865), a general practitioner living at 36 Gay Street, had a dissecting room in a building at the bottom of his garden, indicating that he may have given instruction in anatomy. His son, John Kent Spender, who eventually became a physician to the Mineral Water Hospital acquired his knowledge of anatomy in this building.[171]

The United and Mineral Water hospitals both had a pathology museum and the United hospital had the extensive medical library bequeathed by Caleb Parry and other local practitioners. Both museums have since vanished and much of the contents of the old United Hospital library were transferred to Bristol University Medical School library where they can still be found.

Lectures on some medical subjects took place in Bath. Sir George Smith-Gibbes published a syllabus for a course of chemical lectures in 1799. Dr Charles Wilkinson, who had lectured on experimental philosophy at St Bartholomew's

Hospital before moving to Bath, gave a course of lectures on pneumatics, calories, optics, hydrostatics, electricity and galvanism in 1815. The lectures were open to the public at a cost of one guinea. There do not appear to have been any organised lectures specifically for medical students at any time during the early nineteenth century. As a consequence, any student wishing to pursue the comprehensive curriculum laid down by the Court of Examiners of the Society of Apothecaries in 1815 had to attend lectures elsewhere.

The large increase in numbers of the city's medical profession came at a time when the spa facilities were at a low ebb. Though there was still a large influx of ailing visitors, Bath was becoming a favourite place for retirement and it was this older age group who provided the bread and butter of medical practice. The attractions of the city in the early nineteenth century is nicely summarised by a contemporary writer:

> *Free from the bustle and inconvenience of a manufacturing town with little but little wholesale commerce it is particularly adapted to the quiet repose necessary for the invalids who resort thither for the benefit of the waters. The taste and beauty of its domestic and public edifices, their commanding and elevated situations (the Crescents particularly) exhibit a combination of architectural symmetry and grandeur which aided by the effect of the surrounded scenery presents such an harmonious blending of the beauties of nature and art as no other city in Great Britain can rival.*

Many of the citizens were not only ailing but very wealthy and provided a substantial income for the more successful medical men. George Norman, whose father had founded the Casualty Hospital and who himself had engineered the amalgamation with the City Infirmary to form the new United Hospital, was highly thought of by both rich and poor. He was so successful in his practice that at one point his annual income exceeded four thousand pounds, making him the best paid surgeon outside London. When he retired in 1857, the occasion was marked by a double presentation at the Guildhall which was attended by a huge crowd. He was presented with a bust of himself and two hundred pounds which had been subscribed by his more wealthy admirers. He was also presented with a silver salver and at the end of the presentation an Irish labourer stood up amongst the crowd and exclaimed 'Why sir, I was murdered some years ago and Mr. Norman cured me'.

Some practitioners enjoyed the best of both worlds having made a fortune before retiring to Bath where they continued a successful practice. William Tudor (1769–1845) settled at Bath in 1805 after retiring from the 2nd Dragoon Guards on half pay. As surgeon to the Queen, the Prince Regent and Duke of Cambridge, he continued to practice in the city owning a house in Queen's Parade and a large mansion at Kelston to the northeast of Bath.

Partnerships were rare at this time and most practitioners practised from their homes, although the more wealthy had rooms in the city and retired to a villa on the outskirts. In 1826, out of forty-eight surgeon-apothecaries (i.e. general practitioners) there were only two partnerships, Kitson and Grove, at Queen Square and Spry, Long and Spry at Gay Street. An earlier partnership between Joseph Spry and William Bowen at 1, Argyle Street was formed after Bowen completed his apprenticeship with Spry.

Many physicians working in Bath during the eighteenth century demonstrate a wide breadth of interests and diversity of achievements. From Oliver onwards, Bath doctors represent a human mosaic of tremendous educational accomplishment; in literature, in science, in commerce and in the arts. Thomas Brewster, elected physician to the General Hospital in 1744, became famous for his translation of the six Satires of Perseus. David Hartley, who was elected in the same year as Brewster, is remembered far more as a philosopher then as a physician. His reputation in medicine was considerably stained by his championship of a quack remedy for treatments of urinary stone, a condition from which Hartley suffered. Brewster and Hartley were appointed as supernumerary physicians shortly after the hospital opened, together with Richard Bostock, a recusant who had obtained his MD degree at Utrecht, and William Woodforde, the Regius Professor of Medicine at Oxford. Woodforde, one of the less distinguished professors of physic at the University, seems to have spent a considerable amount of time in Bath as he regularly attended committee meetings at the hospital. The governors may have elected Woodforde as an honorary physician through a desire to give the hospital credibility in the world of academic medicine. He was also a Fellow of the Royal College of Physicians and their Censor in 1733.

In the later years of the eighteenth century, interest in the developing sciences is reflected in the considerable number of names of Bath doctors which appear amongst the founding members of the Bath Philosophical Society, the Bath and West of England Society and the Fleece Medical Society, one of the earliest provincial medical societies in the country. Caleb Parry was a member of all three societies.

Bust of Caleb Hillier Parry. *(Bath Royal Literary and Scientific Institute)*

The Fleece Medical Society was so named because meetings were held at the Fleece Inn at Rodborough, a small village near Stroud in Gloucestershire. It was at one of these gatherings in 1788 that Dr Parry told his audience that angina pectoris was caused by coronary artery disease, though it took another one hundred and twenty-five years for the medical profession to accept his theory. Caleb Hillier Parry distinguished himself both financially and professionally and is reputed to have enjoyed an annual income in excess of seven thousand pounds at the height of his career. He was the author of many perceptive publications, and was a keen naturalist, agriculturalist and balloonist as well as a musician and painter. He was the first physician to describe the association between overactivity of the thyroid gland and the staring gaze known as exophthalmos, though the paper which he read to the members of the Fleece Medical Society was not published for some time afterwards, by which time another physician called Graves had described the condition which came to bear his name.

The Fleece Medical Society had a small and select membership, including the great pioneer of vaccination, Edward Jenner, who was one of Parry's closest friends. The last meeting of the society took place in 1793 and there were no further medical societies launched in the vicinity of Bath until the early nineteenth century.

Parry arrived in Bath in 1779, the year in which the Bath Philosophical Society was founded for discussion of scientific and philosophical subjects and making experiments to illustrate them. There were at least twenty-seven original members which included six physicians and two surgeons[172]. The Society lasted only eight years. It is possible that this early demise was due to members of the Society leaving the district. William Herschel, the astronomer who discovered Uranus, was one of the most active members, contributing thirty-one papers. He moved to Datchet in 1782. The chemist and cleric, Joseph Priestley, had moved from Bowood House in Wiltshire to Birmingham two years earlier. Other members died but enthusiasm was not dampened and three more philosophical societies were formed, the last of which is still extant (The Bath Royal Literary and Scientific Institute).

The Bath and West of England Society also had support from its medical members in the eighteenth century. Formed in 1777, it was instituted for the encouragement of agriculture, planting, manufacturers, commerce and fine arts, and was the brainchild of Edmund Rack, a Norfolk draper who settled in Bath in 1775[173]. At this time, agricultural standards in the western counties were deplorably low with little or no application of scientific knowledge. Edmund Rack's chief interest was in the advancement of agriculture by developing a technology to make the most of farming. He foresaw the need for an agricultural revolution to parallel the advancement in commercial and industrial spheres.

Application of technology was already underway in industry and it is interesting to find that scientific culture in industrial towns took on far more life and potency than it did in the southwest of England where society was centred around a rural economy.[174]

The Bath and West of England Society was the first and longest lasting of the city's scientific societies, later becoming the Bath and West Society. Like the Philosophical Societies, the medical profession were well represented as members in its early days. Why should this have been so? These institutions were not medical societies; indeed, the rules of the Philosophical Society forbade discussion of Law, Physic, Divinity and Politics. Medicine was not universally regarded as a science in the eighteenth century. Medical teachers at Oxford and Cambridge were still influenced by traditional dogma which did little to encourage an experimental approach. To an extent this also applied to the training of surgeons and apothecaries where apprenticeship tended to curb free thought and lead to isolation of its practitioners.

For the physicians, intellectual isolationism was a form of defence whereby the great mystery and elitism which surrounded this branch of the profession could be maintained. In Bath, this attitude also embraced the mysteries of the waters insofar as anyone outside the elite group could not publish the results of his own observations without fear of being harangued out of town. Isolationism was, therefore, a way of protecting business interests. The apothecary who compounded a successful potion or pill was not likely to share the recipe with his competitors. As long as the medical profession in its various branches adopted this attitude there was little hope of their integrating into provincial scientific or medical societies, a situation which still prevailed during William Oliver's lifetime. Within fifteen years of his death, some striking changes had taken place in Bath medical society. The most evident is the almost complete replacement of Oxford and Cambridge graduates by men trained at the Edinburgh Medical School. They came from a wide variety of backgrounds. Caleb Hillier Parry was the son of a non-conformist minister; William Falconer's father was Recorder of Chester; Anthony Fothergill (1732–1813), who moved to Bath in 1784, came from a Quaker family in Yorkshire. What characterises all of them is their diverse interests, enquiring minds and their involvement with technology, applying scientific discoveries to solve everyday problems.

Change was also taking place in the organisation of surgeons and apothecaries. Towards the close of the eighteenth century the latter group began to fragment into chemists and druggists on the one hand and general medical practitioners on the other. This trend continued during the first third of the nineteenth century. In 1800, there are listed in a Bath directory eighteen apothecaries and nine chemists and druggists, while in 1830 the apothecaries' numbers have dwindled to three whereas there are twenty-nine chemists and druggists. The surgeons began to fragment into those

Advert for dispensing chemist from *1837 edition of the Bath Directory (Private collection)*

who undertook the major surgery as opposed to the general practitioners. In the eighteenth century the terms apothecary, surgeon and surgeon-apothecary are often synonymous with the same kind of practitioner. By the nineteenth century, this group was eager to drop its trading image and identify itself within the professional class, a well-defined section of the newly emergent middle classes. Within the medical fraternity, the physician retained his elite position. Sometimes the upper social classes employed the services of a physician whereas the surgeon-apothecaries were consulted on matters concerning their servants.

Provincial apothecaries and surgeons may have also sought intellectual recognition by involvement in their local scientific or philosophical societies. An agricultural society might have interested the profession for another reason. Until the eighteenth century, technological developments in medicine and pharmacy had been minimal. In the latter field, there had been some advances in the application of

Portrait of Dr William Falconer. *(From his 'Dissertation on the Influence of the Passions' 1796)*

chemistry during the seventeenth century but innovation was generally lacking in the field of botany. Simples, a name given to drugs made from medicinal plants and herbs were either collected from an apothecary's physic garden or imported from abroad. It was in this particular field, the cultivation and processing of medicinal herbs, that an agricultural society assumed its relevance. Quite early on in the history of the Bath and West of England Society, the medical members became involved in a study of rhubarb cultivation. In the Society's publication, *Letters and Papers*, correspondence began to appear on the subject.[175] Medicinal rhubarb, *Rheum Palmatum*, was used as a mild laxative, the drug being prepared as a powder from the dried root of the plant. The drug was imported from Turkey, Russia and the East Indies. Though rhubarb of this type could be cultivated in this country[176], there was considerable doubt in the minds of many physicians that the English variety was efficacious. The Society set up a trial to assess the effect of home cultivated rhubarb, directed by Drs. Falconer and Parry and assisted by Mr. Farnell, house apothecary to the General Hospital. The results demonstrated conclusively that English rhubarb produced an effect 'in every respect such as might be expected from the best foreign rhubarb'.[177]

The Society's earlier publications show a distinct preoccupation with chemical analysis, a subject dear to the hearts of certain Bath physicians and apothecaries. William Falconer had a reputation as an accomplished chemist as well as a botanist. Both Falconer and Anthony Fothergill became interested in contamination of food by poisonous metals. The Society published Fothergill's work on lead and copper poisoning in which he identified potential sources of contamination. He described the numerous ways lead could be taken in to destroy the life of man: 'in oil, in wine, in rum, in cider, milk, cream, vinegar, pickles and preserves; tea may be deleterious by being packed in lead; children's playthings are commonly painted with red or white lead [and] many of the paints used in water colours are poison; cosmetics are chiefly preparations of lead, mercury and bismuth'.[178] Of copper he warns against food becoming contaminated by being left in badly tinned vessels, or vessels which have oxidised. There is also a letter from

N°4. Double Cottage with Skillings at the Ends

Falconer's design for cottages, (from *Letters and Papers of Bath and West of England Society, Vol 2.)*

Fothergill on the dangers of drinking too much strong liquor, with an accurate description both of acute alcoholic poisoning and chronic damage due to cirrhosis of the liver. The Society also concerned itself with techniques of cider production and the means by which the drink could be made less of a health hazard. Occupational health of those employed in agriculture is also discussed and in this connection there are several letters about rabies. Falconer's paper on the preservation of health of persons employed in agriculture follows a rather predictable course on the effects of climate, exercise and diet. There are, however, one or two observations and recommendations which display more originality. He warns of the dangers of eating too many pears, particularly when the stones are swallowed. There are useful directions for dealing with frostbite and exposure to extremes of climate. He comments that the small size of farmhouses with their low ceilings 'occasions too many people to be crowded together, a circumstance always very unfavorable to health and the most common source of contagious disorders'. His remark is an acknowledgement of the importance of building design in effecting an improvement in health. In this respect the early work of the Society contributed some useful ideas in the field of preventive medicine which antedated the sanitary legislation of the following century.

Besides the local societies described, a number of Bath medical men were active members of London medical and philosophical societies. It has been said that fellowship of the Royal Society in the first part of the eighteenth century was often determined merely by acquaintance with the secretary. Certainly Jerry Pierce's only claim to fellowship seems to be from contributing a paper on a tumour of the knee and maintaining friendship with Dr Richard Mead. By the end of the century, however, there seems little reason to doubt the merit of the Royal Society fellows. Drs. Parry, Falconer, Watson and Haygarth were all F.R.S. Several medical men were also involved with the London Medical Society, founded by John Coakley Lettsom who was also a member of the Bath Philosophical Society, despite living in London.

No medical society appears to have formed in Bath until 1836 when a branch of the Provincial Medical and Surgical

Association (later the British Medical Association) was established through the enthusiasm of Dr Edward Barlow (1779–1844). Local branch meetings were usually held in the board room at the Mineral Water Hospital and provided the opportunity for exchange of views and discussion of difficult or interesting cases. Any medical practitioner within striking distance of Bath could join. By 1837 there were sixty members including the Regius Professor of Medicine at Oxford. In 1841, the Bath and Bristol branches amalgamated. Members read papers and discussed medical issues, for example the payment of fees by assurance companies requesting medical reports from a proposer's personal medical attendant. Some early papers discussed were 'A case of suspended animation from drowning, a case of neuralgia, empyema of the lung following lodgement of pistol balls and treatment of diabetes mellitus by yeast'. The Association also dealt with ethical issues. Disputes were common between members of the profession and usually concerned the infringement of one practitioner's care of a patient by another practitioner. This usually arose because the patient called in a second opinion without the knowledge of the first practitioner. (An ethical committee of the British Medical Association still exists but few complaints of this kind have been heard since the arrival of the National Health Service which has had the effect of diminishing business competition which existed in the past)

In 1839, a Medical Book Society was started by Dr Thomas Sandon Watson, a physician to the Mineral Water Hospital, who managed to recruit fourteen other local doctors. Each member subscribed to the society's funds which were used to purchase medical books for its members and hold regular meetings to stimulate discussion. After a time, the books were sold to the highest bidder. In 1845 the membership numbered twenty and in 1860 there were forty-five. Compared with other provincial towns, Bath's Medical Book Society was formed at a relatively late date. In Northampton, for instance, a medical book society was inaugurated in 1787, while in Liverpool the medical library was founded in 1779. Many provincial medical societies appear to have evolved from medical book societies or libraries. If physicians were wealthy enough they could afford to build up their own libraries and there is evidence that several Bath physicians owned extensive collections of books. Caleb Parry had a vast library which his son donated to the Bath United Hospital, founded in 1826, four years after his father's death. Anthony Fothergill subscribed to various publications by medical societies to keep abreast of the latest developments and regularly lent his books to younger colleagues.[179]

1845 saw the formation of the Bath Pathological Society which was chaired by George Norman, senior surgeon at the United Hospital. Around five cases were presented at each meeting. By 1882 the society was known as the Bath Pathological and Clinical Society but so far no records of this society have come to light and it may have dissolved by the turn of the century because another Bath Clinical Society was formed in 1908. One of the founding members was Dr Rupert Waterhouse (1873–1958), whose name became associated with acute haemorrhagic destruction of the adrenal glands, known as the Waterhouse-Friderichsen syndrome. Dr Waterhouse qualified at St Bartholomew's Hospital in 1897 and moved to Bath in 1901 where he was appointed physician to both the Royal United Hospital and the Mineral Water Hospital.

Quite often doctors held honorary appointments at more than one Bath medical institution, though not so much in the early days when the Mineral Water Hospital was virtually the sole medical institution in the city. As the number of medical charities grew, so did the opportunity for honorary appointments. In the nineteenth century, appointment to one of the city's dispensaries or small specialist hospitals was often a stepping stone to later election to the staff of the Mineral Water Hospital. After the City Infirmary and Dispensary amalgamated with the Casualty Hospital in 1826, the resulting Bath United Hospital became a principle rival in the attraction of honorary staff and from the end of the nineteenth century onwards, the United Hospital had usurped the Mineral Water Hospital's position at the top of the election hierarchy. Whereas Daniel Lysons (elected physician 1781) was appointed honorary physician to the City Infirmary eleven years before his election to the Mineral Water

Hospital, his successors, a century later, were always elected in the reverse order. This reversal in the prestige of two institutions ultimately had unfortunate consequences for the Mineral Water Hospital which, despite its rightful claim to be a national hospital, has on several occasions been in danger of losing its identity and ending up as a department the Royal United Hospital, a process which has already forced the closure of other specialist hospitals in the city. As Ann Borsay has noted in her comprehensive study of the social history of the General Hospital, this reversal of prestige also affected the hospital's finance. By the 1820s the significant number of new medical charities which had been established in the city caused the General Hospital to lose financial ground in the increasingly competitive arena of benevolence[180]. (History, it seems, is repeating itself in the twenty-first century.)

The literary output of Bath doctors over the past four centuries is impressive. The medical treatises and papers alone would fill many volumes, not to mention poetry by Oliver, musical scores by Harington, philosophical essays by Hartley and Falconer, observations on farming by Caleb Parry and topographical sketches by James Tunstall. Both physicians and surgeons were frequent contributors to the Lancet and British Medical Journal in the nineteenth century. William Falconer and Anthony Fothergill were awarded the Fothergill Gold Medal of the London Medical Society for their essays and Sir George Smith Gibbes gave the Harveian Oration to the Royal College of Physicians in 1817. Several surgeons at the Bath Infirmary and Dispensary published pioneering work on cancer of the bowel and breast. In recent times, physicians have been no less prolific in their authorship and several standard medical textbooks have emanated from the pens of Bath doctors.

Royalty who visited Bath in the nineteenth century sometimes consulted a local practitioner for advice and if they were sufficiently impressed, they might consider rewarding the doctor with a title or other prize. Queen Charlotte consulted Dr George Smith-Gibbes and surgeon William Tudor during her visit in 1817. Despite the queen dying a year later, Gibbes was knighted for his services; Tudor remained a commoner.

During his exile in England, the corpulent and gout-ridden French king, Louis XVIII, visited Bath in 1813, staying at 72 Pulteney Street with his entourage. Louis's doctor in the city was George Gavin Browne-Mill. Born George Browne, of a Lanarkshire family, he added the name Mill in 1803 on the death of a friend, David Mill of Bath. Browne-Mill obtained an M.D. degree from Edinburgh University. He arrived in Bath around 1803, where he remained in practice for the rest of his life. A patient, Lt Col Robert Stewart who died in 1809, left him 'two hundred pounds for a piece of plate as a small mark of my Great Regard and High esteem for him, from whose Valuable friendship and Eminent Medical abilities, I have often derived essential benefit'. He also left him his gold snuff box and a diamond ring. Even Brown-Mill's housekeeper benefitted from being left twenty guineas 'for her great attention to me when sick.' His treatment of Louis resulted in further financial reward and in 1820, the king made Brown-Mill a baron.

Not all work done by doctors was for pecuniary gain. The honorary physicians and surgeons appointed to the Mineral Water Hospital attended the patients at noon on each Monday and Friday[181]. They were conducted on a ward round by the house apothecary to see their respective patients and to recommend their discharge if appropriate. Each week, a particular physician and surgeon were nominated at the Committee meeting to be responsible for the care of all patients admitted during the next seven days. The 'taking-in' physician also had to read through the current batch of letters requesting admission and advise the Committee of their suitability on medical grounds.

On the first Monday of each month, all the Medical Staff who were Governors met in the apothecaries shop and examined the condition of the drugs. Once a year, they had to furnish a report to the Governors about the annual cost of drugs. This insured that the apothecary remained as cost conscious as possible.

The system of having a weekly rotation of taking-in medical staff continued until 1907, after which time the physicians were allotted approximately fifty beds each. However, they were still expected to attend the hospital only two days a week though, by 1912, the Management Committee was beginning to tighten up on the medical staff's obligations. Physicians had to sign an attendance book and as their number had, by this time, increased to five, it was thought expedient to have them visiting on different days, rather than the old traditional gatherings on Mondays and Fridays. The insidious creep of regulatory bureaucracy probably sowed the first seeds of discontent amongst the medical staff which germinated as hitherto unthinkable suggestions of payment. In 1917, with the hospital overflowing with soldiers, the medical staff put in their bid to claim the three pence per day capitation fee which the army was paying the hospital. Rather surprisingly, the Committee approved, though two of the physicians subsequently refused to accept payment.

Further hopes of payment were launched in the 1920s when the medical staff were keen to open a wing to treat patients of 'moderate means' from whom the hospital hoped to recover a fee, but the plan never materialised. With their private 'spa' practices providing a healthy income, the majority of the consultant medical staff were more than happy to gratuitously serve the patients in their hospital right up to the day, in 1948, when it ceased to be a charitable institution and was absorbed into the National Health Service.

The creation of the Health Service profoundly altered the position of the consultant medical staff. For the first time in the hospital's history, they could claim a salary for their work and were no longer entirely dependant on a flourishing private practice. The consultant physicians were now expected to devote a lot more time to the hospital, much of which was taken up doing clinic work. Indeed, there was no outpatient department in the pre-NHS days, as all patients were referred for admission. There was also a much greater distinction between the role of the hospital doctor and the general practitioner, a distinction which had sometimes been blurred before the days of the NHS. With the lost opportunity for general practice and a reduced commitment to private practice, the hospital consultants identified themselves primarily as rheumatologists while the financial security offered by their NHS salaries allowed them to happily shed the 'spa doctor' image. As a result, the spa, although still administered and owned by the city council, became little more than an extension of the hospital outpatient department. At first, this was seen as a great benefit. The council welcomed the financial security of a large annual grant from the NHS. Confidence in the spa's future was boosted in 1966 by publication of a Bath Development Plan in which it was suggested that the city should retain and improve its existing function as a spa. Yet within a mere ten years, Bath ceased to be a spa at all.

On Friday, 6th December 1976, the Physical Treatment Centre in Bath Street was unusually crowded. Media persons, patients and spa preservationists hovered about the foyer like passengers awaiting the final train from a doomed station. That afternoon, the large brass cocks controlling the flow of mineral water were shut down for the last time. Their closure represented the end of an era for Bath. The Mineral Water Hospital's own supply was also compromised at this time by leaks in the Stall Street conduit and the hospital had to make use of heated tap water until 1978 when the repairs were finished. Within a matter of months, the mineral water was cut off again, this time because of the discovery of amoebic contamination. Since that time, all hydrotherapy in Bath has been carried out in heated tap water.

Inevitably, the closure precipitated a flurry of letters in the local press expressing sorrow, indignation and bewilderment. A doctor, visiting from Germany, told the city council they were misguided to throw away their greatest treasure and an eighty-three year old gentleman from Surrey, using the Elizabethan Charter, declared he would sue the Minister of Health and the Bath City Council, maintaining that closure of the baths would be a criminal act! Fortunately for the officers of these institutions, the Surrey gentleman was two hundred and sixty-two years too late to file a successful litigation. Despite the exhortations of a small group of enthusiasts calling themselves the Action Committee for Bath Spa Preservation, there was a general feeling of indifference from the majority of Bath residents and the medical profession. The preservationists came mostly from the ranks of patients, not doctors. Unlike their predecessors, whose prosperity was heavily dependent on the reputation of the waters, present-day local medical practitioners had little to lose by the spa's demise.

The decline of British spas in recent times has been largely due to a scepticism of their worth by doctors. Their

Demolition of the New Royal Baths in the 1980s. Only the facade was preserved. The remainder of the building was converted for use as shops and offices. (*Author's photo*)

image had long been tarnished by the stains of quackery and empiricism. Spas had always been a popular resort for fringe practitioners, and Bath was no exception. 'Empiricks and juggling medicasters do so much abound here,' wrote Dr Guidott in 1669, 'that 'tis almost as hard now to meet with a regular and accomplished physician as it was in former times for Diogenes to meet an honest man.' According to Dr Guidott, quacks not only boasted of curing the impossible, but charged exhorbitant fees for their first consultation. They made unnecessary repeat visits to patients as well as frequenting the baths each morning to advertise their presence. They were usually itinerant. 'Tinker like, yet with more grace, they ride from town to town and from house to house to seek work.'

With the appearance of the Bath newspapers in the eighteenth century, quacks frequently placed advertisements in the papers announcing their arrival and whereabouts. One of the most colourful characters to set up in Bath at this time was a Scot called James Graham, better known as the Emperor of Quacks. At the age of twenty-six, he travelled abroad and practised as an itinerant ear and eye specialist. During his travels, he learnt of Benjamin Franklin's experiments with electricity. The idea of electricity excited him and he saw in it a power that might be used for his own profit when applied to the treatment of diseases in desperate patients eager for something new. He returned to England in 1774 and set up practice in Bristol where he advertised his wonderful cures. In the following year, he moved to Bath but stayed only for the summer season, reasoning that there were greater fortunes to be made in London. In 1777, he returned to Bath and it was there that his fortunes took an upward turn; one of his patients was Catherine Macaulay who afterwards married his younger brother William.

While in Bath, Graham published a book entitled *The General State of Medical and Chirurgical Practice, Ancient and Modern, showing them to be inadequate, ineffectual, absurd and ridiculous.* In it, he advised that his remedies could only be taken with advantage under his own eye, a sure way of guaranteeing a steady income, though his personal supervision of naked mud bathing suggests a more voyeuristic motive. Sometimes he preferred to place his patients on magnetic chairs, or into baths through which he passed electric currents, a technique which was eventually adopted by more orthodox doctors at Bath. What annoyed the established Bath practitioners most was Graham's denunciation of their treatments and implications of his superior abilities. He claimed to have cured paralytic patients who were discharged incurable from the Mineral Water Hospital.

The distinction between quack and the regular practitioner was often unclear. There was no Medical

Register and outside London there was very little regulation of medical practitioners. Those who were elected to honorary hospital appointments were expected to have gone through recognised educational channels; physicians had to obtain a university degree in medicine and surgeons and apothecaries had to serve an appropriate time as apprentices and pupils. Most quacks had none of these educational attainments, although the possibility of buying a medical degree from Aberdeen University's Marischall College on the recommendation of two graduates was observed by one satirical poet of the time:

N'er doubt my pretensions I am a physician
See here's my diploma and in good condition,
From Aberdeen sent by the coach on my honour,
I paid English gold to the generous donor.

If that won't suffice here's my prostitute patent,
To cure all disease apparent or latent
Perhaps you suspected I was but a poacher,
On the right of physicians a frontless encroacher:
But my qualification's like theirs without flaw
And I kill my game fairly according to law.

It would be wrong to suppose that all quacks were dodgy doctors. Some so-called quacks developed highly specialised skills, like the itinerant oculists who operated for cataract and dentists who extracted decaying teeth. By the nineteenth century, dentistry had become respectable in the eyes of the medical profession and by the early twentieth century dentists had separated their training from that of doctors. Oculists had evolved into those taking a medical degree who then trained to became ophthalmologists and those without a medical degree who tested eyes and prescribed spectacles, but did not perform surgery. The ophthalmologists became associated with eye hospitals which appeared in most major British cities during the early nineteenth century. There were two in Bath, the first founded in 1811 and an Ear and Eye hospital which started in 1837. The latter eventually dropped eye work to concentrate on Ear, Nose and Throat conditions. By 1973, both institutions had been absorbed into the Royal United Hospital.

There was one group of practitioners who were regarded with hostility by the city's orthodox medical profession during the nineteenth century. In 1898, the Mayor of Bath arranged a conference with representatives of the medical profession, inviting them to form an advisory committee which could answer medical questions connected with the management of the baths. Certain orthodox practitioners made it quite clear that they had no intention of joining a committee if they had to sit alongside homeopathic practitioners.[182] Dr James Tunstall, resident apothecary to the Mineral Water Hospital from 1843 to 1850 and later honorary physician, was particularly outspoken and led a campaign by the local branch of the B.M.A. to vilify homeopathic doctors.

Hostility towards homeopathic practitioners was exemplified by the case of another Bath doctor, George Newman (c1810–1875). Before coming to the city, Newman had been a Poor Law Medical Officer at Glastonbury where he had come under attack by his orthodox colleagues after he turned to homeopathic methods. As a result the Royal College of Physicians urged the Poor Law Commissioners to dismiss him from his post.

Despite his troubles in Glastonbury, Newman managed to set up a thriving homeopathic practice in Bath which led to the opening of a small dispensary at 4, Green Park, later moving to Chapel Row where a hospital was established. Newman was joined in 1845 by a young German doctor, Johan Christian Luther, who trained under the guidance of Samuel Hahnemann (the inventor of homeopathy) and gained an M.D. degree from St Andrew's University. Unfortunately J.C. Luther died from typhoid fever four years later. His practice was temporarily taken over by his brother, Heinrich Waldemar Luther, until the arrival of a third brother, Carl Wilhelm in 1851. He stayed in Bath for a mere two years before moving to London. The Luther family were influential in spreading homeopathy to the British Isles and Carl was the first person to introduce homeopathy to Ireland[183].

Newman was a thoroughbred homeopathist whose distrust of allopathic treatments was felt as strongly as the disbelief regular physicians had for homeopathy. So when an American doctor, Robert MacLimont, arrived in Bath in the 1860s proclaiming that homeopathic and allopathic treatments could be given alongside each other, and applied for the post of physician to the homeopathic hospital, Newman was outraged. He recommended the hospital trustees turn down McLimont's application unless he pledged himself to practise as a *bona fide* homoeopathiSt[184]

McLimont reapplied and was elected but almost immediately broke his pledge. Newman was so incensed that he posted a letter to the British Journal of Homeopathy asking for readers to make a judgement about McLimont's attitude. Most sided with McLimont's views. This was perhaps the turning point which would eventually cause a reconciliation with the orthodox profession, but even a century later there was still hostility from some orthodox practitioners and, in recent years, a growing number of doctors are discrediting homeopathy as no better than quackery.

Bath residents seem to have been more sympathetic towards homeopathy and in 1893, the Homeopathic Hospital moved to a larger premises at Lansdown Grove. This was developed as a private hospital for persons of moderate means and partly financed by the Jenning's Trust. The first Medical Officer was Dr Percy Roberts Wilde (1856-1929) who was also physician to the West of England Hydro at Limpley Stoke, a village to the south of Bath. This institution, which ran between 1862 and 1899, provided the austere regimen of hydropathic therapy and catered for the masochistic. It was a style of treatment which involved cold baths and wet blankets in remote locations. Hydros were the forerunners of today's health farms. An American patient staying at a Scottish hydro in 1904 remarked, 'We cannot decide whether we are in a boarding school or a theological training-house.'[185]

Wilde published prolifically on homeopathic cures for rheumatic conditions. He was also founding editor of the *Medical Annual*, published by Wright's of Bristol, which gave details of the latest advances in medicine and which survived until the 1980s.

The preoccupation with etiquette and professionalism, and the marriage of science with clinical medicine which obsessed practitioners from the end of the eighteenth to the middle of the nineteenth century, was probably the reason why Bath as a spa went into decline during this time. After 1860 a newly confident profession had emerged ready to take up the challenge of redeveloping the spa. The economic climate had also improved so that money was available to translate ideas into practice. Even after the Municipal Reform Act of 1833, the medical profession had a good deal of influence in the running of the city and was well represented on the City Council. Gradually, this influence has waned and doctors have become more inward looking and preoccupied with their professional duties.

From the mid-nineteenth century until the end of World War II, the organisation of medical practice changed very little. Most of the institutions founded in the Regency and early Victorian eras were still flourishing and the spa was still a going concern. Practitioners worked either singlehandedly or in partnership but it was unusual to have more than two working together. The apothecaries increasingly relinquished their role of dispensing drugs to chemists and druggists and changed their title to general practitioner. Home visiting was common and surgical operations continued to be performed at home as well as in hospital. After the discovery of general anaesthesia in the mid-nineteenth century, more complex surgery was possible and this was increasingly done by hospital surgeons.

Since World War II there has been a radical change in the way medical services in the city have been administered. This is primarily due to the National Health Service. General practice and hospital medicine have become completely separated and economic necessity has brought about closure of the small specialist hospitals which previously existed in the city. Likewise, singlehanded practices have gradually disappeared and most medical partnerships are made up of several doctors working together. Although some practices continue to operate from what were once dwelling houses, the trend has been to move into purpose built premises.

Both the NHS and the regulation of medical practice which began in the nineteenth century with the Medical Acts of the 1860s , has led to greater control over doctors' professional freedom. The result of these two pieces of legislation has been to iron out peculiarities that had previously existed in individual towns and cities. Even the one legacy from the past which seemed at first to defy standardisation, the medical facilities of the spa, has been forced to bury itself largely by pressure from administrative groups outside the city. The Royal National Hospital for Rheumatic Diseases is the city's only remaining tangible link with the medical world of the eighteenth century. Even this historic establishment is threatened with closure, as it was in 1962 when it was only saved by the enthusiasm and campaigning of Dr George Kersley, a physician to the hospital. In the words of Kersley, 'it was felt that every effort should be made to preserve what was best of the old. It is especially important to keep the high morale, the individuality and the personal feeling towards patients as people with individual problems'. It remains to be seen whether economic necessity will overrule these sentiments, so bringing the last medical association with the spa to an end.

Dr George D. Kersley. (1906–1993). Vignette from a photograph by Edward St Maur taken in 1979 when Kersley was mayor of Bath. *(RNHRD)*

Kersley's hospital ward rounds in the 1950s were memorable for the two large Alsatians which he owned. The dogs would follow along behind the retinue and as the doctors and nursing staff entered the ward, both dogs would sprawl themselves on the floor near the door until the round was completed. The patients adored these animals, but the staff were not quite so keen, especially when they needed to get in and out of the ward door. At some later stage the Alsatians were replaced by a Poodle.
(from *Reminiscences of the Min*. Unpublished pamphlet. 1986.)

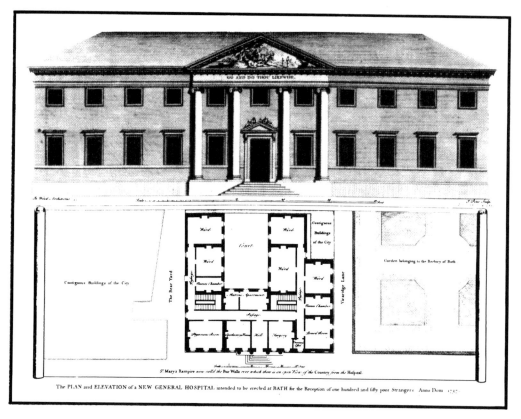

The PLAN and ELEVATION of a NEW GENERAL HOSPITAL, intended to be erected at BATH for the Reception of one hundred and fifty poor Strangers. Anno Dom 1747.

THE Usefulness of HOSPITALS for the Reception of *Sick People*, is so well known, that it is needless to say any Thing of it. The frequent and noble Benefactions to *St.* THOMAS's and *St.* BARTHOLOMEW's in *London, &c.* shew the Conviction People have, after long Experience, that such Donations are *True Charity.* It is upon this general Principle of *Relieving the Poor and Distressed,* that many well-disposed Persons have set on foot, and hope to establish, an *Hospital* at BATH: And what more particularly moved them to promote this Work, was the Consideration, that in many Cases the *diseased Poor* might there recover their Healths, which they could not do from any other Charity, or by any other Means whatsoever. The Care of the *Physician,* the Assistance of the *Surgeon,* and the Medicines of the *Apothecary,* may be had in any other Part of the Kingdom; but the *Benefit of the* BATH *Waters, in their full Virtue,* can only be enjoy'd at the *Fountain-head.* The Expence, indeed, of living at BATH long enough to receive a Cure, is greater than most Parishes are able or willing to defray; and therefore they chuse rather to support their *poor Cripples,* by a small Allowance at Home, than be at the Charge of endeavouring their Relief by maintaining them at BATH. Few Parishes are free from such Persons, who, by the Loss of their Limbs, are become a Burden to Themselves and their Neighbours, and drag on an uneasy Life, which, by God's Blessing on the *Charity* here proposed, might be render'd comfortable to themselves, and profitable to the Publick. It would be endless to enumerate the many different Cases in which the like good Effects of this *Charity* might reasonably be expected; and surely, a Consciousness of having been the Instruments, under GOD, of the Restoration of such Objects from Misery to Ease, from Impotence to Strength, and from Beggary and Want, to a Capacity of getting an honest Livelihood, and comfortable Subsistence, would be so sincere a Pleasure to all good Minds, that they must think it cheaply purchased by a generous Contribution towards so good a Work. But though the Relief of our miserable Fellow-Creatures might be sufficient to induce all good-natur'd Persons to promote this *Charity,* especially those who have themselves felt the Benefit of these *healing Waters;* yet it may not be amiss to mention another very great Advantage that will accrue to the Publick from such an *Hospital* being founded at BATH: All Physicians allow, That the greatest Certainty that can be attained to in the Knowledge of the Nature and Virtues of any Medicine, arises out of the Number of Observations of the Effect it has on *Human Bodies* in *different Circumstances.* The World is indeed greatly indebted already to many worthy and learned Gentlemen of the *Faculty,* who have publish'd their Observations on the BATH *Waters,* and given the Histories of their *Patients* Cases with great Exactness: These Histories are very valuable, and greatly assist the present Practitioners in the Performance of the many Cures which numberless living Witnesses can now testify that they have received upon

the Place: But surely, if the Knowledge of the Nature and Efficacy of these *Waters* could still be render'd more extensive and certain, it would be doing great Service to every individual Person, who may hereafter, in any Country or Age, have Occasion for their Use. Nobody can doubt but that this *Hospital* will greatly contribute towards this desirable End, who considers, that Persons of higher Rank are too often negligent of their own Health; and, by no means, so exact in taking their Medicines, abstaining from Things which hurt them, and staying a due Time, as could be wish'd, and is indeed necessary, in order to give the Physician a sufficient Opportunity either of doing them all the Service their Case would admit of, or of making Observations for the future Benefit of others. Whereas in this *Hospital* every Person will be under his Government and Direction in all Circumstances regarding his Health; so that a few Years will furnish more Histories of Cases, which may be depended upon, (if the Physicians keep due Registers of the *Sick* under their Care) than any Man's private Practice could have done in an Age: And it is to be hoped, that the Success which may reasonably be expected from the Regularity of these *poor Creatures,* may induce others of better Condition voluntarily to imitate them in the Management of Themselves, that they may receive the like Benefits. Every body may therefore see how great an Advantage this *Hospital* will be to the Publick: The *Sick* will be healed, many *Parishes* eased of the Burden of their useless *poor Cripples,* and the Knowledge and Use of the BATH *Waters* will be greatly improv'd to the Benefit of all succeeding Generations.

IT being necessary, for the Promoting, Carrying on, and Supporting this *Charity,* that Persons of Honour and Reputation should take it into their Protection and Guardianship, the Contributors present have agreed, That every Person contributing Twenty Pounds, or any Sum exceeding that, towards this *Charity,* shall be admitted a Governor of this *Hospital.*

IT is proposed by the Contributors present, to build an *Hospital* capable of Receiving and commodiously Entertaining One Hundred and Fifty poor *Distressed Persons.*

THE Expence of Building the said *Hospital,* according to the above Draught, and of Furnishing the same with Beds, and other Necessaries, it is thought, upon the most moderate Computation, will amount to the Sum of Six Thousand Pounds.

ANY Persons inclin'd to encourage this Undertaking, are desir'd to send their Contributions to RICHARD NASH, Esq; FRANCIS FAUQUIER, Esq; and Dr. OLIVER, at *Bath*; or Mr. BENJAMIN HOARE, Banker, at the *Golden Bottle* in *Fleet-street, London*; or leave their Subscriptions with Them for the Use of this *Charity*: And they may be assur'd, that all such Donations shall be faithfully applied to the Purposes intended

by the Donors, and a Monthly Account publish'd by Mr. Ho.. of all such Donations.

EFFECTUALLY to prevent any poor Persons coming to *Bath,* and being burdensome to the Town, under a Pretence of desiring to be admitted into the said *Hospital,* the following Order for such Admission is agreed on, *viz.*

THE Person proposed shall first have his Case drawn up by some Physician or skilful Person in his Neighbourhood, which, being duly attested by the Minister and Church-Wardens of the Parish he resided in, and transmitted to the Physicians of the said *Hospital,* together with the Age of such Person, shall by them be carefully considered and examined; and if they find that the Person is a proper Object of this *Charity,* they shall signify such their Judgment to the Minister of the said Parish; and so soon as there is a Vacancy in the said *Hospital,* shall notify it to him by Letter, for the Person to come within a limited Time, who is to bring back these Letters of the Physicians to the Minister; *by which* he or she is to be admitted into the said *Hospital*; and if any Person shall come to *Bath,* under Pretence of proposing himself to the *Hospital,* contrary to this Order, he shall not only be refused Admittance, but be treated as a Vagrant, with the utmost Severity of the Law.

EVERY Parish sending a Person to the *Hospital,* shall supply him with Thirty Shillings, which, upon his Admission, shall be lodged in the Hands of the Treasurer of the *Hospital,* to defray the Charge of his Funeral, in case he dies in the *Hospital*; or to be returned to him whenever he is discharged from thence, to answer the Expence of his Journey to his own Abode.

WHENEVER any Person is proposed to the Physicians of the *Hospital,* and is adjudged by them to be a proper Object, he shall be immediately minuted down to succeed to the next Vacancy that shall happen; and every Person so minuted, shall absolutely succeed in his Turn, any Interest or Application from any Person whatsoever notwithstanding.

THESE Articles are all that are now thought necessary to be settled by the Contributors present; but as soon as the Foundation of the *Hospital* is laid, (publick Notice whereof will be given in some of the Papers) General Meetings of the Trustees and Contributors will be appointed, for them to consider and settle such farther Regulations as they shall then judge to be for the Good of this *Charity.*

THESE Articles are submitted to the Judgment of the Publick: And all Persons are desired to give their Opinions as to any Alterations or Additions, to promote the Good which is intended by all the Contributors.

176

11. Hospital for the Nation

Hoare's painting depicts a framed illustration of the Bath General Hospital hanging on the wall behind Dr Oliver. It resembles a plan and elevation which still hangs in the hospital and was part of a broadsheet advertising the institution to would-be subscribers. Although the plan fairly closely resembles the final build of the hospital, its original conception was very different.

The General Hospital was established to provide for social needs as much as medical, but it was not the first. In the sixteenth century, the huge annual flux of poverty-stricken invalids became such a headache to the Corporation that the Mayor petitioned Parliament to safeguard the interests of the city.

A great number of poor and diseased people do resort to the city of Bath... for some ease and relief of their diseases at the baths there... The inhabitants are greatly overcharged with the same poor people to their intolerable charge. Therefore no diseased or impotent poor person living on alms….shall resort or repair from their dwelling place to the said city of Bath and to the baths there for the ease of their grief unless such person be not only licensed so to do by two Justices of the Peace in the county where such person doth dwell but also provided for by the inhabitants (of their own parish). The inhabitants of Bath shall not in any wise be charged by this Act with the funding or relief of any such poor people.

This Act effectively transferred the burden of supporting poor persons seeking treatment from the citizens of Bath to the person's own parish. It also helped to control the number of beggars entering the city as anyone who arrived at the gates without a licence could be punished and treated as a vagabond. Removal of 'malingerers' served to focus social awareness on those genuinely in distress through

Opposite: Part of an 18thC broadsheet advertising the Bath General Hospital to would-be subscribers. *(RNHRD collection)*

illness and fostered greater benevolence from charitably minded individuals. Persons with chronic skin disease were particularly unfortunate for they were still branded as 'lepers'. They would have found great difficulty in getting accommodation had it not been for John de Feckenham's beneficence in providing his small 'howse for the poor by the whote bathe', later to be known as the Leper Hospital. Feckenham, ever mindful that physicians' fees were beyond the means of less fortunate individuals, even wrote a book of 'sovereign medicines....chiefly for the poore which hath not at alle tymes the learned phisitions at hand'. He had plenty of advice for bathers:

> When you com to Bathe after your joyrneing, rest and quiet your bodie for the space of a daie or two. If it be not a faire cleare daie, go not into the open bathe, but rather use the water in a bathing vessel in yor own chamber as many men doe.
> The best time in the daie to go into the bathes is in the morning an houre or half an houre after the sunne riseing, or there about, in the most quiet time. You must go into your Bath with an emptie stomake and so to remayne as long as you are in it except great necessitie require the contrarie. Yf at any time you be faynt in the bath then you may drynke some ale.[186]

A few years later, benevolence flowed in every direction from the hand of Thomas Bellott, steward to Lord Burghley. He gave money for the restoration of the abbey chuch and founded and endowed a small hospital which opened in 1609 and bears his name.[187] Bellotts is, in many respects, the embryo of later hospitals in having attached medical staff and a limit on the length of stay, and in being an institution for the accommodation of persons undergoing treatment. This distinguishes it from the other so-called hospitals in the city at this time which were merely hospices for the poor and aged.

The original hospital was built in 1609 as a single storey building arranged around a court and bisected front to back by a central passageway. Ten patients were accommodated during the early part of the seventeenth century. Women were excluded from admission, Mr Bellott having, according to Robert Peirce, 'no kindness for the infirm of that sex, whatever he had for the sound and trigg'. Each

Above: Bellotts Hospital today. The original hospital building was demolished and rebuilt in 1859. *(Author's photo)*

Left: The Arms of William Cecil, Lord Burghley which was transferred from the old building and placed over the front entrance. *(Author's photo)*

patient received a weekly allowance of seven groats and their stay was limited to four weeks.

Admissions were confined to the months of April, May and September. This coincided with the seventeenth century 'bathing season'. A married couple acted as master and matron and were expected to 'curteously welcome and intreate the said poor' and keep the building sweet, clean and in good order. A surgeon was employed on an annual retainer of one pound. He had to examine prospective patients and advise the mayor, who administered the charity, on the suitability of admission. Anyone suffering from contagious disease was turned away. From 1652 onwards, free medical advice from a physician was available to patients at the hospital through a charitable fund provided by Viscount Scudamore (1601–71). The first physician appointed was Dr Tobias Venner (1577–1660). Venner divided his practice between Bath and Bridgwater and is best known for his book *Via Recta ad Vitam Longam* which provides contemporary advice on maintaining good health.

Visitors who could afford to pay stayed at one of several lodging-houses in the city. Many of these were owned or

Portrait of Tobias
Venner from the
frontispiece of his book,
*Via Recta ad Vitam
Longam. 1638*

rented by medical men who ran them like private nursing-homes. The finest of all the lodgings was the Abbey House which stood on the east side of the King's bath and was demolished in 1755 to reveal Roman baths under its foundations.

By the early eighteenth century, beggars were again becoming an irritating thorn in the Corporation's flesh. They began drifting back to Bath in ever growing numbers after 1714 when the old Elizabethan Act effectively regulating their presence in the city expired. The more privileged citizens had to distinguish between paupers with genuine medical needs and malingerers, 'to discriminate real objects of charity from vagrants and other impostors who crowd both the church and the town to the annoyance of the gentry residing here and who ought to be, by the care of the magistry, expelled and punished.'

What was needed was a large hospital for both men and women where the admission procedure could be so tightly regulated that only those with illness deriving benefit from the Bath waters, and who could be vouchsafed by a responsible person as being deserving of charity, would be permitted entry. Idle folk who came to Bath to extort money from fashionable visitors could then be sent packing without troubling the consciences of the rich.

The eighteenth century has the reputation for spawning philanthropists and the growth of organised voluntary effort and care of the sick is one of the better characteristics of the period. Inevitably, a degree of self interest by subscribers and donors underlaid this wave of philanthropy. Self interest has always played some part in social awareness and rich men were neither exempt from ravages of disease nor from financial ruin, two facets of life which must have been all the more evident to visitors at Bath, flanked on the one side by invalids and on the other by gamblers. Gambling was such an important aspect of the city's life that in 1706, fifty known gamesters and sharpers were reported to have arrived in Bath from London.

One of these gamblers was a man called Richard Nash who in time became one of Bath's best known characters. Beau Nash was born at Swansea in 1674. His father, hopeful of giving him a good education, sent him to Oxford where, according to his biographer Oliver Goldsmith, 'he soon showed that though much might be expected from his genius, nothing could be hoped from his industry' and he was sent down. After a rather unsuccessful try at being a soldier and a lawyer, he visited Bath in 1705. Not long after his arrival, the city's Master of Ceremonies was killed in a duel and the persuasive Nash was appointed in his place. Nash wielded tremendous influence on the social behaviour of the city's visitors and had a great propensity for extracting money from people, particularly ladies. Though he grew rich on the proceeds of gaming, not all the money he collected lined his own pockets and he was amongst the initiators of the scheme to found the Bath General Hospital. One can argue that Nash, as the moulder of fashionable Bath, was keener than anyone to rid the city of the beggars who, to use Wood's expression, teased people

Pastel Portrait of Beau Nash attributed to Benjamin Morris. *(RNHRD)*

of fashion, but Nash's considerable efforts in fund-raising were primarily to benefit the sick poor; removal of malingering indigents could have just as easily been effected without the expense of a large hospital.

Restoring the health of working men and women did have economic implications in an age obsessed with material prosperity and commercial success. The early years of the eighteenth century mark the rise of the *nouveau rich* man whose social mobility over two or three generations could transport his family from humble origins to immense social and material elevation; men like Ralph Allen who originated from a quite humble Cornish family and by his own ingenuity and effort became wealthy enough to commission his country mansion at Prior Park, three miles from the centre of Bath. There were many self-made men emerging at this time, benefiting from the growth of manufacturing industries and world trade. They often employed a large workforce with many skilled and semiskilled individuals amongst it. Businesses were dependant on these men and women to work effectively and economically. There was a constant worry that any decline in the health of the working population might create a shortage of available labour and lead to disastrous wage increases. It is therefore not surprising to find the *nouveau rich* well represented amongst the inaugurators of a proposed hospital where working men and women from all over Britain, precipitated into impecunious circumstances by illness, could be rehabilitated from physical handicap and cured of their incapacities.

Beau Nash's London bankers, Henry and Benjamin Hoare and local banker, property developer and colonial trader Richard Marchant, were both involved in the scheme at an early stage. Henry Hoare had been a founder of the Westminster Hospital, the country's first voluntary hospital in 1715. His father Richard, who founded the banking firm, was a frequent visitor to Bath for reasons of health and was in the habit of having several crates of bottled Bath Water delivered to his London house each year. Hoare's enthusiasm for the thermal waters might even have caused him to influence some of his customers to extend beneficence. Lady Elizabeth Hastings (1682-1731), renowned for her philanthropic deeds, and Sir Joseph Jekyll were two more wealthy people who became involved with the Hospital scheme at an early stage. Both were amongst the clientele of Hoare's Bank.

Sir Joseph Jekyll (1663–1738), Master of the Rolls, seems to have been equally possessed of philanthropic zeal but in a somewhat different manner for one feels he was motivated by knowing what was best for the poor. The poor begged to differ and Judge Jekyll, who was also Honourable Member for Reigate became one of the most unpopular politicians of his time. He was the champion of the Gin Act which imposed swingeing duty on the spirit in an attempt to stamp out drunkenness on the streets of London. The mob

Portrait of Sir Joseph Jekyll by Michael Dahl *(Courtesy Government Art Collection)*

were so incensed by this piece of legislation that they threatened to burn down Jekyll's residence and the unfortunate man was obliged to enlist the help of sixty soldiers to protect his property.

His interest in founding hospitals led him to get involved with the inauguration of the General Infirmary at Northampton, near his country seat. Jekyll was an enthusiastic do-gooder to the end. In his will, he bequeathed his entire fortune to relieve the National Debt. Unfortunately, the National Debt stood at eight million pounds while his fortune amounted to a mere twenty thousand. As one wit observed, Judge Jekyll might just as well have tried to stop the flow of water under Blackfriars Bridge with his wig.

In the years between 1716 and 1723, Jekyll got together a number of interested persons to start raising money for a hospital in Bath but their attempts to find a suitable plot on which to build proved fruitless; in 1723, with a fair number of subscriptions already collected, Jekyll and other eminent worthies, including the Lord Presidents of England and Scotland, called a meeting in Bath to announce that funds would be used to 'provide for poor lepers, cripples and other indigent persons resorting to Bath for cure, well recommended and not otherwise provided for.'

The two hundred and seventy pounds so far collected was invested in South Sea Bonds and the income used for renting and fitting up apartments for invalids, and for other incidental expenses. A committee of thirteen was chosen to administer the charity and decide who should receive relief. Paupers who were turned down could expect a raw deal, for the magistrates of Bath were, in the strongest terms, called upon by the contributors (of the charity) to expel and punish vagrants and imposters.

The committee of thirteen were supposed to meet each month to approve requests for relief. Six of the committee were medical practitioners. The eldest, a seventy-three year old Cornishman physician called Richard Bettenson (1651–1724) had made money from property development in the city. His beneficence had already extended to a substantial donation towards a marble case for a drinking fountain in the Pump Room. He had scarcely been elected when he died and his place was taken by an apothecary, Francis Bave, whose physician brother Charles was also one of the committee members, and his sister-in-law, Hester Whitlock, was the hospital's first matron.

The Bave (pronounced Bavey) family were wealthy and influential in Bath and had strong medical connections. The grandfather, Dr Samuel Bave (1588–1668) was a German émigré from Cologne who applied for British citizenship in 1625[188]. After gaining a degree in medicine at Oxford, he set up practice in Gloucester through the influence of a friend who was an apothecary in the city. He remained there for ten years, amassing a considerable fortune, and marrying Hester Robinson, the daughter of a wealthy lawyer. In 1638 he moved to a more lucrative practice in Bath where he bought property in the south western sector of the city. In addition, he and his wife acquired Barrow Court, a manor house in the Somerset parish of Tickenham, and a house called Highfield in Upton Cheyney.

As a physician, Samuel Bave was held in high esteem and corresponded with many distinguished doctors of his day including the royal family's physician Sir Theodore Turquet de Mayerne, Sir Thomas Browne of Norwich and Dr John Bathurst, medical adviser to Oliver Cromwell.[189] He attended a large number of patients who visited Bath to take the waters and had an extensive 'riding practice', making visits into the surrounding countryside. He was the Aubrey family's doctor and attended Richard Aubrey at Kington St Michael during his terminal illness in 1652. Four years later, John Aubrey consulted him about a venereal infection.[190]

Samuel Bave was noted for an excellent command of foreign languages and for his rather extravagant costume, dressing 'day by day in purple velvet and the finest linen, much bedecked with lace'. Not everyone had a high opinion of his medical skills:

'From an old German yclipped Dr Bavie[191]
Whose skill is not half so much as his knav'ry
And ten to one that will rather kill 'ee than save 'ee
Good Mercury defend me'

Samuel and Hester Bave had eight children, including Anthony who was one time vicar of Twerton, and Charles who was the main beneficiary of the family wealth and lived in their Bath property but does not appear to have engaged in any profession. The Bave family owned at least two houses in the city: one stood in Bell Tree Lane and was eventually demolished to make way for the Bath United Hospital, erected in 1824. The other stood on part of the Bave's land next to the Lower Borough Wall and seems to have been the principal residence of the family until its sale in 1774 when it was turned into the Alfred Hotel and, in 1792, the Bath City Infirmary and Dispensary. The local paper reported that some boisterous youths, thinking it was still a hotel, tried to enter the infirmary soon after it had opened. The reporter suggested the matron should give each of them a fever patient as a bedfellow if they tried it again.[192] This very fine building was finally demolished around 1860 to make way for part of the Albert Wing of the original Bath United Hospital. The site was again razed to the ground in 2009 and at the time of writing, is being rebuilt as part of a new hotel.

Charles, like his father, also had eight children, two of whom became Bath medical practitioners. Francis, (b.1678) was an apothecary in the city and served on the council. His

The Alfred Hotel, once the residence of Dr Charles Bave and latterly the first premises of the Bath City Infirmary and Dispensary. *(Author's collection)*

brother Charles (b. circa 1675) followed in his grandfather's footsteps as a physician. In 1699, he married a girl from Marlborough called Winfred Kerr with whom he had a stormy relationship. On one occasion, Charles went looking for his wife in the city and had eventually found her in a street at one o'clock in the morning 'under a gentleman's cloak'. Charles's friends told him they had observed Winifred behaving very indecently and with scandalous familiarity towards several persons. She also ran up considerable debts and Charles had been forced to pay three hundred pounds, the sum owed to mercers and innkeepers. She eventually left him and their daughter Hester and made her way to Jamaica.

His wife's wanton ways did not adversely effect his medical career. He seems to have been held in high esteem by influential physicians in London. He treated Sir John Clopton for 'a scorbutic cutaneous disease' in 1713[193] and he was in correspondence with Dr Richard Mead and Dr John Freind about patients who they referred to him for spa treatment. He was also in correspondence with Dr Herman Boerhaave, the famous Dutch physician whose pioneering methods of medical education at Leiden University revolutionised the training of doctors.[194]

Charles Bave received a glowing testimonial in 1728 from the author of 'An essay against too much reading':

> *Yes, sometimes a new Physician is sent to us, and the poor country souls put their lives in their hands, to give them the practical part; but I will never take any of their prescriptions 'till they have been in the hands, and under the Directions of such celebrated and ingenious Men as Dr Bave; and in all probability, Dr Harington must be a very safe Physician, the World allowing him to be a Man of fine Sense, a regular Liver, and a graduate Physician: besides the vast advantages he has gained in being in so many consultations, and having perpetually his Father's Directions and Rules of Practice for his Improvement.*[195]

The Dr Harington mentioned in the quote was Edward Harington (1696–1757), a descendant of the Kelston family who eventually married Dr Charles Bave's daughter, Hester, on February 6th 1724. After the break-up of her parent's marriage, Hester had been maintained at a boarding school by Charles who paid thirty pounds a year for her education and board.[196] Dr Charles Bave, his brother Francis and his son-in-law Dr Edward Harington, were all members of the original committee of thirteen set up in 1723 to establish the Bath General Hospital; Dr Harington was the only one to see it open in 1742 and served as honorary physician until 1750.[197]

The other medical members of the committee included Dr George Cheyne, Jeremiah Peirce, Dr John Beeston (1674–1725) and Dr John Quinton (d.1743) who published a two volume treatise extolling the virtues of the Bath waters. Cheyne and Peirce were the only two medical men on the original committee who were still alive when the hospital opened.

Surprisingly, only one cleric seems to have been involved with the founding committee, the archdeacon of the city, Dr Hunt. This contrasts with other provincial voluntary hospitals of the period where clergy were often the prime movers of such charities. The foundation of the Bath General Hospital owes more to the enthusiasm and generosity of businessmen like Ralph Allen and Richard Marchant, to property speculators like Humphrey Thayer (d.1737), a London druggist and Commissioner of Excise, who had bought undeveloped land in Bath during the early eighteenth century. Local medical practitioners like William Oliver and Jerry Peirce who themselves were property speculators also played a prominent part in the hospital's foundation. After all, the Bath medical fraternity was the cornerstone of Bath's principle industry, the health trade, and its members were sufficiently influential in the affairs of the city and its rich visitors to ensure the success of the proposed new hospital at Bath, the first truly national hospital in the country. There was only one problem: nobody on the Committee could agree on how or where to build it.

Bath in the early eighteenth century bore very little resemblance to the city as seen today. The mediaeval wall, though in a deplorable state, still bounded most of the city's perimeter. Within these confines lay a city 'of no more than fifteen streets, four inferior courts, five open areas of a superior kind, four terrace walks, sixteen lanes, three alleys, four throngs, and two bridges.'[198] Almost all the houses then standing in the city have since been demolished, many during the eighteenth and early nineteenth centuries when there was a programme of intensive rebuilding. The old walled city has literally gone to ground, following the fate of its Roman predecessor. Except for a short length on the north side of the old town and the east gate, the borough walls remain only as streets.

It was in the spring of 1727 that a twenty-three year old architect, John Wood, quit London to take up residence in this small confined town, its buildings crowded around narrow muddy streets and passageways, its resident population no more than three thousand inhabitants. Wood was a local boy, son of a Bath builder and was educated at the Blue School in the city. He had worked in London for Lord Bingley to assist in the construction of his new town house in Cavendish Square. In 1725, Bingley asked Wood to design the gardens of his country seat, Bramham Park, in Yorkshire, and this has led to a misconception that Wood was a Yorkshireman.

Wood was also employed by the Duke of Chandos, who lived in such splendour that his ninety-strong household included a private orchestra of sixteen musicians. Chandos had also chosen Cavendish Square as a site for one of his town houses and one can imagine that he became acquainted with the promising young architect while he was enjoying the patronage of the Duke's neighbour. There were other London acquaintances who proved useful to Wood after he left the city: a wealthy surgeon called Robert Gay, who became MP for Bath, and Humphrey Thayer. Thayer was treasurer of the Appeal fund for the proposed General Hospital .

Possibly through Thayer and Gay's influence, Wood was chosen to design the hospital and look for suitable ground on which to erect it. He was attracted to an open piece of ground just south of the town near the river, called the Ambrey, a site now occupied by the Technical College theatre but in those days providing a vegetable garden for one Samuel Broad. Wood designed two versions, one quadrangular and the other circular. Both versions incorporated a bath in their design which was to be supplied with thermal water flowing down a conduit from the Hot Bath. The buildings could accommodate a maximum of sixty patients, but there were unexpected problems and the site was never used.

Seven years passed before the trustees could agree on a new site. Ironically, it was as a result of legislation introduced by Sir Joseph Jekyll, who was then MP for Reigate, that the new site became available, though his Bill had nothing to do with hospitals. An Act was passed in 1737 which required all playhouses to be licensed by the Lord Chamberlain. Many small provincial theatres failed to obtain a licence and were closed, including the old Bath Playhouse, built in 1705. The building occupied a desirable piece of undeveloped land just inside the city's northern boundary and enjoyed open views across the fields which then sloped upwards towards Lansdown, providing a panorama of open countryside: the ideal site for a hospital.

By June 1738, the site was ready for the foundations to be excavated. John Wood's designs for the new hospital had already been made public in February when a broadside appealing for donations was engraved. This showed the front elevation and ground floor plan of the proposed building. The final design adopted had a ground plan in the shape of a trapezium, the east and west side being skewed at an angle of four degrees with the north front. This angulation was necessary to prevent an incursion onto Vicarage Lane which meets Upper Borough Walls at an angle.

Wood's original hospital, 'a magnificent pile of building in the Ionic order,' had three storeys, the entrance on the north side being to the principal, or first, storey as is usual in Georgian architecture. The north front has a tetrastyle frontispiece in its central elevation which supports a pediment, the tympanum of which was to have been decorated with a bas-relief of a scene depicting the parable of the Good Samaritan. The Trustees engaged a sculptor called Vincent Matthysens to execute the design and, although he was paid thirty pounds for his services, the committee got no more than a model and some drawings. Perhaps his fee for the real thing exceeded the budget.

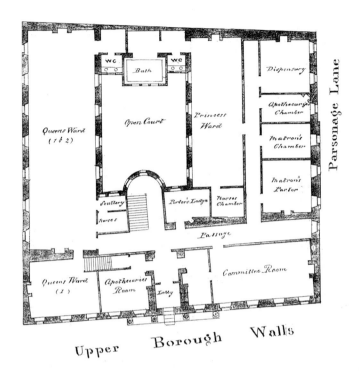

Ground plan of the
General Hospital
before the west wing
was added.
(RNHRD)

The north side, at least below the level of the cornice, has the least since the hospital was first built though much of the original stonework has been replaced. The first cornice had largely crumbled away by 1850 and had to be restored. The original windows had sashes with thick Georgian glazing bars. Two of the original sashes survive on the west side but the rest have been replaced by plate glass. Some of the side windows were heightened at this time and the reveals splayed to allow more light in. The west side was altered considerably in 1860 by the abutment of the bridge which connects the old hospital with the new west block. The east side was partially hidden by the Bear Inn which occupied the site of Union Street. The Bear Inn was demolished in the 1790s .

The hospital took over three years to be built. The foundations were dug and the first stone was laid in 1738 by the Right Honourable William Pulteney, Earl of Bath. The stone blocks and lime were donated by Ralph Allen. The interior of the hospital today bears scarcely any resemblance to the original. In 1742, when the hospital first admitted patients, they entered by the doorway in the centre of the building, now blocked off. Beyond the entrance vestibule, they would have been greeted by the porter who occupied a small room near the staircase.

The resident apothecary and matron each had a bedroom and a sitting room on this floor and the apothecary's shop, later renamed the dispensary, was also here. There were separate rooms for the physicians and surgeons but, in view of their rather infrequent visits, their rooms were converted to other uses quite early on. Most of the women patients were accommodated on the ground floor in Queen's and Princesses' wards.

The original staircase ascended in an apse overlooking the rear courtyard, but all trace of this has disappeared and the present concrete staircase on the east side is of recent construction. Upstairs, there were four more wards and a large storeroom which was converted into a ward in 1754. The basement provided accommodation for the maids and other servants of the hospital as well as a kitchen, a bakehouse and brewhouse, a pantry, wash-houses for the patients, a laundry and a laboratory for compounding medicines. There was probably a mortuary on this level. Access to the basement was gained either by the main staircase or through a side door in Vicarage Lane. This was the entry for delivery of provisions and fuel. The lavatories, known variously as the houses of offices, necessary houses and privies, were also on this level and there were frequent complaints that they stank; hardly surprising when one considers that all the hospital waste was swilled away along a drain which terminated in the ditch beyond the city wall.

The upper floors were kept relatively free of bad odours by the installation of a bellows ventilator, a piece of up-to-the-minute technology 'erected in the most commodious place in the house' and invented by an ingenious country parson, Dr Stephen Hales (1677–1761), whose interests lay in as diverse subjects as measurement of horses' blood pressure and clearing mud from harbours. The terrible scourge of typhus, which earned itself the name 'hospital fever' because of its predilection for these institutions, was almost eliminated by Hales' inventions. It was never a problem in the Bath General Hospital and, apart from several outbreaks of smallpox, the hospital seems to have been a reasonably healthy place. There were no cases of cholera in the building when the disease broke out in Bath in 1832 even though 74 people died of the disease in the lower parts of the town. The hospital was less fortunate with bloodsucking insects: in May 1751 a committee was convened to consider 'the most proper method to destroy and prevent bugs in the hospital.' Their deliberations do not seem to have stemmed the flood of these small but voracious parasites. Three years later the apothecary, Mr Morris, was asked to investigate how the nurses' room might be altered 'in such a manner as may best prevent bugs from harming them'. Bugs were not the only parasite causing consternation and both staff and patients were frequently afflicted with *the Itch*, caused either by scabies or body lice.

In its early days the building was heated by open coal fires. The house steward had the duty of measuring the quantity delivered to guard against fraud. Light in the hospital was provided by oil lamps and candles. In 1749 a total of one hundred and forty-nine gallons of rape seed oil was used in lighting the building at a cost of nineteen pounds, seven shillings and three pence farthing. The ubiquity of candles and open fires constituted a considerable fire risk. The building was insured with the Sun Fire Office for three thousand pounds and its contents for one thousand. Just before Christmas 1784, a fire broke out which was eventually brought under control by the chairmen.

No patient could be admitted unless the local doctor first sent a referral letter describing the patient's case. A minister or churchwarden of the parish was required to vouch that the person was deserving of charity. The hospital medical staff relied entirely on the clinical information given in the referral letters to make a decision on the suitability of each case. Because of the variable abilities of the patients' practitioners to accurately describe cases, a significant number of patients had to be prematurely discharged as 'improper.' Some practitioners had a particularly black reputation. In 1854, the Committee complained about a

Trowbridge doctor called Stapleton of whom it was stated that there was 'invariably much difficulty in obtaining from that gentleman fair and satisfactory reports of the numerous cases which he sends to the hospital.'[199]

There has always been a waiting list for admissions since the earliest days of the hospital. In 1818 there were forty two patients on the list. The Committee was always eager to keep the numbers low but, like the present day waiting list, its length reflected the state of the hospital's finances. The rules forbade queue jumping: 'Every person minuted [for admission] shall absolutely succeed in his turn, any interest or application from anybody whatsoever notwithstanding.'

In 1868, the Committee, disturbed by the length of the male waiting list, suggested several novel ways of reducing it. One was to reduce the time allowed for people to arrive at the hospital after they had been summoned. It was suggested that patients coming from neighbouring counties should arrive within two days, while those coming from further afield could take five. Even allowing for the increased speed of travel after the advent of the railways, these limits proved totally impractical. Finding this proposal unworkable, the Committee then asked the medical staff to tighten their criteria on what constituted a 'proper' case. This certainly weeded many patients waiting for admission who were sent a circular telling them that their cases were no longer appropriate for Bath water treatment. Unfortunately, the Marquis of Westminster was most displeased by this ploy, as his agent had applied for the admission of a patient subsequently removed from the waiting list in this way.

Patients living within the city of Bath were excluded from admission because it was assumed they could avail themselves of treatment at the baths whilst living in their own homes. If they were sufficiently impoverished, they could apply to the Bath Pauper Charity, set up around 1747. This provided the free services of a local medical practitioner and medicines supplied from a small dispensary in Wood Street. In 1792, the charity enlarged to provide in-patient facilities and became known as the Bath City Infirmary and Dispensary. By this time it was recognised that 'in acute and critical diseases, medical advice, attendance, drugs and other necessaries can only be administered with certain advantage when patients are properly accommodated and collected together.'[200]

Poverty was the one common denominator in all patients admitted to the General Hospital in its early days. Some patients arrived in such a ragged state that they had to be given clothes by the hospital merely for the sake of decency. Others were filthy and it was the matron's job to inspect and to 'cause new patients to be made clean.' There was a bath tub in the basement for this purpose, and the hospital seems to have ordered a liberal supply of Best Bristol Soap in its earlier years, as well as plenty of 'flesh' brushes for scrubbing the skin, though both of these may have been intended primarily for therapeutic use; the soap to make linaments and enemas and the flesh brushes as instruments of massage. The frequent immersion in the hot baths during their stay would have ensured that patients in the hospital were a good deal more savoury than many a person of quality lodging in easier circumstances a few streets away.

The book of referral letters for the 1750 decade gives some indication of patients' social circumstances. The age distribution reflects that of the general population at this time and there are relatively few patients over sixty. The patients' occupations are infrequently recorded in the letters but the information available suggests that many of the male patients were agricultural workers and domestic traders - farm hands, gardeners, barbers, butchers, tailors, carpenters. Some patients were involved in manufacturing industries – brass-founders, glaziers and glass-grinders, pewterers, shoemakers, potters. Of the latter group, exposure to lead and other heavy metals was often the precipitating cause of their illness. Painters and plumbers frequently appear for the same reason. Only a third of all admissions were female. Those women who were single were mostly in service but many were married and, with physical disability, were incapable of looking after their families.

Not infrequently, the patient's illness was itself the cause of impoverished circumstances and some of the referral letters dwell as much on the patient's financial misfortunes as on their medical details. James Ward, a fifty year old surgeon, had once enjoyed a thriving practice at Bodmin, but years of ill health had greatly reduced his circumstances. He was struggling to maintain his practice when he fell from his horse and broke his leg. After that, he could no longer walk unaided and, with meagre savings and no work, he could not even entertain the prospect of a trip to Bath where he might find the most efficacious treatment. Fortunately, he was accepted for admission by the hospital and was able to scrape enough together for the journey.

Soldiers also appear quite frequently amongst the early records, particularly when the British army was engaged in military action. Large numbers were admitted in 1745 after receiving injuries in the Jacobite uprising. In the following century, the hospital played its part in rehabilitating soldiers wounded in foreign campaigns, notably in the Crimean and Boer wars. During both world wars, the hospital was commandeered by the military services to provide treatment for the many service men whose injuries had left them with chronic physical disabilities.

Although the majority of patients admitted in the eighteenth century lived within a day's journey of Bath, some came from the far flung corners of the British Isles. Sometimes a request to retain a bed was sent on ahead of a patient delayed on the road.[13] The cost of transporting poor patients frequently had to be borne by their parishes and the hospital demanded three pounds 'caution money' for each patient admitted.[143] This was retained until the patient was discharged and it indemnified the hospital against the cost of providing transport home. When an Irishman, John Commerford, was discharged in June 1743, it cost £2–9s–6d for his passage to Cork. The higher cost of long journeys determined the Governors to recommend an increased rate of five pounds caution money for patients coming from Ireland and Scotland. In the nineteenth century the railways transformed travel, making it easier and cheaper to get to Bath from distant areas of Britain, but in earlier years the colossal expense of long distance travel probably deterred many patients from coming to the hospital. A Leicester doctor, referring a poor patient for admission in 1754, wrote that the man's equally poverty-stricken friends were desirous that the patient should go to Bath to take the waters and were trying to raise money to convey him to the hospital 'with great difficulty - even that of begging.'

We forget, living in an age of helicopter rescues and escorted ambulances, that patients in the eighteenth century had to accept life on an entirely different time scale. This is well illustrated by the case of one Thomas Francis who was admitted to the hospital in February, 1785. The man was a sailor, apprenticed to the captain of a merchant ship which was on a trading voyage to

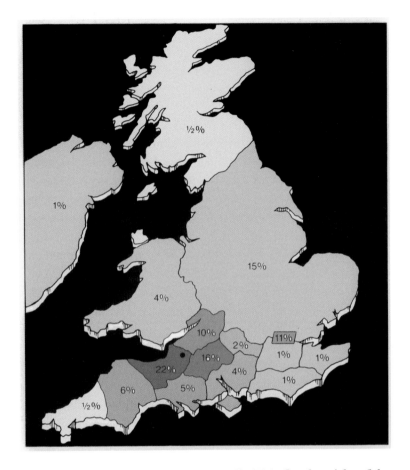

Geographical origins
of patients admitted
to the General
Hospital during the
eighteenth century.
(Author's analysis)

Gibraltar bay where he arrived in April 1784. On the night of the
sixteenth, whilst the ship was lying at anchor, Francis was about to
the rigging when a flash of lightning dashed him to the deck. He
was carried senseless to the captain's cabin where he remained
unconscious for a further three hours. His arm was badly
scorched where he had gripped hold of the rope. His neck was
wounded and a hole had burnt through his woollen hat,
singeing his hair. He recovered consciousness but was found to
have lost all use of his limbs. The day after the accident, the ship
resumed its planned itinerary, first to Russia and then back to
Dublin with a further cargo. During the four months of this
voyage, the injured sailor remained on board and it was not until
autumn that he was able to get back to his home in Glamorgan.
By this time he had recovered some use to his arms but was still
unable to walk. He was referred to the Bath General Hospital for
treatment, nine months after his injury.

In recent times, with the growth of rheumatological departments in district general hospitals, far fewer patients come from remote parts of the British Isles, but the catchment area extends well beyond the limits of the Bath health district. Nobody pays caution money now: the last collection was made in 1937.[17] Caution money was used to defray other expenses, such as clothing, or extra wages paid to nurses who looked after patients with smallpox. Those who arrived suffering from infectious diseases were turned away, as was anyone whose case was thought to be venereal. Expectant mothers were also barred from admission, although women recently confined were accepted. In such cases, a nursing mother was sometimes employed at extra expense as a wet nurse. Occasionally, women patients were accepted for admission and subsequently found to be pregnant. The medical staff sometimes missed quite obvious symptoms of early pregnancy. It took them over a month to realise that a patient admitted in 1754 with abdominal discomfort, vomiting and missed periods was becoming 'big with child.'

If a patient had the misfortune to die in hospital, caution money provided a means of defraying the funeral expenses. Eighteenth century funerals, like those of today, were not cheap. When a patient died in 1756, it cost thirteen shillings 'for breaking the ground,' five shillings for a shroud and ten shillings for a coffin. Deaths were uncommon; out of five hundred cases admitted between 1752 and 1754, only twenty-four died in hospital. This is all the more remarkable, remembering that Bath was often the last resort for the chronically ill and injured. Quite a few patients had already received treatment without any benefit in other voluntary hospitals, particularly in London.

The hospital had its own burial ground situated across the street on the far side of the city wall. It is first mentioned in 1743 when Mr Emes, the hospital's builder, was employed to 'make a passage through the town wall and a staircase down to the burying ground', though the city council did not officially grant use of the land for burial until 1767. Only then would the Bishop of Bath and Wells agree to consecrate the ground. There seems to have been some trouble getting coffins through Mr Emes' doorway and in 1783 a Mr West offered to widen it at his own expense.

By the mid-nineteenth century, the ground could accommodate no further bodies and was closed. For a while it was used as a refuse tip for a nearby shop then, in 1887, a Mr Taylor of Trim

Hospital burial yard. Once this area was in the town ditch outside the city wall, visible on the left.
(*Clive Quinnell*)

Street requested permission to keep his ducks there. In 1954, the hospital proposed turning it into a car park but was declined planning permission.

The wards contained beds, arranged at intervals along the two long walls, and a long table down the middle. The first bedsteads were wooden and made by a local cabinet maker, Gracious Stride, at a cost of thirty shillings each. The design was copied from those used in London hospitals and each bed was draped around with blue check curtains matching those at the windows. The luxury of the inter-sprung mattress, indeed even bed springing itself, was not a feature of these eighteenth century beds; patients slept on mattresses supported on sack cloth. Pillows and bed linen were provided and Matron was expected to put clean sheets on the beds of new patients, though the bed linen was only changed once a month. From 1752 onwards, the wooden bedsteads were gradually replaced with iron ones. In 1846, the hospital bought a hydrostatic bed, invented by a Scottish doctor, Neil Arnott, to overcome bedsores in immobilised patients. The mattress was essentially a water-filled, rubberised canvas bag, rather like a modern water bed.

Life on the wards has always stirred at an early hour, a tradition perpetuated since Georgian times when patients were aroused from their slumbers at the crack of dawn. The first task of the able-bodied patients was to help the nurses clear up the wards. The bare oak boards were cleaned by scattering sand and ashes about the floor and then sweeping them up. Matron visited the wards every day to supervise the nurses and make sure the patients were behaving in a proper manner. By modern standards, patients had to adhere to a relatively restrictive set of rules. They were not allowed to play cards or dice, nor curse and swear. Nothing

Discharge letter dated 1809, giving details of expenses deducted from the £3 'caution money' which would have been paid on admission. The hospital charged for two flannel waistcoats and a shirt, and for the patient's carriage home. The patient was given a small amount of cash for the journey. (*RNHRD collection*) is mentioned about smoking until 1854 when a patient was caught smoking in the street and the medical staff were asked to inform the Governors 'whether it be injurious to allow patients to smoke whilst under treatment.' Their decision is not recorded.

Men and women were not supposed to visit each other's wards without special permission from Matron. This was not rigorously enforced in the early days, as at least two patients were recorded as having eloped. In the Victorian era, the preoccupation with sexual segregation reached such obsessional heights that the corridor which connected the two wings of the hospital had to be divided along its length to prevent male and female patients catching sight of each other.

Patients who wrote letters were also viewed with suspicion. In 1742, the Committee exhorted 'officers of the house [to be] diligent in discovering any correspondence that may be carried on between patients in the house or [with] any person of the house whatsoever, by letter or otherwise, and if any letter be suspected of holding an improper correspondence, such letter will be delivered to the House Visitors at their next visitation.' Patients were even forbidden to lend or borrow money, though this would not have bothered them much as there was nothing to spend it on except food, and they were not allowed to have extra provisions.

Even today, admission to hospital is accompanied by a small loss of personal liberty, but this pales into insignificance compared to the no-nonsense attitudes of a century ago when patients were treated like irresponsible schoolchildren. In this respect, the Victorians were far more pernickety than the Georgians who seem to have been quite tolerant of other people's foibles. When no one owned up to a misdemeanour, the Victorian Committees would punish every patient in the hospital. In 1873, when obscene graffiti was discovered in one of the outside toilets, all patients were barred from leaving the hospital until the culprit had owned up. Graffiti writers posed such a threat to the hospital that the Committee ordered the outside walls of the building to be rusticated. Reprimands and expulsions were common. In the space of one week (August 1871), the porter nearly lost his job for lending his violin to a patient who played it in the ward and another patient was ordered to pay for damaging a door whilst racing his wheelchair around the hospital.

Meals were eaten in the wards and all patients who could walk were expected to sit at the tables. The food was sent up from the kitchen and was not always as hot as the patients would have liked. The wards were supplied with saucepans and a kettle for boiling tea, a drink available only on prescription until the late nineteenth century when tea replaced gruel as the breakfast beverage. As connoisseurs of the drink will know, nobody ever makes a decent cup of tea using hard water, so a small cistern of soft water was kept on each ward for making tea.

Plenty of beer was available, brewed on the premises, and even some house wine, made from Malaga raisins obtained at Bristol. The wine was supposedly drunk for its medicinal value. The Governors were only too aware of the problems of inebriation and publicans in Bath were forbidden to serve patients with intoxicating liquor, on pain of losing their licence. Patients were issued with brass identity badges when they were admitted and were not allowed out of the hospital unless they were wearing them.

The choice of patients' diet was the responsibility of the medical staff and the apothecary had to prepare a diet list for each ward. By modern standards, the diet was monotonous, though reasonably nutritious. Meals consisted principally of meat broth, bread, rice and cheese. No greengrocery was ordered until 1844 when the Matron was instructed to add a little oatmeal and vegetables to the broth 'by way of experiment.' Preservation of food would have been a problem before the appearance of refrigerators. The hospital kitchen was not equipped with a fridge until 1889.

During the eighteenth century, bread was made in the bakehouse below stairs. Towards the end of the eighteenth century, some experiments were made with different flour mixes in an attempt to cut costs. In 1796 the hospital bought a milling machine so that the expense of paying a miller could be avoided, though five years later it was cheaper to buy ready-ground flour imported from America. After 1836, bread was bought from outside contractors and the hospital's baker was made redundant. The patients ate from wooden plates called trenchers and took their broth in elm bowls. China and earthenware were too fragile and expensive. Drinks were served in enameled pint mugs.

At nine o'clock each morning the apothecary started his ward rounds to check on the patients' condition and

administer medicines. Once a fortnight, he recited the list
of Hospital Rules for the benefit of patients who could not
read and as a reminder for those who could. Another daily
round was done by two of the hospital Governors who were
elected each week to be House Visitors. It was their job to
investigate complaints from patients and staff and inspect the
quality of the provisions and food. Major complaints were
brought to the attention of the Committee. These mostly
related to allegations of ill-treatment by the hospital staff.
There were a whole spate of complaints lodged in the mid-
nineteenth century, often made by a representative of the
patient rather than the patient themselves. In 1844, the
Committee received a letter from a woman in Bristol
complaining about the treatment her servant had received
while a patient in the hospital. The physician in charge of the

Prince Ward, Bath
Mineral Water
Hospital during the
World War I
(Detail from a postcard)

case was questioned about his management and the Committee was pleased to find the allegations were totally unfounded and unreasonable. This seems to have been the conclusion in virtually every case. When one Thomas Hammond died shortly after he was discharged, his friends complained that he had not received proper assistance. The Committee's verdict: complaint groundless. If the patients complained while in the hospital, they risked expulsion and if they complained after their discharge, they could not expect to be re-admitted if their condition worsened. In 1855, notices were hung up in the wards warning patients that any complaints made after they had left Bath would automatically be considered groundless! This appears to have stayed the flood of complaints for two years until a patient tried to claim compensation for an injury he had received when a rope broke while he was being lowered into the bath. Although he subsequently developed an abscess, the hospital refused to pay him a single penny.

Very few complaints were made against the medical staff, but several incidents occurred a year after the hospital opened which eventually led to one of the surgeons being suspended. It was the sort of case which editor's of today's popular newspapers would have found totally irresistible. But when Archibald Cleland was relieved of his post as assistant surgeon in 1743, the world had not experienced the phenomenon of sensational journalism. The only notice the public received was the appearance of a broadsheet in the Pump Room, announcing that an enquiry was about to be held to investigate charges of indecent practice brought against the surgeon by two women patients in Princess Ward: Mary Hudson, afflicted with hysterical fits, and Mary Hook, who was suffering from leprosy.

The enquiry took place on September 21st 1743 when Cleland appeared before a court of eighteen Governors, amongst whom was the Mayor, Ralph Allen. Cleland was accused of professional misconduct as a result of performing repeated vaginal examinations on the two women. Evidence was also brought against him in connection with another patient, Sarah Appleby, who had died at the hospital the month before. She had been admitted for treatment of hysterical fits and venereal disease. Witnesses told how Miss Appleby had been examined several times by Cleland who used a vaginal douche in an attempt to improve her fits, supposing them due to disease of her uterus. In the process he brought down blood and 'pieces of placenta,' suggesting that the woman had miscarried. Cleland did not deny making the examinations which he claimed were a necessary part of the treatment: he did not do so to procure a miscarriage. However, the Matron and nurses were suggesting that Cleland's douching had caused the patient's death and they had observed her condition worsen after each treatment. A post-mortem examination proved not only had the woman never been pregnant (her womb was too small and the cervix tightly closed) but that her death was caused by a ruptured ovarian cyst.

Mary Hudson's case was similar and Cleland's purpose for performing vaginal examinations 'when she was in fits' was to discover if the uterus was the 'seat and cause of this and her other complaints.' In the case of Mary Hook, the examinations were more difficult to justify. Miss Hook was noted to have a large belly and complained of difficulty in passing water. Cleland examined her, 'taking oil on his hands whilst she was standing all the while' because he suspected she might be pregnant. Certain Governors at the enquiry thought it unlikely that a woman who was pregnant would have consented to such an examination for fear of discovery and expulsion from the hospital. They questioned the need to do such an examination at all.

In reply to cross-examination, Cleland maintained that the complaints had been trumped up by women who were little more than common prostitutes. He had evidence to prove this. One of the women, Mary Hook, was known to a physician in Cheltenham called Baptiste Smart who testified she was of ill-repute. Just before the trial, Dr Smart and Mary Hook's mother arrived in Bath. Cleland arranged for them to meet at the Carrier's Inn, but Mrs Hook failed to keep the appointment, claiming later she had forgotten the name of the inn. She had visited her daughter in hospital and had been waylaid by the house apothecary who, Cleland claimed, had prevented her from meeting Dr Smart. A suggestion arose from the Governors that the meeting at the inn was contrived with the view of bribing Mrs Hook into persuading her daughter to retract the accusations against Cleland. The Governors later published an affidavit sworn by Hook's mother to this effect. In his defence, Cleland insinuated that some of the physicians and surgeons, together with the house apothecary, had colluded to do all they could to get him suspended from the staff of the hospital. While he admitted performing several vaginal examinations on Hudson and Hook, he insisted that the examinations were necessary for clinical reasons. He denied that he had told a nurse to leave the room during examinations, or that he had bolted the door, despite a sworn affidavit by the nurse.

After considering all the evidence, the seventeen Governors present were unanimous. Cleland's actions amounted to 'indecent practice,' and the majority (thirteen to four) voted for his dismissal from the staff of the hospital. Cleland may well have been genuinely guilty of improper behaviour but many observers at the time, including the novelist Tobias Smollett, were convinced that the surgeon was victim of professional jealousy which had exaggerated some indiscreet, yet well-intentioned examinations. Whatever the truth, the case illustrates the vulnerability of male doctors then, as now, to accusations levelled by female patients undergoing vaginal examinations. After the hearing, one of the Governors was heard to say that if he had been a surgeon he would be reluctant to examine any woman 'above the shoestrings or below the necklace.'[201]

Able bodied patients were expected to help clean the wards, lend a hand in the laundry and aid the nursing of their fellow patients whose infirmities confined them to wheelchairs or bed. The hospital provided crutches for those needing them, and special chairs which were designed by the medical staff for paralysed patients. The absence of nearby lavatories in the eighteenth century made provision of urinals and close stools a necessity on each ward for the convenience of those unable to get downstairs to the 'Houses of Office.' It was therefore just as well that another of the apothecary's duties was to check that the wards were properly ventilated. When the philanthropist, John Howard, visited the hospital in 1787 on one of his yearly investigative tours, his olfactory sensibilities were so offended that he was relieved to report in the following year that at least a few of the windows opened. The physicians had always been in favour of keeping the windows closed for fear that the patients would risk catching cold after returning from the baths.

Throughout the week, the patients went to the baths for treatment. On Sundays they were able to go to one of the churches or chapels in the city, but only if they wore their badges. A visitor to Bath in 1766, the Rev. John Penrose, witnessed a party of patients attending a service at the Abbey.

It was a very affecting sight to see all the patients ranged in two lines, men on one side, women on the other, making a lane from the outer door of the Abbey to the door of the inner part where the service is performed, for the Mayor and Magistrates and all the congregation to pass through. Eight beadles in a Uniform Dress - Brown Greatcoats with yellow capes and sleeves turned up with yellow - with a staff in hand with a brass knob on top, attended them. And when they went from church, they all walked two and two, very orderly, four beadles with staves preceding, then the men patients, then two more beadles, the women patients, then the two other beadles closing the procession.[202]

During the week, prayers were read on the wards. Before a chaplain was appointed in 1755, this task fell upon any nurse who was literate enough to read the prayer book. Patients were also allowed out to 'take the air' in the meadows beyond the town wall, presumably upwind from the ditch where the sewage discharged. All patients had to return in time for supper and were not allowed out at night. There are several instances of patients being discharged for breaking this regulation. Considering their long length of stay, on average ten months, it is not surprising to find patients' frustration venting itself. Fighting amongst persons was much more commonplace in those times; even medical staff sometimes settled disputes with their fists if they disagreed with each other.[203] Fighting and swearing by patients were frequently reported in the House Visitors' books.

Patients had little with which to amuse themselves in the early days. The whitewashed walls were devoid of pictures and the only reading material was a bible and a prayerbook. In the mid-nineteenth century, newspapers were allowed but the Registrar was ordered to withhold the *Weekly Despatch* and other 'notoriously objectionable publications.' By this time, the need for more recreation was being recognised. 'The medical board are unanimously of the opinion that if the hospital contained the means of placing patients through many hours of the day in well-ventilated room where they might be provided cheerful occupation such as a well-chosen library, they would derive far greater benefit than that obtained by general permission to leave the hospital which the closeness of the rooms they now occupy renders absolutely necessary.'[204] Books were more easily obtainable than extra room. The 'well-chosen' library included such edifying tomes as *Bible Quadrupeds*, *Jesse's Gleanings* and *The History of Common Salt*. Charles Empson donated a further three hundred and eight volumes in 1858, observing that 'such an addition to the institution would while away many an hour that must otherwise drag heavily.' In a lighter vein, amateur dramatics and concerts were frequently performed for the patients' amusement.

With the library stocked, the Committee turned its attention to providing more room within the hospital precincts. Throughout the first half of the nineteenth century, there was increasing concern about the way patients might behave when let loose on the town. When the Committee wrote to the Duke of Cleveland in 1852, seeking permission to use the Sydney Hotel[205] as a new hospital site, they begged to assure his Lordship that the patients, being wholly confined to the hospital and gardens 'under strict surveillance,' would be rarely, if ever, seen by neighbours. Ironically, it was the hospital patients who, two years later, complained that their sleep was being disturbed

Sampler done by a patient, Mary Wise, in the early 19thC showing the hospital with the porter standing in the front door way. *(Private collection)*

by the foul language of drunkards roaming along Upper Borough Walls (a feature of the city's night life which still prevails!).

The practice of addressing patients as numbers seems to have arisen during Victorian times, as part of a rhyme written by a patient in that era indicates:

On every bedstead a brass badge is hung,
On state occasions round our neck is slung.
Upon the surface are the numbers shown,
By which instead of names we are here known.[206]

There is no evidence of such anonymity in the early years of the hospital. The wholesale regimentation of patients in the nineteenth century, and even in the early part of the twentieth, reflects a changing attitude in society towards the underprivileged. Patients who accepted charity at this time were totally patronised by the governing structure of the hospital and, as such, could not expect many rights or privileges. Today's patients fortunately enjoy a rather more relaxed atmosphere.

The modern image of a hospital nurse conjures up a busy, efficient and intelligent young woman, dressed in clean neat uniform, whose long training concludes with exacting examinations. Not so in the eighteenth century. Nurses then were more like domestic servants and had a reputation for being rough and coarse, as well as immoral and inebriate. Nursing has never been easy work and still requires great stamina and dedication. The Bath General Hospital Rule Book of 1782 instructed nurses to 'behave with tenderness to the patients, submit to their superiors and show charity and respect for all strangers.' Moreover, they had to preside at the servants table, clean the wards by seven each morning and were not allowed to drink tea without consent of a physician.

In 1990, the Mineral Water Hospital employed the equivalent of seventy full time nurses, but there were only four when it first opened. They each received eight pounds a year, with free board and lodging. Two of them, nurses Powell and Hubbard, worked in the hospital for two years and were then laid off. Nurse Hubbard seems to have been rather lacking in tender behaviour because several patients lodged complaints of ill usage. The other two nurses managed to remain in employment for seven years before being dismissed for stealing money from patients. New nurses were taken on and the total complement soon reached nine. The replacements were as motley a group of women as the first. One of them was so lame and disabled that the House Visitors mistook her for a patient and promptly admitted her. Another two had to be dismissed after patients complained about their behaviour. The situation was no better at the Bath United Hospital. In 1833, a night nurse was dismissed for stealing, but nurses' wages were pitifully low and their accommodation and conditions of work were deplorable.

Each ward was staffed by one nurse whose duty was to look after the patients and ensure that 'decency and good order prevailed.' An hour after she finished her cleaning, the nurse would be busy serving breakfast sent up from the kitchen below stairs. Evidently the breakfasts did not always arrive very promptly, so that patients on Duke's ward had cause to grumble that cook was abusing them by failing to provide their meal hot.

Nurses slept at one end of their respective wards in a small apartment screened off by curtains. One can assume they must have been disturbed at night on occasions, although the hospital's chairmen were employed to sit up with very ill patients and paid eight pence a night for their trouble. Night nurses were not employed until 1891. Before then, the hours of duty for nurses had been long and tedious and it is not surprising that these women became bad tempered and turned to the bottle. They could not even leave the hospital without permission from Matron. Even in 1931, the nurses were working more than the fifty six hours per week recommended by the Royal College of Nursing.

The Matron was in a much more fortunate position. She was provided with two rooms of her own on the ground floor and paid an annual salary of twenty pounds, a sum exceeded only by the incomes of the Registrar (thirty pounds) and the resident apothecary (sixty pounds). The first matron, Mrs. Whitlock, was elected on Christmas Eve 1741 and remained in office for nineteen years. Her credentials are not recorded but she would have been chosen for a capability in efficient housekeeping and management, not for any special skill in nursing. It probably helped that her sister was the wife of one of the governors (Francis Bave). Her duties were more akin to a matron of a boarding school than of a modern hospital. The Matrons in the eighteenth century appear to be widows or spinsters, though at least two of them retired to get married. (Elizabeth Whiting in

1777 and Martha Down in 1785). Elizabeth Morris, appointed in 1791, had been a housekeeper to a Mr. Daniel of Belmont for twenty years. According to her testimonial, she could 'write in a good hand and do accounts.'

Between them, the Matron and the house steward were responsible for running the hospital's domestic affairs. The Matron was given an allowance by the treasurer to purchase all the household linen, to order provisions for the kitchen and keep a stock of things like candles and soap in store. The Committee frequently exhorted Matron to be prudent and frugal. Linen was never thrown away until it was threadbare and even then it was cut up and used by the surgeons for dressings. A cloth-woman was paid two shillings and sixpence a week to mend linen and patients' clothes, though the patients themselves did much of this work.

It was the Matron's job to supervise the staff and patients. She reported any misdemeanours to the House Visitors. There was a particularly troublesome patient called John Harpur who was one of the first patients to be admitted in 1742. Matron caught him 'behaving indecently in the bath and quarreling with his fellow patients.' In later years this would have resulted in immediate expulsion but as this was the very first complaint brought to the House Visitors' notice, the man was merely given a reprimand. A week later there was more trouble. Several patients on King's ward, 'notwithstanding the orders of the house being read to them, insisted on going out and were with difficulty restrained by ye porter.' Patients, like staff, were not allowed to leave the hospital without Matron's permission and she locked the outside doors at nine o'clock each evening to deter anyone slipping in and out under cover of darkness.

The patients in King's ward continued to be a thorn in Matron's flesh. She discovered that 'Will Hagget did goe out to drink a pot of ale' and the errant Harpur was still making a nuisance of himself. Even the staff were in disgrace. When Matron sent one of the chairmen across the river to Bathwick mill for some oatmeal, he took five hours to get it. This so affronted the good lady that she had him dismissed by the Committee.

During the eighteenth century the number of nurses varied from four to nine, depending on the state of the hospital's funds. In 1773, a post of Head Nurse was created. This woman was paid a higher salary of ten guineas a year. As well as attending to her own ward, she had to supervise the female patients when they visited the baths and 'preside at the servants' table and see decency and order was preserved.' On the whole, the nurses during this time seem to have been dependable and remained in employment for an average of seven years, ranging from a few months to twenty years. Quite a few died in office. A minority were dismissed, primarily for drunkenness or insolence, while in 1772 it was reported that Nurse Woodward would be replaced because she had eloped, though with whom is not recorded. Occasionally there was a general reshuffle of staff so that a nurse became the cook, the cook became the housemaid and so on. Not all indiscretion led to dismissal. Despite Nurse Waters 'obstructing ye charity of the house by advising a person not to put his benefaction into the [contributions] box but give it to the porter,' she was retained on the staff for a further eighteen years.

The standard of nursing seems to have reached an all time low in the 1820s . Patients frequently had to pay nurses secret bribes to get attention. The medical staff regarded them as incompetent.[207] The Committee was also embarrassed to find the majority of nursing staff more aged and infirm than the patients. They were rapidly pensioned off and a rule was introduced restricting the appointment of new nurses to single women aged between thirty and forty-five. To encourage an improvement in standards, nurses had their wages increased by one pound a week after completing two years service to the satisfaction of the Committee.

The working conditions of the nurses changed little in the first hundred years. Until 1829, when they were provided with their own bedrooms, the nursing staff slept on the wards. There was no separate accommodation provided until 1883 when the hospital purchased the Sedan Chair Inn, to the rear of the west wing, for its first nurses home. Further properties were bought in Trim Street, opposite the hospital, between 1913 and 1918. In the early part of the nineteenth century, the nurses had the most meagre food and beer allowance of all the staff. Despite patients having mixed vegetables with their meals from 1830 onwards, nurses had to make do with potatoes alone until 1871.

Nurses pay remained at eight pounds per year between 1741 and 1828, whereas other staff saw an increase in income during this period. The Committee, conscious of the need to improve the standard of nursing, elected to increase nurses wages to twelve pounds a year with biennial increments of one pound, up to a maximum wage

	Bread	Meat	Cheese	Butter	Beer
Menservants	28 oz	14 oz	8 oz	?	4 pints
Chairmen	28 oz	14 oz	8 oz	?	8 pints
Washerwomen	21 oz	14 oz	4 oz	2 oz	6 pints
Maids	21 oz	14 oz	4 oz	1 oz	3 pints
Nurses	14 oz	14 oz	3 oz	1 oz	3 pints
Patients	14 oz	4 oz	0.5 oz	0.5 oz	1.5 pints

Daily food allowances for staff and patients. 1827, excluding potatoes and rice. *(RNHRD)*

of fifteen pounds. In return the Committee expected all prospective nurses to be able to read and write. For some reason, married women whose husbands lived in Bath were ineligible to be appointed. In 1898, the Committee reported difficulty in obtaining efficient nurses and reluctantly agreed to another wage increase, bringing the maximum wage to thirty pounds a year. Probationers were also taken on at this time. Though beer was no longer supplied by the hospital an allowance of 'beer money' continued until 1903. Properly trained, fully qualified nurses were first employed in 1910 as ward sisters but the only requirement for ordinary nurses was an ability to read and be fit enough to pass a medical. They were given no formal training apart from a course in sickroom cookery at the Bath Technical College.

With the foundation of the hospital's school of massage in 1912, nurses were encouraged to enroll on the six month course in massage, anatomy and physiology and sit the examination of the Incorporated Society of Masseurs. Though outsiders could also enroll on this course, the majority of these embryonic physiotherapists were nurses working in the hospital. Other skills like plastering, now performed by specialised technicians, were formerly carried out by nurses.

Massage became popular in the early nineteenth century. In 1820, the senior physician, Dr Edward Barlow, lamented how the hospital nurses were so inept at shampooing,[208] a term then used to describe frictional massage on any part of the body. This was a task which nurses were expected to perform in the early days. They used firm bristled instruments called flesh brushes, though there are no details of how often this happened, or who instructed the nurses in this delicate art. By 1852, it had become a sufficiently specialised occupation to warrant the hospital engaging a 'rubber', Mary Isles, who remained in office twenty-seven years before being dismissed for providing alcohol to patients.[209]

With the completion of the Massage Baths in 1889, an advert was placed in the British Medical Journal for a masseur and masseuse. Perhaps the Baths Committee hoped to attract a higher calibre of person by using French terms, though the lady who had replaced Mary Isles was retained on the staff as the 'general rubber and shampooer.' Dr Murrell, an eminent authority on the use of such terms, likened the difference between massage and shampooing to 'playing a difficult piece of music as opposed to striking the keys of a pianoforte at random.' [210] Not all masseurs could be classed as such virtuosos. Mr Donovan, masseur to the Mineral Water Hospital in 1902, had to be relieved of his duties after breaking a patient's elbow and generally administering his massages in a most unsatisfactory manner.[211]   Despite such catastrophes, massage became increasingly important as an adjunct to hydrotherapy. One Bath physician thought massage so important that it was 'nothing short of bigotry to refuse to

The Massage Baths, completed in 1889, were demolished just under a century later and replaced by the present ediface which houses the museum shop. *From: Tunstall's Rambles About Bath.*

214

employ so potent an agent for the relief of human suffering.'[212]

Before 1904, the masseurs only spent six hours a week visiting the hospital to treat patients, but the governors, by making the ward mistress redundant, were able to increase the weekly hours to fifteen. This was still considered insufficient and the masseuse was asked to give instruction to some of the nurses. Training was probably given quite informally until 1912 when Miss Margaret Clements, a local masseuse recommended to the hospital by the Incorporated Society of Trained Masseuses, (the forerunner of the Chartered Society of Physiotherapists), was engaged to teach nurses the theory and practice of massage, together with a course of lectures on anatomy and physiology. There were two lectures a week for six months and the first pupils sat the Society's examinations in May 1913.[213]

The four years of the Great War was a huge stimulus to the development of physiotherapy at the hospital, though the term was not generally used until 1921.[214] With so many war casualties on the wards, the number of trained masseurs was increased to five. Preference was given to blind therapists, many of whom had lost their sight on the front line. Guided by touch, they were often particularly skilled at massage.

The war also stimulated increased expenditure on gadgets. In 1917, a Shanks whirlpool bath was added to the hospital's paraphernalia, providing patients with what is now popularly called a Jacuzzi. This proved particularly effective in treating the chronically infected wounds sustained on the battlefields of Flanders. Other pieces of apparatus, which in these days are more familiar to frequenters of health clubs than to hospital departments, were purchased in rapid succession: radiant heat lamps, solaria, and Zander machines. The latter, named after the inventor of mechanotherapy, J.G. Zander, allowed patients to exercise weak limbs by treadling or cranking weighted levers and wheels.

Much of the physiotherapy equipment from this time is now obsolete. Impressively named gadgets like Leduc's Pulsating Current Generator, the Plurostat and Smart and Bristowe's Faradic Coil are all but forgotten. Today's Health and Safety inspectors would be horrified by electric baths, and galvanotherapy is seldom used. Short wave diathermy was prone to cause havoc to pictures on people's television sets, unless it was operated inside a wire cage. Ultrasound and Megapulse are no

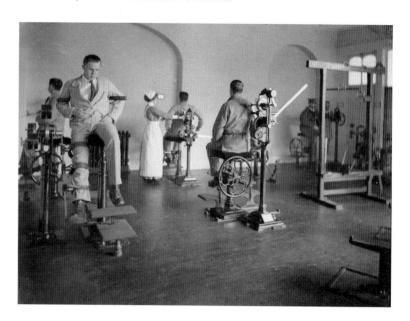

Patients exercising on
Zander
mechanotherapy
apparatus
(RNHRD collection)

longer in vogue, as they appeared to be no more effective than
placebo treatments. There are far fewer sparks flying about these
days and the therapy is more comfortable. Modern physiotherapy
is less likely to strike terror into the hearts of patients than it was
in the days of humming, buzzing and flashing contraptions, but
ironically, fear may have played a part in the success of past
treatments, at least in rheumatoid arthritis. Stress causes an
increase in the hormone ACTH which in turn stimulates the
adrenal glands to produce more corticosteroids. Before the 1950s,
when an extract of the hormone became available for therapeutic
use, physicians at the hospital tried to increase the natural output
of ACTH by giving 130 volt shocks to patient's heads after
administering an anaesthetic and a muscle relaxant drug.[215]

The Mineral Water Hospital's long association with physical
treatments made it the obvious place in which to develop a school
of physiotherapy. After the Great War, the hospital's School of
Massage and Electrotherapy, under the guidance of Miss
Clements, became well known. In 1918, it was advertised in
Methuen's *Handbook of Massage* and the *Journal of the Incorporated
Society of Trained Masseuses.* It issued its own embroidered badge
and in 1921, admitted male students as well as women. Miss
Clements resigned as superintendent in 1926 and the school
seems to have subsequently gone into decline. In 1933, John
Hatton, one of the most enthusiastic Spa directors the city
council has ever employed, proposed that a hydrotherapy

training school should be set up as a joint venture between the council's spa department and the hospital, but plans to rebuild the hospital on a new site, and then the second world war, served to delay matters. The war, like its predecessor in 1914–18, emptied the hospital of its usual clientelle and filled the wards with servicemen requiring rehabilitation from their injuries.

Such was their need that, in 1943, a Rehabilitation Department was created under the management of Dr George Aldred Brown (1897–1946) offering hydrotherapy, massage, electrotherapy, physical training and curative workshops. The hospital's first occupational therapist, Miss Hick, was appointed at this time to give instruction in the curative workshops, and physical training was provided by Miss Toley. In the following year, the Rehabilitation Department was completed by the addition of a Welfare Officer, Miss Catherine Cox, who provided a service akin to the present-day medical social workers.

In recent years, the hospital has become increasingly focussed on rehabilitation. As rheumatology services have opened in hospitals throughout the South West, Bath is no longer the first choice for rheumatic disease patients and their referring doctors.[216] The hospital has had to diversify and it saw a niche in the provision of rehabilitation for patients with ankylosing spondylitis and those recovering from head injuries. More recently it has developed services to help patients suffering from chronic fatigue and for the rehabilitation of women suffering from radiation injury after treatment for breast cancer. But the hospital's reducing income and high level of operating costs experienced in servicing a small foundation trust from an old and expensive building has meant it can no longer retain its operational independence. In July 2012, the management committees of the RNHRD and the Royal United Hospital agreed to work towards combining.

Whereas Bath's hospitals have progressively distanced themselves from the thermal springs, spa facilities have been re-established at the new Thermae Bath Spa. The centre, which offers hot baths and douches, steam rooms and complementary therapies, provides an effective means of promoting exercise and relaxation, and the integration of leisure and healthy living. Although the emphasis is now on prevention of disease rather than treatment, the physiological effects of hydrotherapy and massage can still provide some of the rationale for advocating spa treatment in several conditions. The utilisation of naturally heated water coupled with the historic reputation of healing springs and a milieu of a modern treatment centre can produce a powerful placebo effect, even if subsequent research fails to demonstrate any special therapeutic quality of the water itself. Spas are currently not on the menu of British orthodox medicine despite their continuing popularity elsewhere in Europe.

It remains to be seen if, and to what extent, therapeutic bathing will ever be resurrected by the medical orthodoxy at the Bath spa.

Opposite: The Cross Bath in 1829. (Detail of an engraving from *Bath & Bristol - A Series of Views. London .1829*)

Below: The Cross Bath in 2010 (*Photo: Edmund Sumner, courtesy of Themae Bath Spa*)

Notes and References

Abbreviations:
MB: Minute Books of Bath General Hospital; DNB: Dictionary of
National Biography; BMJ: British Medical Journal

[1] http://www.bathintime.co.uk/

[2] For an account of Roman medical bathing practice see
Fagan, G.G. *Bathing in Public in the Roman World*. Univ. of
Michigan 1999. pp. 85-103

[3] Genesis

[4] *Gesta Stephani, Regis Anglorum etc*. ed Sewell, R.C. London
1846. p.38

[5] Turner, W. *A Booke of the Nature and Properties as well of the
bathes in England as of other bathes in Germanye and Italye.*
Arnold Birckman. Cologne 1562

[6] Jones, J. *The Bathes of Bathe's Ayde*. London. 1572

[7] Gabriele Falloppia, *De medicatis aquis atque de fossilibus*.
Venice,1564

[8] Wood, J. *Description of Bath*. Reprinted by Kingsmead
Press, Bath. 1969

[9] Harrison, W. *'Description of England'*. Ed. F.J.Furnival.
London. 1887. Also ed. by George Edelen. Ithaca. N.York.
1968

[10] DNB. See also D. Thorburn Burns *Thomas Guidott
(1638–1705): Physician and Chymist, Contributor to the Analysis
of Mineral Waters*. Analytical. Proceedings, 1981, 18, 2-6

[11] Ward, Ned. *A Step to Bath*. London. 1700

[12] DNB

[13] Oliver, William. *A practical dissertation on Bath-Waters.* London 1716

[14] Saunders, W. *A treatise on the chemical history and medical powers of some of the most celebrated mineral waters.* London 1800

[15] Much of the paraphernalia of this business can be seen in the *Museum of Bath at Work.*

[16] Peach,R.E.M. *Street lore of Bath.* Bath 1893 p153

[17] Lecture by Mike Chapman on *'Dr Charles Hunnings Wilkinson-Early 19th century Science in Bath'*

[18] *The Improved Bath Guide.* Wood and Cunningham. Bath 1810. p. 20

[19] Freeman, Henry W. *The new methods of cure at the hot mineral springs of Bath : with special reference to the Nauheim system as practised at the baths of Bath.* Bath 1897

[20] Stevens, J.N. , *A Treatise on the Medicinal Qualities of the Bath Waters* (Bristol, 1758), pp.76-8

[21] Davidson,S *Report on a visit to Harrogate. 23 Jan 1945.* Pamphlet published by Harrogate Council

[22] See Osbourne,B *The twentieth century decline of the British Spa.* www.thespasdirectory.com: Thomson, W.A.R. 'Spas that Heal' Black, London 1978

[23] Ernst E; Pittler MH *How effective is spa treatment? A systematic review of randomized studies.* Dtsch Med Wochenschr, 123(10):273-7; discussion 278 1998 Mar 6

[24] O'Hare, J P, Heywood, A, Summerhayes,C, Lunn,G, Evans,J M, Walters,G, Corrall,R J M, Dieppe,P. *Observations on the effects of immersion in Bath spa water.* BMJ vol 291 p 1747ff

[25] Take H et al. *Activation of circulating platelets by hyperthermal stress.* Eur J Med Res, 1(12):562-4 1996 Nov 25

[26] Grossman E et al. *Effects of water immersion on sympathoadrenal and dopa-dopamine systems in humans.* Am J Physiol, 262.
(6 Pt.2) 1992 Jun

[27] Kubota K et al. Department of Medicine, Kusatsu Branch Hospital, Gunma University School of Medicine, Japan. Life Science, 51(24):1877-80 1992

[28] Green RG, Green ML. *Relaxation increases salivary immunoglobulin A1.* Psychological Reports 1987;61:623-9

[29] Heywood, A. *Lead, Gout and Spa therapy.* p 84, published in 'Hot Springs of Bath' Ed. Kellaway, G. Bath. 1991

[30] Strec Vet al. Vyskumny ustav humannej bioklimatologie Bratislava. Vnitr Lek, 38(2):148-54; Feb 1992

[31] Ammer K, Melnizky P. *Medicinal baths for treatment of generalized fibromyalgia.* Forsch Komplementarmed;6(2):80-5; Apr 1999

[32] Mirolo BR et al. Hennessy JM.Ward LC. Jones LC. *Psychosocial benefits of therapy.* Cancer Nursing 1995; 18:197-205

[33] Article on Aix-les-Bains in B.M.J. July 23 1921 p118

[34] Ryley Scott, G. *The Story of Baths and Bathing.* p59-62.;London 1939.

[35] King, Preston.'*Bath Waters*' Arrowsmith. nd. p124

[36] Wilde,P. *The physiology of gout, rheumatism and arthritis as a guide to accurate diagnosis and efficient treatment.* Wood & Co , New York. 1922

[37] MB 4. 232

[38] C Tei, *Thermal therapy for congestive heart failure: estimation by TEI index,* J. of Cardiology Supplement , (Japanese Coll. of Cardiology) 37(1):155-159.; 2001

[39] M Imamura et al. *Repeated thermal therapy improves impaired vascular endothelial function in patients with coronary risk factors,* J. American College of Cardiology, 38(4):1083-1088; 2001

[40] Hannuksela, M.L. et al. *Benefits and risks of sauna bathing.* American Journal of Medicine , 110(2):118-126.; 2001

[41] Tomasik M. *Effect of hydro-massage on changes in blood electrolyte and lactic acid levels and haematocrit value after maximal effort.* Acta Physiologica Polonica 1983;34:257-61

[42] Bowerman SB. *The effect of empathic touch and expectations on mood change during a therapeutic massage treatment.* Dissertation Abstracts International 1990;50:4763.

[43] Booklet produced by Macmillan Practice Development Unit, Centre for Cancer and Palliative Care Studies, Institute of Cancer Research/Royal Marsden NHS Trust, Fulham Road, London SW3 6JJ

[44] Ferrell Torry AT, Glick OJ. *The use of therapeutic massage as a nursing intervention to modify anxiety and the perception of cancer pain.* Cancer Nursing 1993;16:93-101

[45] Day JA, Mason RR, Chesrown SE. *Effect of massage on serum level of beta-endorphin and beta-lipotropin in healthy adults.* Physical Therapy 1987;67:926-30

[46] Vickers A. *Yes, but how do we know it's true? Knowledge claims in massage and aromatherapy.* Complementary Therapy Nurs Midwifery;3:63-5; 1997

[47] Cady SH, Jones GE. *Massage therapy as a workplace intervention for reduction of stress.* Perceptual & Motor Skills; 84:157-8.1997

[48] Garzon P, Eisenberg, *Variation in the mineral content of commercially available bottled waters: implications for health and disease.* MJ Am J Med, 105(2):125-30; 1998 Aug

[49] Scalabrino A et al. *Clinical-epidemiological study of the efficacy of thermal therapy in gastroenterologic diseases* (Trans), Clin Ter, 149(2):127-30; Mar-Apr 1998

[50] Garrison, F.H. *An Introduction to the History of Medicine.* 4th ed. Saunders, London and Philadelphia. 1929. p328.

[51] Charleton, R. *'An Inquiry into the Efficacy of Bath Waters in Palsies'.* 2nd ed, in *Three Tracts on Bath Water* (Bath, 1774), p34

[52] MB 10.298.

[53] *Narrative of the efficacy of the Bath Waters in various kinds of Paralytic Disorders admitted into the Bath Hospital.* Cruttwell. Bath 1787. p59

[54] Chapman, R.W. (ed) *Jane Austen's Letters to her Sister Cassandra and Others.* Oxford.1932, vol.1, p.20

[55] Spry, J.H. *A Practical Treatise on the Bath Waters.* London. 1822, p.292

[56] MB 27.453

[57] Kersley, G.D. Personal communication. 1987.

[58] MB 16.253

[59] MB 20.39

[60] This is an extremely rare book and the only known library copy is in Yale University

[61] Freeman, H. *The thermal baths of Bath.* London 1888. p. 238-9

[62] Marjot,R. *The first anaesthetics in Bath.* Proceedings of the History of Anaesthesia Society. Vol 41. May 2009

[63] Bouter, L.M. Article in Dutch in Ned Tijdschr Geneeskd. 2000 Mar 11;144(11):502-5.v

[64] McNulty,M. in *Hot Springs of Bath* ed. Kellaway,G.A. Bath 1991. p69.

[65] Franke A, et al. Long-term efficacy of radon spa therapy in rheumatoid arthritis--a randomized, sham-controlled study and follow-up. *Rheumatology (Oxford)* 2000 Aug;39(8): 894-902

[66] Heberden, William *Commentaries on the History and Cure of Diseases.* Boston 1818 p60

[67] Saunders, W. op.cit. p. 178-9

[68] Wilkinson, C.H. *Analytical researches into the properties of the Bath Waters, etc.* Wood & Cunningham 1811

[69] Granville, A.B. The invalids and visitors handbook to the Hot Springs of Bath. Bath 1841 p76

[70] Peskett, G. and Raiment, P. : Archives of Medical Hydrology, August, 1925.

[71] Smollett, T. *Expedition of Humphrey Clinker* Ed L.M Knapp. London 1966. p45

[72] Peirce, R. op.cit

[73] Hembry,P. *The English Spa. 1560–1815. A social history.* Athlone Press.London 1990. p62.

[74] Peirce, R. Bath Memoirs Bristol. 1697. pp 32-34.

[75] Quinton, John. *A treatise of warm Bath water, in which is [sic] more than two hundred cures made at Bath , etc.* Oxford. 1734

[76] Case descriptions from Bath General Hospital Letters Book

[77] Falconer, W. *An account of the Use, Application and Success of the Bath Waters in Rheumatic Cases.* p.20. Bath. 1795

[78] ibid. p.26

[79] Swift, H.H.et al.*Rheumatic Fever as a Manifestation of Hypersensitiveness (Allergy or Hypallergy) to Streptococci.* Paper read at the Bath Conference. 1928.

[80] Charleton, Tr.3. pp. 56-7

[81] ibid p.60

[82] Charleton, Tr.3. p.60

[83] Lane, H. *Differentiation in Rheumatic Diseases* 2nd Ed. 1892. Churchill. London. p.80

[84] Kersley, G.D. Personal Communication.

[85] Plan in possession of the Guildhall Archives, Bath

[86] Lowe, T.P. *Treatment of senile Rh. Arthritis by forcible movements.* BMJ. 1894

[87] MB 31.433. Bye-law 13 was amended to allow the appointment of a fourth surgeon who was designated *orthopaedic*.

[88] Spender, J.K. *Osteo-arthritis*. London. 1888

[89] Letters Book p114

[90] Letters Book p99

[91] Falconer, W. (1795) op. cit.

[92] Spender (1888) op. cit.

[93] MB 26. 204

[94] Hugh Lane's career as a pioneer rheumatologist was cut short by his untimely death in 1895. His co-author, C.T. Griffiths, was resident medical officer between 1885 and 1890, and subsequently moved to Birmingham where he continued in private practice.

[95] Tunstall, J. *The Bath Waters: their uses and effects in the cure and relief of various diseases.* Churchill. London. 1850.

[96] In 1975, the Government introduced a law making charitable donations to universities free of tax to the donor but this did not apply to donations given to NHS hospitals, hence the advantage of having a research unit affiliated to Bath University

[97] Bannatyne, G.A. *Rheumatoid Arthritis; its pathology, Morbid Anatomy and Treatment.* Bristol. 1896. p. 71.

[98] Dr Frank. R. Blaxall was latterly bacteriologist to the Vaccine Department of the Ministry of Health. He established the Government Lymph Institute at Hendon.

[99] Bannatyne, G.A., Wohlmann, A. S., Blaxall, F.R. *Lancet,* 25.04.1896.

[100] *Bulletin of the Committee for study of Special Diseases.* Vol 2. p. 106. Cambridge. 1907.

[101] MB. 28.145/6.

[102] This mortuary room, in the 1860 wing, became the dispensary in 1915 (MB. 28.297).

[103] Morris, Emily H. *Report on the Clinical and Bacteriological Examination of the vagina in sixty cases of rheumatoid arthritis.* Bulletin of Committee for Study of Special Diseases, Vol. III, Dec., 1910, p. 83.

[104] Routsias, J.G. et al. *Autopathogenic correlation of periodontitis and rheumatoid arthritis.* Rheumatology (Oxford). 2011. 50(7).pp 1189-93

[105] MB 28.221 (Sept 1909).

[106] MB 28. 194

[107] MB 28.461/2

[108] Turner. E. *A Brief History of the R.M.W.H.* Bath. 1921. p. 9.

[109] Turner, E.A. *A Brief History of the Royal Mineral Water Hospital.* Bath. 1921.

[110] MB. 32.63. (1932)

[111] MB. 34.227 (1938)

[112] Kersley, G. *The Three R's'* Bath. n.d. p.11.

[113] Peter Maddison subsequently left Bath to set up a rheumatology service in Bangor, North Wales and was appointed to the Chair of Musculoskeletal Medicine at Bangor University. He was replaced at Bath by Professor David Blake. The Postgraduate Medical Department was rebranded in 2003 as the School for Health and in In 2010 the School was subsumed into the Faculty of Humanities and Social Sciences where it became the Department for Health. There is no longer a chair of Bone and Joint Medicine but Professor Neil McHugh, a consultant rheumatologist at the RNHRD, holds an honorary university chair.

[114] At the time of writing research is being carried out into connective tissue disease, including lupus and scleroderma, spondyloarthropathy, including psoriatic arthritis and ankylosing spondylitis, complex regional pain syndrome, chronic fatigue syndrome/myalgic encephalomyelitis, pain management and neuro-241rehabilitation.

[115] Verhagen AP, de Vet HC, de Bie RA, Kessels AG, Boers M, Knipschild PG. *Balneotherapy for rheumatoid arthritis and osteoarthritis*. Cochrane Database Syst Rev 2000; (2):CD000518

[116] For a review of contemporary ideas on the Devonshire Colic see Waldron,A *The Devonshire Colic.* Journ. Hist Med & Allied Sci.1970; XXV: 383-413

[117] Charleton, R. *Three Tracts on the Bath Waters*. Bath 1774

[118] Charleton, R. Tract 2 p84

[119] Charleton, R. op cit

[120] Charleton, R. op.cit

[121] Oliver, W. *A Practical Essay on the Use and Abuse of Warm Water in Gouty Cases.* 2nd ed. (Bath, 1753), pp.62-63

[122] Ball, G *Two Epidemics of Gout* Bull. of the History Of Medicine' No 5 p. 407.

[123] Oliver, W *Practical Essay on the Use and Abuse of Warm Water Bathing in Gouty Cases* p36 Bath 1751

[124] *ibid* p39

[125] Eisinger, J. *Lead and wine*. Med. Hist. 1982.26:279-302

[126] Barlow, E. *An Essay on the Medical Efficacy and Employment of the Bath Waters*. Bath. 1882 pp 81-2

[127] *ibid*.p113

[128] *ibid*.p113

[129] Lysons, D. *On the effects of a decoction of the inner bark of the common elm in cutaneous disease*. Med. Trans. ii. 203 (1773)

[130] White, W. *Observations and experiments on the broad leaf willow bark*. Bath. 1798.

[131] Coates, V. and Delicati, L. *Rheumatoid Arthritis and its treatment*. London. 1931. This textbook reflects hospital practice during the 1930s. Leo Delicati was Medical Officer at the hospital and later moved to Buxton where he was MO at the Devonshire Royal Hospital.

[132] Hill, L. *Review of Gout*. 1939–1946. Annals of Rh. Diseases.5. pp. 171-176

[133] Kersley, G.D. *Gout*. Clinical Journal. Sept. 1936.

[134] http://www.buildinghistory.org/bath/medieval/outcast.shtml

[135] Rawcliffe, C. *Leprosy in Medieval England*. Boydell Press. 2003.

[136] Leland, J. *Itinerary*. Ed.Hearne,T. Oxford 1768/69

[137] Possibly Elizabeth Strode c1669–1715

[138] Tunstall,J. *Rambles about Bath* Bath 1847 p.59

[139] Charleton

[140] Brabazon, A.B. '*Bath Thermal Mineral Waters: their uses and abuses*' Part 3. BMJ. Mar 23 1878

[141] Shepherd, Rev. W., *The Life of Poggio Bracciolini*, Liverpool; 1837; p.67.

[142] Blackmantle,B. *The English Spy* London 1825 p 373.

[143] Mansford, J.G, *The Invalid's Companion to Bath*. Bath 1820, pp. 90-1

[144] Peirce, R. Op.cit

[145] http://www.twickenham-museum.org.uk/detail.asp?ContentID=182 There is information about Sir Joseph and Sir James Ashe at Twickenham museum.

[146] Book of case referrals to the Bath General Hospital now in Bath City Archives

[147] The General Hospital (later the Mineral Hospital) never had any paediatric wards. They were provided at the Royal United Hospital in Bath when it was enlarged in the 1860s .

[148] Tatler. 78. 8.10.1709

[149] Holland, E. *Citizens of bath : occupations in Bath in the Reign of James I* Widcombe Press. Bath 1988. pp 7-9.

[150] Anon. *Diseases of Bath- A Satire* London. 1737. Copy in Bath & Northeast Somerset Main Library, The Podium,Bath.

[151] Thought to be written by Mary Chandler

[152] Oliver,W. *A practical dissertation on Bath waters; to which is added a relation of a very extraordinary sleeper near Bath.* London 1707

[153] Letters to and from Henrietta, Countess of Suffolk, London: John Murray, 1824 vol2.246–50

[154] *An Account of Some Cases of Dropsies, Cured by Sweet Oil: In a Letter from William Oliver*, M. D. F. R. S. Philosophical Transactions, Vol. 49, 1755 - 1756, pp. 46-48

[155] *An Account of a Very Extraordinary Tumour in the Knee of a Person, Whose Leg Was Taken off by Mr. Jer. Peirce, Surgeon at Bath; Communicated in a Letter to Dr Mead, Physician to His Majesty, and Fellow of the College of Physicians, and of the Royal Society, London.* Jer. Peirce. Philosophical Transactions, Vol. 41, 1739 - 1741, pp.56-59

[156] Wood, J. *A Description of Bath* p.235. Bath. 1765.

[157] Spence, C. 'For True Friends: Jerry Peirce's Patriot Whig Garden at Lilliput Castle' *Bath History* Vol. XII. publ. Bath Preservation Society. pp 25-43

[158] For a full account of Cheyne's life and works, see Guerrini, A. '*Obesity and Depression in the Enlightenment- the life and times of George Cheyne*' Univ of Oklahoma Press. 2000.

[159] Worman, I. *Thomas Gainsborough*. Dalton. Suffolk.1976. p. 76.

[160] Pallet, *op. cit.* p. 54.

[161] *Letters between Charles Lucas and William Oliver. 7.11.1757.* Published at Bath.

[162] Pallet, P. *Bath Characters* Bath. 1807. PP. 48-9

[163] Eaves, T.C.D. and Kimpel, B.D. *Samuel Richardson - A biography.* Oxford. 1971.

[164] Wallis, P.J., Wallis, R.V. and Whittet, T.D., *Eighteenth century Medics.* Newcastle. 1985.

[165] *Dictionary of National Biography.*

[166] Baylies, W. *An Historical Account of the Rise Progress and Management of the Bath Hospital.* Bath. 1758. p. 121/2.

[167] *Bath Journal* 10 Apr 1758

[168] Genest, Rev. J. *Some account of the English stage* vol. 10 pp. 562 - 3 Bath. 1832.

[169] *Rules of the Bath United Hospital* 1850

[170] Poynter, E L N *Evolution of Medical Education in Britain* London 1966 p122

[171] Obituary notice for J.K Spender B.M.J. 22/4/1916 p 606

[172] Physicians: William Falconer, John Coakley Lettsom, Caleb Hillier Parry, John Staker, William Watson, Charles Blagden. Surgeons: Harry Atwood, John Symonds

[173] Hudson, K. '*The Bath and West: a bicentenary history.*' Moonraker Press. 1976

[174] Neve, Michael. '*The Medical Profession and the Bath Waters in 18th century Bath*' Unpublished paper.

[175] Letters and Papers of the Bath and West of England Soc. vol. 2 passim 2nd edition (abridged). Bath. 1802

[176] In 1760, Robert Dossie (1717 - 1777) persuaded the Society for Encouragement of Arts, Manufactures and Commerce, to encourage production of medicinal rhubarb in this country, see Hudson, D. and Luckhurst, K. W. *The Royal Society of Arts 1754–1954* p. 94, London 1954

[177] Letters and Papers of the Bath and West of England Society. First edition vol 3. appendix.

[178] Letters and Papers 2nd edition op. cit. vol. 2 p.102

[179] see *Take time by the forelock- the letters of Anthony Fothergill to James Woodeforde 1789–1813*. Medical History Supplement No 17.

[180] Borsay, A. *Medicine and Charity in Georgian Bath- A social history of the General Infirmary*. Ashgate. Aldershot 1999. p241

[181] Originally, honorary medical staff attended on Mondays and Saturdays. This was changed to Monday and Friday in 1743

[182] BMJ 29.1.1898. p.326

[183] Chonaire, Rhoda Ui. *The Luther Legacy: homeopathy in Ireland in the 19th Century* Journal of the Irish Society of Homeopaths - Anniversary Issue October 2010. pp.17- 24.

[184] Editorial in the Western Homoeopathic Observer. St Louis. Nov 15 1864 p.40

[185] Hembry, P. *British Spas from 1815 to the Present*. Athlone Press. 1997. p. 214

[186] Gasquet, F.A. *The Last Abbot of Glastonbury and other Essays*. London. 1908. pp.218-22.

[187] For a fuller history of Bellott's Hospital, see Manco, J. '*The Spirit of Care*' Bath. 1988. pp. 74-78

[188] House of Commons Journal Volume 1: 27 February 1626, *Journal of the House of Commons: volume 1: 1547–1629* (1802), p. 825. URL: http://www.british-history.ac.uk/report.asp?compid=6163.

[189] British Library Manuscripts Add.46378

[190] Powell, Anthony 'John Aubrey and his friends'. Hogarth Press, London. 1988, p71 and 82

[191] The final *e* of Bave was pronounced, hence the rhyme

[192] *Bath Chronicle* 15/11/1792

[193] Quinton, J. *A Treatise on Warm Bath Water Oxford.* 1734. p.62

[194] British Library Manuscripts op.cit

[195] MacKinnon, Murdoch, *An unpublished consultation letter of Sir Thomas Browne,* Bulletin of the History of Medicine. 1953, 27: 503-11

[196] Court of Arches *Bave versus Bave.* op.cit..

[197] Rolls, R. *The Hospital of the Nation.* Bird Publications. Bath 1988. pp12-13.

[198] Wood *op.cit.*

[199] MB 20. 341

[200] Broadsheet advert for the Pauper Charity. 1792 Reproduced in Baly, M. *Nursing and Social Change.* 3rd Ed Routledge London 1995 pp 76-9

[201] For details of the Cleland Affair see: Cleland, A *An Appeal to the Public.* Bath 1743; Cleland, A. *A full vindication of Mr Cleland's Appeal.* Bath & London 1744; *A short Vindication of the Proceedings of the Governors of the General Hospital.* Bath & London. 1744.

[202] Penrose, J. *Letters from Bath. (1766-67)* Alan Sutton. Gloucester. 1983 p.59

[203] Fighting between medical staff at the Bristol Royal Infirmary is recorded in *History of the BRI* by Monroe Smith

[204] MB. 19. 547

[205] This building is currently the Holburne Museum of Art

[206] Part of a poem written by an anonymous patient, circa 1865. (Boodle Collection, Bath Central Library)

[207] Barlow, E. *An Essay on the Medicinal Efficacy and Employment of the Bath Waters*. Bath. 1822.

[208] Barlow, E. '*An Essay in Medical Efficacy and Employment of the Bath Waters*' Bath. 1822. pp. 130-131

[209] MB. 24.350.

[210] Douglas Kerr, J.G. '*Popular guide to the use of the Bath Waters*' Bath. 1891. p.47

[211] MB. 27. 230

[212] Douglas Kerr op.cit. p.86.

[213] MB. 28. 416

[214] Turner, E.A. *A brief history of the Royal Mineral Water Hospital* Bath. 1921. p.23.

[215] Kersley, G. D. et al. '*Insulin and ECT in the treatment of Rheumatoid Arthritis*'. B.M.J. 14.10.1950. p.855

[215] Dixon, A. St J. *Rheumatology in the United Kingdom*. Troutbeck Press. 2000. p.89

TERMS FOR DRINKING THE BATH WATERS,

Either at the KING'S,
Or HETLING COURT PUMP ROOMS:

For One Week..£0 2 6 | For Three Months, £1 1 0
For One Year £2 2 0

NO CHARGE FOR A SINGLE GLASS.

PUBLIC BATHING.

KING'S and QUEEN'S BATHS.

GENTLEMEN: Monday, Wednesday, and Friday.
LADIES: Tuesday, Thursday, and Saturday.

CROSS BATH.

GENTLEMEN: Tuesday, Thursday, and Saturday.
LADIES: Monday, Wednesday, and Friday.

Terms: One Shilling each Person, from Six to Eleven in the Morning.

TEPID SWIMMING BATH.

Daily, *(Sundays excepted,)* from Six to Eleven, on payment of One Shilling each Person, or 15s. per Quarter.

HOT BATH.

WOMEN: Monday, Wednesday, and Friday.——MEN: Tuesday, Thursday, and Saturday, from Six to Eleven, on payment of Sixpence each Person.

PRIVATE BATHING.

HOT BATH and CROSS BATH.

Two Shillings and Sixpence each Person, from Six in the Morning till Ten at Night.

KING'S and QUEEN'S BATHS.

One Shilling and Sixpence each Person, from 6 in the morning till 10 at Night.

Two Children of one Family, under 12 years of age, using the same Bath, to pay for one only.

In the Private Baths any desired temperature can be afforded, below and as high as 108° Fahrenheit.

A Shower Bath, (at the Hot Baths,) One Shilling and Sixpence.

A Vapour Bath, (at the King's Baths,) Two Shillings and Sixpence.

A Lavement, of admirable construction, with every convenience, (at the King's Baths and Hot Baths,) two Shillings and Sixpence.

PUMPING.

Pumping, out of the Bath, (300 Strokes, or any less number,) One Shilling.

For every additional 100, Threepence.

Pumping in the Baths, per 100 Strokes, Threepence.

☞ Persons frequenting the Baths and Pump Rooms are particularly requested not to offer any Gratuity to the Attendants, who will be immediately dismissed for accepting it, and are already adequately remunerated for their services.

Charges for spa facilities at Bath. *(from Bath Directory 1837)*

Index

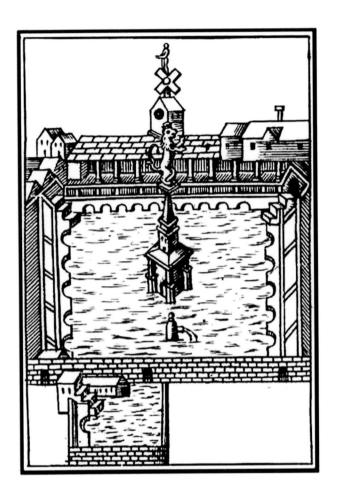

The King's Bath *(From Speed's Map of Bath 1676 edition)*

About London Publishing Partnership

The London Publishing Partnership is a publishing services company that specializes in working with researchers, learned societies, research institutes, think-tanks and also individual authors. We can provide the following services.

- Consultancy on editorial, production and marketing strategies for books at the individual-title and whole-programme levels.
- High-quality and speedy production work (copy-editing, typesetting, proofreading, artwork, indexing, project management).
- Management of the printing, order fulfilment and distribution of books, or the production and distribution of eBooks and downloads.
- Tailor-made marketing and publicity campaigns (either for individual publications or for an entire programme).

Our emphasis in all that we do is on quality and efficiency. We specialize in working with first-rate academic and professional research organizations and we fully understand their concerns. The company was founded in 2010 and our institutional client list includes the Centre for Economic Performance, the Paul Woolley Centre for the Study of Capital Market Dysfunctionality, the International Growth Centre, and the Centre for Economic Policy Research. Books for these institutions have been published by us, but under the imprints of our clients. Under our own London Publishing Partnership imprint we have published for Neil Monnery (*Safe as Houses? A Historical Analysis of Property Prices*), Peter Westin (*In From the Cold: The Rise of Russian Capitalism*) and Diane Coyle (*What's the Use of Economics: Teaching the Dismal Science After the Crisis*).

See: www.londonpublishingpartnership.co.uk for further details.